T0247371

Dave Chappelle and Philosophy

Pop Culture and Philosophy®

General Editor: George A. Reisch

For full details of all Pop Culture and Philosophy® books, and all Open Universe® books, visit www.carusbooks.com

Pop Culture and Philosophy®

Dave Chappelle and Philosophy

When Keeping It Wrong Gets Real

Edited by

MARK RALKOWSKI

OPEN UNIVERSE
Chicago

Volume 1 in the series, Pop Culture and Philosophy®, edited by George A. Reisch

To find out more about Open Universe and Carus Books, visit our website at www.carusbooks.com.

Copyright © 2021 by Carus Books

All rights reserved. No part of this publication may be reproduced, stored in a retrieval system, or transmitted, in any form or by any means, electronic, mechanical, photocopying, recording, or otherwise, without the prior written permission of the publisher, Carus Books, 315 Fifth Street, Peru, Illinois 61354.

Printed and bound in the United States of America. Printed on acid-free paper.

Dave Chappelle and Philosophy: When Keeping It Wrong Gets Real

ISBN: 978-1-63770-002-0

This book is also available as an e-book (978-1-63770-003-7).

Library of Congress Control Number: 2021941775

FOR MY POSSE:

Avery Alford
Kyell Andrade
Kourtney Buckner
Fryda Cortes
Hailey Figur
McKenzie McManaman
Alejandro Medina
Bawi Par
Joshua Robinson
Emmanuel Zelalem

I should only believe in a God that would know how to dance. And when I saw my devil, I found him serious, thorough, profound, solemn: he was the spirit of gravity—through him all things fall. Not by wrath, but by laughter, do we slay. Come let us slay the spirit of gravity!

—NIETZSCHE, *Thus Spoke Zarathustra*

There's no snakes.

— DAVE CHAPPELLE, *The Midnight Miracle*

Contents

Why You Can't Cancel Dave Chappelle

MARK RALKOWSKI

When *Sticks and Stones* was first released, Rotten Tomatoes, the influential American review aggregation website for movies and television, gave it a zero percent score.

That's what critics thought of it. Fans felt differently. As soon as it was opened up for an audience score (initially it was closed to the public), *Sticks and Stones* received 99 percent from thousands of user ratings.

As this book goes to press, *Sticks and Stones* has been rated by 40,945 users and maintains a 99 percent audience score. Talk about a difference of opinion between elite progressives and ordinary people!

Since these early days of peak negativity, the critics' score has risen a little bit—it is now at 35 percent—but the overwhelming response has been negative. As *Slate* put the point, watching Chappelle's recent comedy specials "is like dropping in on a rascally uncle who doesn't know, or doesn't care, how much he is disappointing you" (8/27/19). *The Atlantic* said that *Sticks and Stones* "registers as a temper tantrum, the product of a man who wants it all—money, fame, influence—without much having to answer to anyone" (8/28/19). And *Salon* suggested that Chappelle's special was regressive, offering "low-bar yucks to anyone yearning for validation of their anti-PC stance. Indeed, it may end up being one of the defining comedy specials of our time. Because our time is defined by cruelty" (9/5/19).

When Joe Rogan looked at the disparity between critical and public opinion of Chappelle's special, he thought he saw clear evidence of the progressive Left's inclination to "cancel" anything and anyone it finds objectionable. It was not enough for critics to write and publish their reviews at opinion-shaping venues like *Slate, Salon*, and *The Atlantic*; the cultural gate-keepers at Rotten Tomatoes went a step further in trying to control public perception of *Sticks and Stones* by letting it earn a zero percent from critics while closing it off to fans. But, as Rogan said, "You can't cancel Dave Chappelle" (*The Joe Rogan Experience*, 9/5/19). And judging from the fact that Chappelle received the Mark Twain Prize for Humor just two months after the release of *Sticks and Stones*, as well as one Grammy and *two* Emmy Awards for the special, it looks like Rogan had a point.

Why is this? Why is Dave Chappelle un-cancelable in today's otherwise unforgiving cultural climate? Is it a kind of moral credit he has in reserve thanks to *Chappelle's Show* and his decision to walk away from fifty million dollars in 2005? Or is it just that people adore him and so will forgive him for things that would condemn others to the sidelines of pop culture?

The answer is that it's probably neither of these things, or it's a special kind of adoration that saves him. I think Dave Chappelle is un-cancelable because he's the most talented comedian in the world, and humor is one of the most valuable things in life. You can't cancel him because his comedy feels like a cool bandage on an open wound; he makes life feel better, no matter your politics and sometimes in spite of them.

When Keeping It Wrong Gets Real

Let's look more closely at Chappelle's critics to get a better sense of what they found so objectionable about *Sticks and Stones*. They've raised a wide range of objections to his recent shows, but there are three main points. The first is that Chappelle is on the wrong side of history. We can see this in his arguments against cancel culture and political correctness: instead of siding with victims of sexual assault and acting as an ally to transgender people, Chappelle has mocked the LGBTQ+ community, come to the defense of disgraced celebrities like Louis C.K., and joked about not believing Michael Jackson's accusers, Wade Robson and James Safechuck.

In a statement to *TMZ* on August 27th 2019, Safechuck responded to Chappelle's bit from *Sticks and Stones*, expressing heartbreak "for all those children who look to see how they will be received when they finally find the courage to speak out about their sexual abuses." Chappelle's humor isn't just provocative trolling of white progressives, as he seems to think;

it is hurtful to marginalized people and empowering for people who are already powerful. As Eric Deggans put this point on NPR, "for Dave to turn to his audience and say . . . you're doing something awful when you're looking at these people and banishing them from pop culture because they've been abusive for a long time in secret, that doesn't make sense to me."

The second objection is related to the first, but it drills down on Chappelle's jokes about trans people and argues that he is not just on the wrong side of history with his politics; his comedy is dehumanizing and perhaps best skipped (*Vice*, 8/26/19). These jokes may be "a giant middle finger" to Chappelle's critics (*The Federalist*, 9/6/19), but they're also dangerous for trans people of all races who face unusually high levels of housing insecurity, employment discrimination, unmet healthcare needs, police brutality, social alienation, poverty, and violent crime. As a matter of fact, a trans woman who is mentioned in *Sticks and Stones* committed suicide after the show's release (*New York Daily News*, 10/12/19).

You might say, as Chappelle does often, that his jokes don't matter—he's just a comedian—and people should change the channel if they don't like what they hear. But this underestimates the power of cultural influencers (jokes become stereotypes and implicit biases over time) and callously ignores the specific concerns of people who have asked Chappelle to stop deadnaming and misgendering trans people like Caitlyn Jenner, expressing disgust at trans women's bodies, using slurs like "tranny" instead of "trans," and spreading transphobic tropes, all of which contribute to a comedy that is "regressive, exclusionary, and cruel" (*Medium*, 1/2/18).

The final objection is the most philosophical of the three. Here the point is that Chappelle is not the countercultural truth-teller that he and his fans think he is. Or, if he once was, he isn't any longer. "Like so many other comics, Chappelle sees himself as countering conventional wisdom with hard realities the audience doesn't want to hear, cushioned by a laugh. But Chappelle's takes don't defy establishment thinking at all; they simply channel it" (*The Ringer*, 8/29/19). Chappelle doesn't challenge the way people think or liberate them from their prejudices and biases; he reinforces the grip of both on his audiences. In fact, one of the most likely reasons for his popularity is that it relieves people of the burden of critical self-reflection. It lets them go on thinking what they've always thought while casting today's social critics as the real problem. Far from being a public intellectual like Lenny Bruce or George Carlin who can help us reimagine our world, Chappelle has become a reactionary guardian of the status quo, an enemy of social justice who postures as a truth-telling critic of culture.

Reactionary politics, cruelty, and bad faith—these are very tough allegations. And it's hard to argue with any of them. Chappelle *has been* slow to learn the lessons of the #MeToo movement; his jokes *have been* transphobic; he *has shamed* the victims of sexual assault; some of his bits *do feel* tired; he often *works against* today's social reformers; and he *hasn't been* leading the way in social justice comedy for many years, although his most recent special, *8:46*, and his benefit concert for the victims of the mass shooting in Dayton, Ohio on August 4, 2019, are notable exceptions. What makes Chappelle such an interesting character is that his comedy can have all of these flaws *and we are still drawn to him*. His many Grammy Awards and Primetime Emmy Awards speak for themselves.

> Boy, this comes as a complete surprise. I mean, I read all the reviews and they said so many terrible things: that they were embarrassed for me; I had lost my way; it wasn't even worth watching. I hope all you critics learn from this. This is a teachable moment. Shut the fuck up forever. (Emmys Acceptance Speech, September 19th, 2020)

Some people might prefer that he change his politics, and others will continue to hope that he eases up on jokes about trans people. But many of us (I think even the critics who've given him the hardest time in their reviews) will be excited to watch his next special. Matt Stone, one of the co-creators of *South Park*, has even questioned the sincerity of these public criticisms: "I feel bad for television critics and cultural critics," he said to *The Hollywood Reporter* (9/12/2019).

> They may have laughed like hell at *Sticks and Stones*, and then they went home and they know what they have to write to keep their job. So, when I read TV reviews or cultural reviews, I think of someone in prison, writing. I think about somebody writing a hostage note. This is not what they think. This is what they have to do to keep their job in a social media world.

Some critics may end up feeling disappointed all over again by the next Netflix special, but there's something about Chappelle's unusual mix of "Afrocentric black hip-hop intelligentsia and the skater/slacker/stoner ethos of suburban life" that allows him to speak to an extremely wide range of Americans, including people at opposite ends of the political spectrum (*Laughing Mad*, p. 179). He may not always challenge us to think differently or be more compassionate, but his universal appeal lets him "remix cultural boundaries in ways that others cannot" (*The New York Times*, 4/19/17) and function as a mirror in which we can see our prejudices staring back at us. It also lets Chappelle be a source of comic relief and consolation for everyone. In a country as polarized as the United States, this feels like something worth cherishing and learning from.

Letting Comedy Be Itself

Do critics expect too much from Dave Chappelle? That's what some comedians and writers would say. Chappelle's critics often argue that he used to be a "subversive countercultural voice"—he used to be what we now call "woke"—but today he's behind the times and refusing to evolve, which is disappointing and changing our overall perception of him.

These critics assume that comedy can and should serve *a cause*; they think it is supposed to be an instrument of social justice, and so Chappelle is letting us down and tarnishing his legacy by not punching up at the powerful and contributing to the goals of progressive politics. Judging from his 2020 Emmy Awards acceptance speech, it's clear that Chappelle strongly disagrees with this view of comedy. He doesn't just invite his critics to "shut the fuck up forever"; he also addresses the opinion that he has let anyone down: "It's a special night because comedy gets to be itself. It's all we ever wanted. I hope the war's over. We good?"

For Chappelle, the Emmy Awards were confirmation that his critics were wrong. They were wrong about his show, and they were wrong to think that comedy had any obligations to a political agenda. It was a victory for him personally, yes; these awards celebrated his talents and his show. But more importantly, it was a victory for comedy itself because its radical freedom was affirmed.

Chappelle's critics aren't the only people who have expressed concerns about the anti-social characteristics of today's comedy. In what *The New York Times* has called "the most discussed comedy special in ages," Hannah Gadsby presents an argument against comedy *as a whole* (*The New York Times*, 7/13/18). She challenges the idea that humor is a vehicle for truth-telling and existential therapy. She argues that, far from shedding light on our lives, humor is used to *mask* important truths. Stories have three parts—a beginning, a middle, and an end—while jokes have just two, a setup and a punchline. To end jokes on laughs, comics practice an emotional con artistry. They build tension with the joke's setup, and then they release that tension with the catharsis of a surprise resolution, which is far less emotionally challenging than the audience had expected (*Nanette*, 2018).

Gadsby's point is not just that a comedian is emotionally manipulative; it's that jokes work by directing us *away* from pain and the most important parts of people's stories. In this way they hide the truth and undermine its moral urgency. In her own case, she spent the first ten years of her career telling self-deprecating jokes. She made fun of her sexuality and her appearance, of being mistaken for "a bloke," and she developed many successful bits about the difficulties of being a lesbian in Tasmania, Australia, where gay sex was not decriminalized until 1997.

Her experience provided lots of well-liked "lesbian content," but she did not want to do that material anymore. "Do you understand what self-deprecation means when it comes from somebody who already exists on the margins? It's not humility. It's humiliation. I put myself down in order to speak, in order to seek permission to speak." At this early stage in her career, she did not triumphantly turn suffering into hard-fought wisdom, and she did not use humor to punch up at misogynists and homophobes. She stopped her stories at their punchlines and froze "an incredibly formative experience at its trauma point and sealed it off with jokes." She did this because that's what comedy does: it either deals with the trivial and unimportant, or it takes what is important and makes it trivial.

Hannah Gadsby's *Nanette* has had enormous cultural impact, changing the way comedians and journalists think and talk about comedy. A *Vulture* review concluded that Gadsby's "discovery" went well beyond the limitations of jokes for telling people's stories. Her darker message was that jokes are "more conservative than progressive" because they "can't really challenge or change anything." They reinforce "what we already believe rather than entertaining new information or unfamiliar philosophies" (*Vulture*, 7/12/18). Others have reached similar conclusions about the social and political inefficacy of humor from observing current affairs in American politics. In an essay for *The New Yorker*, Emily Nussbaum argues that jokes won the election for Donald Trump in 2016, and she concludes that the role of humor in our culture deserves careful reconsideration.

Growing up a Jewish kid in the nineteen-seventies, in a house full of Holocaust books, giggling at Mel Brooks's "The Producers," I had the impression that jokes, like Woody Guthrie's guitar, were a machine that killed fascists. Comedy might be cruel or stupid, yet, in aggregate, it was the rebel's stance . . . Jokes were a superior way to tell the truth . . . But by 2016 the wheel had spun hard the other way: now it was the neo-fascist strongman who held the microphone and an army of anonymous dirty-joke dispensers who helped put him in office. Online, jokes were powerful accelerants for lies—a tweet was the size of a one-liner, a "dank meme" carried farther than any op-ed, and the distinction between a Nazi and someone pretending to be a Nazi for "lulz" had become a blur. (*The New Yorker*, 1/15/17)

These pessimistic views about humor are increasingly common. Even the indie rock musician Father John Misty was down on humor after watching its role in the 2016 election. "In that moment, it was like all of the Gen-X humor that I was weaned on had this very cruel orgasm in my mind. In that moment, satire died. We're now living in a post-satire world" (*The Guardian*, 3/30/17).

Chappelle is aware of these issues, but he isn't worried about them. He even embraces the meanness of comedy in *The Bird Revelation*: "Sometimes the funniest thing to say is mean . . . It's a tough position to be in. So, I say a lot of mean things. But you guys gotta remember, I don't say them because they're mean; I'm saying it because it's funny. And everything is funny until it happens to you." For Chappelle, the far bigger worry is our country's inability to communicate about important issues. As he told David Letterman, we have lost the ability to just sit and talk, as "countrymen." We have so much to "unpack," so many social and political problems to work on and disagreements to sort through, and we need to "leave some room for redemption . . . and definitely some forgiveness." That is the only way for people to be honest about who they are, what they think, and what they have done. But instead of that, thanks to the way ideas spread on social media, "it's like a baby running around with a gun. Somebody gotta get that gun away from that baby, or at least [*laughs*] not be afraid that the baby has a gun." Chappelle has clearly opted not to be afraid of the baby with the gun, and he is challenging us, provoking us, with specials like *Sticks and Stones* that push the boundaries of what's considered appropriate.

Chappelle's critics expect more from him. They want less "cruelty" and more countercultural truth-telling. They think comedy has this power, and Chappelle simply hasn't been using it in his recent specials. On the other hand, people like Hannah Gadsby and Emily Nussbaum have argued that humor is *inherently* conservative and regressive; it may even stunt our emotional intelligence by allowing us to laugh at issues that call for critical self-examination and activism. Both of these views express a progressive's point of view on the politics of comedy; they differ only in their assumptions about the value of comedy's impact on our culture. And Chappelle disagrees with both of them. As he says in *The Bird Revelation*, "I didn't come here to be right. I came here to fuck around." He isn't trying to be a thought leader for the American Left, at least not on their terms. He makes this crystal clear in *8:46* when he says of his lack of leadership in the Black Lives Matter movement that it is not his role to "step in front of the streets and talk over the work these people are doing."

But Chappelle also denies that comedy is regressive. Lorne Michaels captures this aspect of Chappelle's spirit as an artist better than anyone in his account of how Chappelle helped the *Saturday Night Live* cast heal after the 2016 election. Michaels says the mood was bleak at the readthrough on the Wednesday after the election. People were "feeling tense and very vulnerable. It was a mess," until Chappelle sat down next to Michaels at the head of the table, sensed the emotion in the room, and read a famous quote by Toni Morrison: "This is precisely the time when artists go to work. There's no time for despair, no place for self-pity, no need for silence, no room for fear. We speak, we write, we do language. This is how civilizations heal" (*Mark Twain Prize*). Michaels says he knew at that point that things would be okay. Chappelle has a similar message for students at his old high school.

> I hope you guys remember this. You are very necessary now. This is a season for artists. Secretly I am building an army of artists. I want all of you guys to get out there and fight in the army. It's not a violent fight, but it is a revealing one. You've got to reveal people to themselves by exposing yourself through your art. Honestly, looking at y'all inspires me. I feel like I was just you. If I could go back and talk to myself, I would tell myself what I'm telling you guys: be nice and don't be scared. (Chappelle talking to students at the Duke Ellington School of the Arts, *Mark Twain Prize*)

These are not the views and actions of a man who believes comedy is regressive and harmful to society. They may not be what progressive critics want from Dave Chappelle, but he doesn't care. He seems to think that his critics don't expect too much from comedy; they expect *too little*. They want to make comedy a political tool; Chappelle wants it to be a tool for revealing truth. "I figured out why they want to hear from me, and it's serious. The only reason people want to hear from people like me is because you trust me. You don't expect me to be perfect, but I don't lie to you. I'm just a guy, and I don't lie to you. And every institution, every institution that we trust, lies to us" (*8:46*).

In a world so full of misinformation, Chappelle thinks an artist's truth is more important than any political values. His art may be mean at times, but that's not all it is. When we let comedy "be itself," Chappelle thinks we bring people together in laughter. He calls the comedy club "sacred ground" and suggests that it may be the last safe space in America to say what you want and laugh when you want (*Mark Twain Prize*). And his advice to his critics seems to be something like this: "forget about politics. Let's 'fuck around'; and in fucking around, let's cut through all of the rhetoric that divides us and discover the things that hold us together." That is how civilizations heal: with an "army of artists" capable of revealing people to themselves. Not with more of the same politics.

Standing Back from the Elephant

At the end of *Equanimity*, Chappelle tells the story of Emmett Till, the fourteen-year-old African American boy who was lynched in Mississippi in 1955 after flirting with a young white woman outside of a grocery store. Chappelle explains how Emmett was abducted, horribly beaten and mutilated, and shot in the head by two white men from the white woman's family. They tied Emmett's body to a wheel and left it to sink in a creek, where it was discovered a few days later. "And luckily for everybody in America . . . his mother was a fucking gangster . . . If you can imagine, in the very midst of a mother's worst nightmare, this woman had the foresight to think of everybody." She made sure Emmett's casket was left open so that everyone could see "his horribly bloated body," images of which appeared in newspapers all across America following the funeral service.

In Chappelle's telling of the story, the dissemination of these photos was a defining moment in American history and a turning point in the Civil Rights Movement. "Every thinking and feeling person was like, 'Yuck! We gotta do better than this.' And they fought beautifully, and here we all are." Chappelle tells Emmett Till's story because his accuser had recently admitted to lying in her court testimony. "You can imagine, when we read that shit, we was like, 'Ooh! You lying-ass, bitch.'" Chappelle says he was just furious, until he was able to put things in perspective. As we get older, he explains, we recognize that our initial reactions to things are often wrong or "more often incomplete."

It's the ancient problem of standing too close to an elephant. "The analogy being that if you stand too close to an elephant, you can't see the elephant. All you see is its penis-like skin." You have to stand back to get a better look, to see the whole animal. Chappelle says that as he stood back and thought about the full significance of Emmett Till's death and the white woman's false testimony in court, he realized that he was grateful that the woman had told the truth before she died—because it's an important truth and the country needed to know it, so "thank you for telling the truth, you lying-ass bitch"—and he was humbled upon seeing the whole elephant: the woman lied, and her lie caused a murder. But that murder "set in motion a sequence of events that made my beautiful life possible. That made this very night possible." How could it be true that this heinous lie could make the world a better place? "It's maddening."

All of this is a setup for the extraordinary climax of Chappelle's show. He says that the story of Emmett Till's lynching, and all of the good that his death helped bring into the world, is related to how he feels about the era of Donald Trump. "I feel like this motherfucker might be the lie that saves us all. Because I have never felt more American than when we all hate on this motherfucker together . . . When it happens, I can see everybody's struggling," which puts everything else in perspective. And so, if Chappelle tells jokes that make you want to beat up a transgender person, "then you're probably a piece of shit and don't come see me anymore." And if you cannot understand that when football players take a knee during the national anthem, they are standing up for all Black people, including Chappelle himself, "you might not want to fuck with me anymore."

Chappelle closes the show by telling his audience that, "no matter how bad it gets, you're my countrymen, and I know for a fact that I'm determined to work shit out with y'all." If Carolyn Bryant, Emmett Till's lying accuser, were alive today, "I would thank her for lying. And then I would kick her in the pussy." This last line makes more sense in the full context of *Equanimity*, but even if you don't have that context you can see what Chappelle is up to here. He brings us face to face with Emmett Till's dead body, one of the greatest icons of the Civil Rights Movement, and he lets us feel his mother's heartbreak. But then he reminds his audience of suffering that most of them share, the nightmare of the Donald Trump presidency. It is a pain that lets Chappelle empathize with all Americans, and it taught white progressives an important lesson about disenfranchisement: "It's tough when your horse doesn't win the race. It's even worse if you don't have a horse" (*New York Times Style Magazine*, 8/19/17).

This is a whirlwind of provocations and profound ideas that pull an audience through a wide range of emotions, only to be released suddenly and triumphantly from the gravity of these reflections by the thought of Chappelle kicking Carolyn Bryant with justifiable contempt. This is a virtuosic example of what philosophers call "relief humor." Chappelle builds an almost unbearable tension over racial injustice and Trump, and then sets us free with a punchline that feels like justice.

We all know what comic relief feels like, and if you've watched *Equanimity* from beginning to end you may have felt it when Chappelle concludes his show with this *tour de force*. He provides relief from the emotional weight of Emmett Till's story, but he also gives his audience relief from other sources of tension in American life: politics, race relations, and moral confusion about the social construction of gender and sexuality. His whole show builds tension around these issues that this climax releases.

Hannah Gadsby might say that this is just a comedian's manipulative practice, and that it doesn't do us any good because it shuts down critical thinking before it even begins. But Chappelle's accomplishments in *Equanimity* call Gadsby's view into question. Isn't there something undeniably beneficial, and even noble, about providing a diverse audience with emotional relief from their *lived experiences* of tension around issues of race and gender? Hasn't Chappelle done something significant if he can bring such people together in cathartic laughter about our polarized politics? This laughter doesn't solve our problems or answer our questions, but at least for a moment it lifts us out of the everyday binaries that divide us: Black and white, male and female, oppressor and oppressed, Republican and Democrat. As Chappelle says during his *Mark Twain Prize* special, "we gotta let some air out of the ball, man." More now than ever, comedians have "a responsibility to speak recklessly," to protect the "sacred ground" of the comedy club, and to "reveal people to themselves."

Letting Some Air Out of the Ball

Charlie Chaplin once said that "life is a tragedy when seen in close-up but a comedy in long-shot." This idea is related to Chappelle's suggestion that we stand back from the elephant and treat our "initial reactions" to most things in life as either wrong or incomplete. He doesn't say there's anything funny about Emmett Till's story; in fact, it makes him feel wonder that so much good could come from something so bad, and gratitude for the "beautiful life" that he enjoys. But when he looks at the things his critics say about him, like his alleged transphobia and victim blaming, or white America's complaints about Black athletes kneeling during the National Anthem, or even the presidency of Donald Trump, they all look trivial by comparison. And there's relief in looking at them from that perspective. It's liberating because the ordinary weight of life is lifted. When a comedian can do this for us, it feels like they have magical powers because they make our suffering disappear.

Sigmund Freud (1856–1939) had a theory about why humor has this impact on us. He thought comedians talk to the "intimidated" part of our psyches, and they give us "kind" and "comforting" guidance through our troubles. Jokes are like the consolations of a loving parent. The Buddha said life was suffering (*dukkha*), and the existentialists said the task of selfhood was characterized by anxiety (*Angst*). According to Freud, *humor* says, "Here is the world, which seems so dangerous. It is nothing but a game for children—just worth making a jest about." The ability to bring about this shift in perspective, from *Angst* and *dukkha* to existential triumph, is a "rare and precious gift" because it is "liberating" and "elevating."

Freud famously thought the mind had three parts, the id, ego, and superego. In humor, the superego—the internalized voice of the parent—looks down on the ego from an elevated perspective, the way a parent looks at a child's concern, and finds it ridiculous. When we laugh at ourselves, we stand outside of our narrow, egoistic perspective on our lives and recognize how small and insignificant we are, how trivial our problems look when put in perspective. This is how humor elevates us above our ordinary judgments, what Chappelle might call our "initial reactions," and this is why it liberates us. As humor shifts us from "the child's" perspective to "the parent's," we are freed from pain and elevated above a hostile world. Freud described this as the "victorious assertion of the ego's invulnerability . . . against the unkindness of the real circumstances." It is a rebellious attitude, not a resigned one, because it protects the ego against the "provocations of reality," refusing to let it suffer. Even the "traumas of the external world" become occasions to gain pleasure ("Humour," pp. 161–66).

Freud's relief theory of humor provides a possible explanation of why we can't cancel Dave Chappelle. It doesn't matter how good our lives are; everyone wants to "let some air out of the ball." As Seneca (1 B.C.E.–65 C.E.) famously wrote, "What need is there to weep over parts of life? The whole of it calls for tears." With a comedian like Dave Chappelle, those tears are turned into laughter. Life is absurd; we age; we get sick, and we die; the world is full of injustice, natural disasters, and disease—and none of it matters, all of it is laughable, at a Dave Chappelle show.

We can't cancel Chappelle because his comedy is a source of consolations that we would rather not live without. The same is true for any great comedian, which is why even someone as disgraced as Louis C.K. continues to sell out live shows and make a living by selling his material through his website. But Chappelle's ability to provide comic relief across lines of race, class, and culture makes him unique in American life. The fact that he can provide equal relief to Black and white people, liberals and conservatives, explains both why he is so widely loved and why his shows are so controversial: his relief for one group often comes at a cost to another. Sometimes we wonder whether he plays this game with us on purpose.

Chappelle opens *Sticks and Stones* by singing the first few lines of Prince's pre-apocalyptic "1999" and talking about the fact that Anthony Bourdain killed himself. Prince faces his destruction and judgment day, not caring and partying like it's 1999, while Bourdain, who "had the greatest job that show business ever produced . . . hung himself in a luxury suite in France." We must never forget it, Chappelle says. That man with that job—flying around the world, eating delicious food, and spending time with interesting people—killed himself. For contrast, Chappelle mentions an acquaintance from high school, an "urban genius" who went "from the hood" to an Ivy League university and a top law school before losing everything, getting divorced from a woman he loved, and going to work at Foot Locker. "Dressed like a referee, the whole shit. This motherfucker is forty-five years old!"

Chappelle says that when he recently got drinks with this old friend, he learned that he had been living with his mother for ten years as he got back on his feet. "The point of the story is . . . never occurred to this n***a to kill himself. He's alive and well in DC. I even suggested to him that he should try it out." Nobody's life is perfect, Chappelle explains. It doesn't matter how they look on the outside. You never know what people are going through on the inside. "I have a great life, but it's not a perfect life. But it's good . . . My shit's an above ground pool. You ever seen one of them? Eh, it's *a pool*!" This is how Chappelle sets the stage for his withering attack on cancel culture.

It may seem like a non sequitur. What do Anthony Bourdain and Prince have in common with cancel culture? But Chappelle is showing us his hand: his recent shows are not for his critics; they are *about* his critics. What we need is more art, more revelation of people to themselves and more patience with each other, not more cultural policing and "celebrity hunting." We need to "let some air out of the ball" if we have any hope of actually improving our polarized country.

> We [comedians] watch you guys fight, but when we're together we talk it out. I know comics that are very racist, and I watch them on stage and everyone's laughing, and I'm like, "um, that mothafucka means that shit." Don't get mad at 'em. Don't hate 'em. We go upstairs and have a beer. Sometimes I even appreciate the artistry that they paint their racist opinions with. Man, it's not that serious. The First Amendment is first for a reason. The Second Amendment is just in case the first one doesn't work out. (*Mark Twain Prize*)

Chappelle sings Prince's "1999" and talks about Bourdain and his acquaintance from high school because the misguidedness of cancel culture—the parts that over-reach—as well as our need for genuine spiritual and cultural healing, are clearest in the context of life as a whole. Bourdain had power, celebrity, and wealth; he was as "privileged" as a person can be, but he took his own life in spite of it all. Kevin Hart's homophobic Tweets don't look like much to worry about in *that* context (*Sticks and Stones*). They are disappointing and hurtful, and they may change the way we think about Kevin Hart and his comedy. But instead of gathering the masses for another social media show trial, Chappelle advises us to put on a Prince album and keep our minds open to the possibility that there's more to people, especially our artists, than our polarizing politics lead us to believe.

In his now infamous *Saturday Night Live* monologue after the 2016 election, Chappelle tells a story about a party he had recently attended at the Obama White House. It was sponsored by BET and everyone there was Black, "except for Bradley Cooper." Chappelle says that at one point he stood back and looked at the pictures of the past presidents on the walls, and he thought about how few Black people had been invited to the White House during the long history of the United States. One of the first few Black guests came during FDR's Administration, and afterward Roosevelt got so much flak from the media that he said he would never have "another n****r in this house."

> I thought about that and I looked at that room, and I saw all of those Black faces (and Bradley) and I saw how happy everybody was, these people who had been historically disenfranchised. And it made me feel hopeful. And it made me feel proud to be an American. And it made me very happy about the prospects of our country.

It was in this spirit that Chappelle wished Donald Trump luck and promised to give him a chance. In telling this story, Chappelle uses his own practice of "standing back from the elephant" to look beyond the 2016 election at the overall trajectory of the country. From that perspective (at that time), the country appeared to be moving in the right direction, despite the outcome of an election that felt like a "moral 9/11" to so many Americans—this was Chappelle's consolation to the brokenhearted liberals in the audience. His vision is honest about American slavery, racism, and white supremacy, but it also invites people to recognize how much has changed in the country since FDR's presidency.

Chappelle was not a "n****r" in a racist white President's White House; he was a rich and beloved celebrity guest of Barack and Michelle Obama in *their* White House, surrounded by other invited Black guests and celebrities. Chappelle offered his audience this consoling vision of the United States in an effort to help heal the country, to "elevate" and "liberate" progressives from the pain of that moment, and to signal to Trump and his supporters that there was hope for unity in the future. However, just a few months later, Chappelle had to apologize to his liberal fans: "I fucked up. Sorry" (*Vanity Fair*, 5/16/17). To activists on the Left, Chappelle's hopeful vision of racial progress and national unity was intolerable, an offense against sacred anti-racist principles, and further evidence that Chappelle would never be a reliable soldier in "the great awokening." Chappelle's critics worry that he gives relief to the wrong people, for the wrong reasons. In Freud's terms, when Chappelle defends celebrities or wishes President Trump luck, or jokes about victims of child abuse and the bodies of trans people, his message appears to be this: "Here are the concerns of these progressives, which seem so urgent and alarming. But they are nothing but a game for children—just worth having a laugh about." In most cases, when Chappelle hears these complaints, he responds in two ways: first, by claiming absolute freedom in the comedy club—it is "sacred ground," the only "safe space" left in the country where people truly speak and laugh freely—and second, by provoking more criticisms from the Left by deliberately offending their sensibilities with new jokes about the same controversial topics. And he isn't going to back down in this fight. As the Kendrick Lamar lyrics say in the epigraph to *Sticks and Stones*: "You mouthafuckas can't tell me nothin' / I'd rather die than to listen to you" (Kendrick Lamar, "DNA").

When Don Lemon questioned Chappelle's leadership in the wake of George Floyd's murder, Chappelle responded differ-

ently. He released *8:46*. In addition to explaining why it is not
his place to "step in front of the streets" at a world-historic
moment like the Black Lives Matter protests of racial injustice
in 2020, Chappelle returns to the story he told during his
Saturday Night Live monologue and corrects the record. He
does not apologize for his comments about Trump; he clarifies
that his information about the history of Black guests at the
White House was incomplete. Chappelle's great grandfather,
William David Chappelle, visited Woodrow Wilson's White
House in 1918 to protest a wave of racial violence accompany-
ing the Great Migration. He was born a slave in 1857, and later
became president of Allen University, a historically Black university in South Carolina in 1897.

> These things are not old. This is not a long time ago. It's today. It's
> today! That man's wife was the woman that my father called on, on
> his deathbed. And they were slaves! Are you out of your fucking mind
> if you can't see that? And these n***as say, "Why isn't David
> Chappelle saying anything?" Because David Chappelle understands
> what the fuck he is seeing, and these streets will speak for them-
> selves whether I am alive or dead.

This is not meant to comfort white people, and it is not a
defense of the status quo. It is an example of James Baldwin's
concept of a love that "takes off the masks that we fear we cannot live without and know we cannot live within" (Baldwin,
The Fire Next Time, p. 95). Chappelle's *Saturday Night Live*
monologue was meant to provide a despairing audience with
consolation shortly after a traumatizing election, and on that
night in that moment Chappelle looked at history to describe
an optimistic vision of this country's past and future: he felt
proud and hopeful while partying with the Obamas because of
what it revealed to him about the country's possibilities.

The 2016 election was disappointing, but the overall trajectory of the country was good; we were bending the long arc of
the moral universe toward justice. In *8:46*, as Chappelle looks at
the Black Lives Matter movement and thinks about the murder
of George Floyd, he takes a new look at the same history and
describes it with a different purpose. "All that can save you now
is your confrontation with your own history, which is not your
past, but your present," Baldwin said in his 1968 *Esquire* interview. This is also Chappelle's message to his audience at the end
of *8:46*. Our history led us to the Black Lives Matter movement;
it is a reflection of who we are and have been. Chappelle "stands
back from the elephant" here in order to relieve his audience of

the lies that white Americans are taught to tell themselves—
"that their ancestors were all freedom-loving heroes, that they
were born in the greatest country the world has ever seen, that
Americans are invincible in battle and wise in peace," as
Baldwin says—the lies that we cannot afford to live within any
longer (Baldwin, *The Fire Next Time*, 101).

And it literally was an offering of love: "I trust you guys. I
love you guys," Chappelle says as he concludes. He is proof of
the country's promise—just look at his success—but his family's history is a reminder of how unlikely his "beautiful life"
was. His great grandfather was born a slave, and less than one
hundred years after William David Chappelle visited Woodrow
Wilson's White House to protest racial violence in the south,
our Dave Chappelle was the guest of America's first Black president. This past is our present. That is what Chappelle sees in
the Black Lives Matter movement. Black history isn't merely
something that we read, and it is not primarily about the past.
"The great force of history comes from the fact that we carry it
within us" ("The White Man's Guilt," p. 47).

Chappelle's *Saturday Night Live* monologue in November
2016 upset his liberal fans, who weren't interested in national
unity and didn't have any interest in giving Trump a chance—
to them, he was an unabashed racist and a misogynist who had
bragged about sexually assaulting women; just the thought of
him in the White House felt like a personal nightmare and a
national disgrace. Why would Chappelle want to extend an
olive branch to someone like that? And why was he telling a
version of Black history, in his story about socializing with the
Obamas, that helps white Americans spread the lie that,
thanks to the Civil Rights and Voting Rights Acts, racism is
over and the United States has perfected its union?

"People who imagine that history flatters them," Baldwin
said, "are impaled on their history like a butterfly on a pin and
become incapable of seeing or changing themselves, or the
world" ("The White Man's Guilt," p. 47). In a word, Chappelle's
critics thought he had "impaled" himself and his audience with
this *SNL* monologue, regardless of his intentions; and *8:46* was
Chappelle's response to this worry. He isn't trapped in myths
about America's inherent goodness, what W.E.B. Du Bois called
"lies agreed upon" ("The Propaganda of History," p. 714). His family's story is an embodiment of the full truth of Black history in
America: his great grandparents were born into slavery, and his
dad called to his great grandmother as he died. In November 2016,
Chappelle told the story about his own recent trip to the White
House because it was so extraordinary in light of these facts. Yes,

Trump was a nightmare and a disgrace, but Chappelle's family had been through far worse and look where he was.

Chappelle's critics don't just think too little of comedy, wanting it to serve the narrow ends of today's social media virtue signaling; they think too highly of themselves and too little of their artists. They are so sure of their own moral superiority that they cannot let comedy be itself. With all due respect to the writers at *The Atlantic* and *Slate*, they don't have Chappelle's vision. And so, they often miss the deeper meanings of his specials and public appearances. Part of Chappelle's point in *8:46* was that he hadn't betrayed Baldwin's call for history as a study of what we carry "within us." He had exemplified it.

This channeling of James Baldwin was an act of love for everyone, and a reminder to us all of who Chappelle is as an artist and how he thinks about his art. "We'll keep this space open," he tells his audience; he will never relent in the fight for a comedian's absolute artistic freedom. "This is the last stronghold for civil discourse." It is a space of revelation where very different people can come together in laughter. This can be mean; humor is rarely gentle. But Chappelle says the truth is at stake, not more politics. He is an artist, not a "moral or intellectual" leader. People may want him to tell them what to think, but he insists that we need to "cut our own meat"; we need to do our own work and think for ourselves.

Comedy *reveals* transphobia in people; it *reveals* their misogyny; it doesn't create it in them. Laughter is a form of honesty, and that honesty can provide space for "redemption." The alternative is our collective "tightrope walk" through the unforgiving spaces of American cancel culture, which "just makes everybody not want to get caught" (*My Next Guest*, Season Three, Episode 3).

Chappelle has been trying to tell his critics for years that they need to let comedy do its own unique work, because it has powers of "pressure relief" that progressive cultural critics will never have. And Chappelle thinks we *need* to let some air out of the ball if there is any hope for a better future. If we can't do that, "it's just rat-a-tat-tat-a-tat-tat-tat-tat-TAAAAT!!" (*8:46*).[1]

---
[1] I would like to thank Ashok Kaushik, Elizabeth Johnson, Ethan Gettes, Nikki Tyler, Ethan Weatherdon, Emmanuelle Dyer Melhado. Anastasiia Frizner, Leo Kehagis and Elijah Moyo for comments on earlier drafts of this Introduction.

I

When Keeping
It Real
Goes Wrong

1
My Money, My Choice

Luis Felipe Bartolo Alegre

In his *Sticks and Stones* special, Dave Chappelle declares to be neither for nor against abortion. "It all depends," he says, "on who I get pregnant." However, he states that the right to carry out an abortion can only be a woman's right.

> I'll tell ya right now, I don't care what your religious beliefs are or anything, if you have a dick, you need to shut the fuck up on this one. Seriously, this is theirs. The right to choose is their unequivocal right. Not only do I believe they have the right to choose, I believe that they shouldn't have to consult anybody, except for a physician about how they exercise that right. Gentlemen, that is fair. (*Sticks and Stones*)

That abortion presupposes an intervention into a woman's body and that only she can decide what to do with it, gives support to the feminist motto, "My body, my choice." From this, and in an unexpected twist, equally worthy of comedy and philosophy, Chappelle concludes that, if a woman can abort her fetus without consulting the father, then a man can choose to take no responsibility for his offspring.

> And ladies, to be fair to us, I also believe if you decide to have the baby, a man should not have to pay. That's fair. If you can kill this motherfucker, I can at least abandon him. It's my money, my choice. And if I'm wrong, then perhaps we're wrong. Think that shit out for yourselves. (*Sticks and Stones*)

Unexpected twists are usually celebrated in both comedy and philosophy. An unexpected joke is usually funnier than an expected one. On the other hand, a counter-intuitive philosoph-

3

ical idea is more likely to get attention and be more quoted, even if only for criticizing it. Furthermore, some twists of comedy and philosophy can be celebrated both for being funny and philosophically insightful, and I think that's also the case for this joke.

Is it true that women's unilateral right to abortion, a mainstream feminist idea, implies men's unilateral right to abandonment, an idea at odds with mainstream feminism? Does men's right to abandonment follow logically from women's right to end their pregnancies?

It's Not (Only) What's Gotten into Me!

Biological parenthood used to be very straightforward. A *biological parent* is one who by virtue of a biological function has made it possible for his or her child to be born. Before modern advances in reproductive technology, the biological parents of a child were always a man and a woman who engaged in sexual intercourse causing the pregnancy of the woman. Here, a biological mother was always a *genetic* mother since her genes were passed down to her offspring. But the typical biological contribution of the mother isn't restricted to passing her genes. Through pregnancy or gestation, she also makes it possible for the embryo to develop (in her womb) into a child, which means she is also the *gestational* mother.

Thanks to *in vitro* fertilization, pregnancy can now be carried out by a surrogate who need not be a genetic parent of the fetus inside her. In such a case, the surrogate would be the gestational mother, but not a genetic mother of the fetus in her womb. Moreover, future technologies could complicate things even more. For example, thanks to human cloning the gestational mother could be the only genetic and, hence, biological parent of her child. Genetic manipulation could enable that three (or more) persons share genetic parenthood, same-sex genetic parents, and even the conception of a human being with a DNA sequence so unique that no genetic parenthood could be distinguished. Artificial womb technologies might allow a man to be a gestational father or even make gestational human parents unnecessary.

Regardless of these complications in the concept of parenthood, though, the case presupposed in Chappelle's joke is a straightforward one. We're dealing with a woman who becomes pregnant from having sex with a man, where there was no explicit previous agreement as to what to do if she gets pregnant. Hence, the genetic and the gestational mother are the same person. Furthermore, we're presupposing that the biological parents have the initial presumption of parental rights and responsibilities. In other words, biological parents are presumed to be legal parents of their offspring—unless they give them up into adoption.

My Show, My Choice

In *The Punchline*, the epilogue to his *Sticks and Stones*, Chappelle comments on the reaction of a woman to some #MeToo jokes he made in a show. "You can't say that!", the woman told Chappelle, to which he answered: "Yes, I can, it's my show. I'll say whatever the fuck I want." Was Chappelle's answer fair?

In order to answer this, we must try to understand what the woman meant with, "You can't say that!" She must not have meant that Chappelle doesn't have the power to do so. Whether Chappelle has the power to make #MeToo jokes in his show depends on two things. First, that there's no legal prohibition that he makes those jokes, and second, that the place where he's performing doesn't prohibit such jokes. Clearly, there's no legal prohibition to make #MeToo jokes, and Chappelle has been able to make these jokes in many places.

She more likely meant that it's unethical for him to tell those jokes. This would change the picture since her statement could be charitably interpreted as some kind of ethical advice to Chappelle. That there's no legal or contractual prohibition to do a joke doesn't necessarily mean that doing it is ethical. In fact, this is part of the reason why he left *Chappelle's Show*. In spite of the fact that neither law nor Comedy Central prevented him from doing his racially charged sketches, he felt that something was probably wrong with them, as he told Oprah Winfrey.

> CHAPPELLE: I was doing sketches that were funny, but socially irresponsible. I felt like I was deliberately being encouraged, and I was overwhelmed. So, it's like you're getting flooded with things, and you don't pay attention to things like your ethics or when you get so overwhelmed. . . . Like, there's this one sketch that we did that was about this pixie that would appear whenever racist things happens. . . . I mean, I don't want Black people to be disappointed in me for putting that out there.
>
> OPRAH: No, you didn't want to be disappointed in yourself.
>
> CHAPPELLE: You know what, Oprah? [*laughter*] You're right. (*The Oprah Winfrey Show*, 2/3/06)

Although there was no legal or contractual issue preventing Chappelle from doing such sketches, his ethics prevented him from doing them. It doesn't matter if we agree or disagree that the *Stereotype Pixie* sketch was socially irresponsible. Chappelle thought it was, and to keep doing them would have disappointed his public and himself. (The *Stereotype Pixies* skit and a very interesting set of comments on this subject by the public can be found in the second of *The Lost Episodes* of *Chappelle's Show*.)

In this context, Chappelle can't simply answer that he can do "whatever the fuck" he wants in his show. Unless he wants to "disappoint," he has to justify that telling these jokes isn't unethical or demand that the woman justify why it is. On the other hand, Chappelle's answer might also be interpreted simply as a clarification that he's exercising his legal right to do those jokes, and that he'll continue his show disregarding the ethical concerns that may be raised, even if those concerns are valid. More or less in the way a woman may defend her having aborted in spite of accepting that it was ethically wrong to do so.

For What You're Worth

There's an analogy between the previous case and the argument for women's unilateral right to abortion. So-called *pro-choice* advocates don't necessarily claim that abortion is never wrong or that the father isn't ethically entitled to oppose it. Instead, women's right to abortion is usually justified by the human right of bodily autonomy suggested by the motto, "My body, my choice."

In one of the most important philosophical arguments for abortion, Judith Jarvis Thomson makes her case with the following thought experiment. Suppose you wake up and find yourself in a hospital bed. The hospital director explains to you that the person in the bed next to yours is a famous violinist who has a deadly kidney disease, and that his circulatory system is plugged into yours in a way that'll allow him to recover from his ailment. The director further explains that you're there because, after having searched through all the medical records available to them, the Society of Music Lovers found that you, and only you, have the right blood type that could help him, so they kidnapped you and plugged him into you. Finally, the director tells you:

> Look, we're sorry the Society of Music Lovers did this to you—we would never have permitted it if we had known. But still, they did it, and the violinist now is plugged into you. To unplug you would be to

kill him. But never mind, it's only for nine months. By then he will have recovered from his ailment, and can safely be unplugged from you. ("A Defense of Abortion," pp. 48–49)

Thomson argues that, although it would be nice of you to accede to this, you're in no way obligated to, even if you only needed to be connected for some minutes. In the latter case, "it would be indecent to refuse," but you're still in no obligation to do it. If you were, this would clash with your right of bodily autonomy.

But should the right of bodily autonomy be more important than the right to life? For Thomson, the issue isn't whether one right is more important than the other, but "what it comes to, to have a right to life" (p. 60). In other words, does my right to life entail any (ethical or legal) obligations in other persons? For example, were the friends of the violinist obligated to help him? Are you obligated to stay for even one minute to help him live? The answer to these questions may be "No," regardless of how much we value life. Hence, if the analogy is appropriate, the mother would have no obligation to carry her pregnancy to term, even if we accept that the fetus is a person with the same right to life as the mother's.

Now, to make sure we're on the same page, no argument based on bodily autonomy can justify making sure that the fetus is dead, let alone infanticide or so-called *post-birth abortion*. After delivery, the baby is no longer inside the mother's body, and his or her existence is no longer in conflict with the bodily autonomy of the mother. After all, if the violinist were to survive after being unplugged, you would have no "right to turn round and slit his throat" (p. 66). However, note that Thomson concedes that the fetus has a right to life for the sake of the argument, rather than because she believes this to be true. Her argument is an attempt to justify the right to abortion even if a fetus is a person.

A very similar conclusion is reached by *evictionism*, which departs from the idea that life begins at conception, as so-called *pro-life* supporters defend, but also recognizes women's right to bodily determination, that's defended by pro-choice supporters. Evictionists recognize the mother's right to *evict* the fetus from her body, but not that of securing its death (Block and Whitehead, "Resolving the Abortion Controversy.")

A Moment in Hookup History

Now we can tackle the argument underlying Chappelle's joke, which can be reconstructed as follows. Suppose Dave gets Shonda pregnant and consider the following four possible scenarios. In the first one, both want an abortion. In the second one, Shonda wants to abort, but Dave doesn't. In the third one, it's Dave who wants the abortion, but not Shonda. In the last one, neither wants the abortion. Scenarios one and four are very straightforward since Shonda's decision matches Dave's decision, and no conflict would occur.

Conflict does occur in the other two cases. In the second one, Shonda's decision to abort overrules Dave's wish to have the child. This, surely, may be a great loss to Dave, but at least frees him from parental responsibilities towards that child. In the third case, though, not only does Dave get to have a child he doesn't want, but he also gets parental responsibilities, or at least the obligation to pay child support. Although Shonda is able to effectively renounce parental responsibilities through abortion, Dave isn't. In fact, this holds for all four scenarios. Regardless of what Dave's wishes may be, he gets parental responsibilities if Shonda wants to have the child, and he's free from them if she wants to abort it. This is the point of Chris Rock's remark that abortion is a women's issue.

> The abortion issue, it's a woman's issue. A woman gets pregnant, she don't wanna hear shit from the man. "Fuck you! I don't need you! Motherfuck you!" Unless she decides to have the baby. Then she's like, "Where's my cheque?" (*Never Scared*)

The relation between this and ethical responsibility can be seen in the light of the *principle of alternate possibilities*. According to this principle, an individual is ethically responsible for an action and its foreseeable consequences if and only if he or she could've done otherwise. Although this principle has been fairly criticized on several grounds, discussing that criticism would unnecessarily extend this chapter. The reader will have to trust that this account of ethical responsibility is adequate and sufficient for our purposes.

It seems clear that, in the second scenario, Dave isn't responsible for Shonda's child, since he couldn't have chosen not to have him. That's Shonda's prerogative! Hence, it seems fair that Dave "shouldn't have to pay," since it isn't his responsibility anyway. Moreover, this argument doesn't only free him from the legal obligation to pay, but also establishes that he is not ethically obligated to do so. In scenario three, on the other hand, Shonda may be ethically obligated to have the child, even if she's still granted the legal right to abort.

Nevertheless, there's an important flaw in this argument. Chappelle says that, if the mother decides to have the baby, he can decide to abandon him. However, "having a child" is not a decision that a woman can make alone since, in the case we're considering, this requires a man who agrees to engage with her in sexual intercourse. Such a man would be choosing to participate in an action where begetting a child is a foreseeable consequence, which would make him responsible for that child. A charitable reading of the pro-choice stand would be, instead, that *only women can decide if the fetuses in their wombs become newborns*, which is a different statement. But still, is it fair that men are considered responsible for a child that they didn't want?

Another Moment in Hookup History

Say Dave and Shonda are now partying at a friend's house, but they get bored and decide to borrow a computer from the house to watch porn. Instead of using a safe paid website, though, they enter free websites likely to contain malware and viruses. After some time doing this, Dave decides to leave the party. Shonda stays, but later she discovers that a virus, which could seriously damage the computer, has been spreading through a website they've visited. The good news is that an easily accessible antivirus could prevent any damage from being done if used on time. She then calls Dave to tell him about the situation and discuss what to do.

As in the case of abortion, we can also picture four scenarios. In the first one, both Dave and Shonda decide to use the anti-virus. In the second one, Dave decides not to use it, but Shonda does. In the third one, Dave decides to use it, but not Shonda. In the last one, neither wants to use the anti-virus. Again, the first and fourth scenarios are unproblematic, since Dave's decision matches Shonda's. In scenario one, Shonda will use the anti-virus freeing her and Dave of any responsibility resulting from the computer being damaged. In scenario four, they would both be responsible for the damage caused, and would probably have to pay for it.

Although Dave isn't interested in making things right in scenario two, Shonda's action would still free him from his responsibility, since no damage will be caused. Finally, in scenario three, Shonda's decision would make them both responsible for the damage caused, even when Dave wanted to use the anti-virus. Can we say here that Dave "shouldn't have to pay" just because it wasn't in his power to use the anti-virus? The answer is clearly "no," since his actions (as well as Shonda's) lead to the computer getting the virus. Moreover, Shonda is in no way obligated to free him from his responsibility, even if she'll also suffer the consequences. This holds even if Shonda decides not to tell Dave what is going on. Although she surely is ethically obligated to tell him, failing to do so doesn't free Dave from his share of responsibility.

Abortion is clearly very different from using an anti-virus. You don't get any rights over the infected computer and you couldn't think of it as a person. However, in both situations, Dave and Shonda agreed to do something that risked causing a circumstance where they had to assume responsibilities. That only one of them had the power to prevent it at some point doesn't mean that the other person isn't responsible for its consequences.

First World Girls Gone Wild

In spite of all that's been said, women's unique right to abortion seems to go against the *parity principle*, according to which the mother isn't more of a parent than the father, nor vice versa ("Are You My Mommy?"). This is often interpreted as both parents having equal rights and responsibilities towards their children. This principle justifies, for example, that a parent has to pay child support in case of abandonment, since this somehow compensates for his or her legal obligations as a parent, which are still performed by the other parent.

However, wouldn't this principle entail men's right to participate in the decision of abortion? Moreover, doesn't women's unilateral right to abortion affect men's reproductive rights? More generally, shouldn't birth control be a problem of both parents instead of a problem of the mother alone? This latter issue was debated more than one hundred years ago in the *Birth Control Review*, where Mary W. Dennett answered affirmatively arguing that, since it "takes a man and a woman to produce a child," both parents "should be equally responsible for its birth and rearing."

Other answers concede that "theoretically" this should be a problem of men and women, but that "in practice" this is a women's problem. A very compelling argument is made by Margaret Sanger, the editor of the *Review*, from the idea that humankind's freedom depends on women's freedom, which in turn depends on her freedom to control her body. "No woman," she says, "can call herself free who does not own and control her body," and "until she can choose consciously whether she will or will not be a mother." Furthermore, women's power to control their bodies results in their power to shape the world and "express the feminine spirit," instead of just preserving a "man-made world."

For Sanger, birth control can turn women's burden of pregnancy into their power as selector of the species. In words of Lily Winer, another contributor to the debate: "Bearing children has been her Great Problem. She will make it her Great Privilege—her Great Prerogative."

Women's function as selector of the species is also described by Louis C.K. in his second argument for abortion.

> Women have to decide who lives and dies. That's because they're the female of the species. In the reproductive arena, that's what the female does. They are the selectors. They have to decide this. We give them this responsibility when we fuck them. . . . Men just want to spray the world with their cum, just mist. "More of me. More of me." [*mimicking explosions*] It's her job to go, "That's enough of you, I think. No, that's really enough." . . . And that's why abortion is the last line of defense against shitty people in the species. So, we need them to abort every shitty baby. (2017)

On the other hand, only women are guaranteed to go through what Sanger calls "the valley of the shadow of death" each time they give birth. Even when a man can, and often does, undergo hardships caring for the mother during pregnancy, nature doesn't force him to do any job for his offspring after fertilization is done. In some accounts, this labor performed by the mother results in her having more parental rights than any genetic parent. As Susan Feldman has argued, if parental rights and responsibilities are to be gained in a labor-basis, the standard case would make the mother more of a parent than the father, since she'd add her gestational parental rights to her genetic parental rights ("Multiple Biological Mothers").

When Keeping It Real Ain't Enough

The problem with the previous considerations, though, is that parental rights and responsibilities are there derived from first principles, disregarding the strongly conventional character of how these are assigned in different societies. Not all cultures make biological parents assume a social parental role. For example, among the Trobriand from Melanesia, fatherhood is exercised not by the biological father, but by a brother of the biological mother.

In modern Western societies, paternity is often presumed of biological parents. In some jurisdictions, though, it's common that a man be presumed the legal father of the children of his wife, even if he isn't the biological father. Furthermore, parenthood is often morally earned even when no biological nor legal attachments exist. This is precisely what happens in *The Fresh Prince of Bel Air*, where Uncle Phil is more recognized as Will's father than Lou (Will's biological father).

However, none of these conventions is necessary, nor are they dictated by nature and ethics. It's true that pregnancy is women's great problem and privilege, but historically, men and women have negotiated for sharing these problems and privileges. Monogamy, for example, is a convention that has facilitated this negotiation. Where monogamy works, it forces men to share the burden of pregnancy that nature has imposed only to women, and women's odds to go through a pregnancy alone are seriously reduced. This results in decisions like having a child or an abortion often being made by couples, and not only by women. In that way, men and women have shared the privilege of shaping the world, instead of quarreling about who has this or that right.

Monogamy isn't the only way to make pregnancy (and relationships) work fairly. Nature doesn't force us in one way or another, it just sets the initial conditions to which we, as a species, need to creatively adapt. In doing so, we have to share some burdens and privileges differently forced upon us by nature. The disparity affecting women is that of being the ones guaranteed to take responsibility for their offspring, and we found some perhaps suboptimal solutions to this. A disparity affecting men, is that they cannot legally decide whether or not to renounce parental responsibilities of the offspring they don't want, since abortion isn't something a man can (or should) legally decide. This is no trivial disparity since it means that they'll be legally compelled to pay for child support for several years of their lives. This often causes great hardships to men with low economic resources, who in some jurisdictions can even go to jail for not paying—which further victimizes his child, whose legally recognized father is now in jail.

In order to overcome this disparity, it has been proposed that a father should have the right "to obtain an injunction against the abortion of the fetus he helped create" (*New York Times*, 12/1/05). This proposal certainly conjures horrible "images of women chained to a bed forced to continue a pregnancy against their will" (*Slate*, 6/8/05), which is why I don't endorse it. However, even after one such enforced pregnancy, women often have the option to give up their offspring and their parental responsibilities through anonymous or confidential birth services. Hence, perhaps men's legal obligation to pay child support should also conjure images of men forced to work to maintain a child they didn't want. Isn't this a burden to men similar to that of unwanted pregnancy to women?

Should fathers be granted the legal right to give up their offspring in the same way mothers can abort their fetuses (and even give them up into adoption after birth)? Or is Chappelle perhaps focusing on the wrong issue when he just pushes this right to abandonment, and doesn't address the broader issue of how men and women do and should negotiate their reproductive privileges and burdens?

I'm not quite sure what the answers to these questions are, so you can *think that shit out for yourselves.*[1]

---

[1] I want to thank Fabiola Valeria Cárdenas Maldonado, whose insightful comments helped me improve the ideas and arguments of this chapter.

2

Is Dave Chappelle a Good Role Model?

ANDY WIBLE

Dave Chappelle is a brilliant comedian. He has a deep under-standing of stereotypes and an ability to pinpoint their uncomfortable, insidious, and hilarious implications. Parodies such as Tyrone Biggums's Red Balls energy drink capture our own discomfort with using caffeine and with Black crack addicts like Tyrone (*Chappelle's Show*, Season Two, Episode 5).

Red Bull may get us through a test, but it isn't the miracle drink that the "It gives you wings" advertising suggests. Red Balls gives Tyrone superpower "wings" but it doesn't make him a benevolent superhero. His acute hearing allows him to hear a baby locked in a car from far away, but when he comes to the rescue he steals the car radio rather than saving the baby. He then lifts a city bus to retrieve a quarter. Such incredible insight on drug use, racism, and stereotypes in one thirty second commercial made *Chappelle's Show* beloved by millions.

A diverse audience looked up to Chappelle as a comic genius and a role model. Yet, some of his more recent jokes that seem to defend sexual assaulters and bully the LGBTQ+ community have tarnished his legacy. Now many of his biggest fans consider him insensitive, mean, and spiteful to the most vulnerable in society.

Is Dave Chappelle a good role model? The question isn't whether he should be imitated by someone who wants to be famous, to make lots of money, or even to be funny. The question is whether Chappelle is a virtuous human being who should be emulated. A quick response by some might be, "No, Chappelle drinks, smokes, and recreationally uses drugs. These are all things no role model should do." These are characteristics popularly not thought to make a good role model, especially for children.

While these activities are unhealthy, they are peripheral misdeeds. Virtuous persons are not perfect and can smoke and do drugs in moderation as long as they are morally considerate of others. Nonetheless, role models should not be your normal immoral, faulty, bad decision-making person. They should be overall exemplary persons. They are the MVPs of society such as Gandhi and Jesus. They are moral superheroes.

Chappelle does joke that our fictional superheroes are not good role models on *Just for Laughs*, at age nineteen. In a quick set-up he says, "not because they never help out Black people." An ironic comment comically pointing out the prime reason. He goes on to say that women superheroes are not role models for children due to the way they are dressed. Wonder Woman has hooker boots and sexy blue underwear, and women super-heroes have bad weapons such as a golden lasso that makes you tell the truth.

Superheroes are reflections of society's racism and sexism. They have looks and special abilities that feed into society's popular warped sense of how a good woman should look and behave. Chappelle says that the golden lasso will likely cause a captured male to say, "nice tits" (*Just for Laughs*, 1993). In many ways society's role models are going through the same reassessment. Many Founding Fathers in the United States previously thought to be good roles models are now considered bad due to their owning slaves and promoting slavery and other injustices. Role models and superheroes must not have serious flaws.

A good role model is someone whom others should copy. As Gatorade said, we should "be like Mike" and emulate the great Michael Jordan. They are worthy of being followed. A role model should have expertise and a good character. Such people can exist in a variety of settings. There are special-interest role models for things such as a sports model, career model, faith model, or parent model. Chappelle says his comic role model was Eddie Murphy. Chappelle today could be considered a good role model for other comedians due to his creativity, work ethic, and . . . . . timing. In the *Block Party* movie Chappelle tells of the importance of timing while playing "'Round Midnight" by Thelonious Monk. He says, "One of my favorite musicians because his timing is so ill. Every comedian is a stickler for timing, and Thelonious was off-time and yet perfectly on time. You should study it if you are an aspiring comedian."

Chappelle was never praised more by fellow comedians for his wisdom, honesty, courage, support, and abilities than when he won the 2019 Mark Twain Prize. The irony of the Twain prize was also addressed. Sarah Silverman may have said it best, "It's perfect you are getting the Mark Twain Prize. Because you both love using the N-word in your masterpieces." After 150 years as America's comedy and literary role model, Twain's status is now being questioned. While some excuse his words due to the time he lived and that his words were for comedic irreverence, others see him as a racist who should not continue to be adored.

Bill Cosby was a comedic genius, like Chappelle, but is clearly disqualified from being a good role model due to having assaulted sixty-two young women. A necessary requirement of a role model of any kind is that they be a moral person. The comedian Jerry Lewis was a great comic from his teens to ninety and was known for decades as the host of the Muscular Dystrophy Association Telethon. His legacy was tarnished because he was considered difficult to work with; he made gay slurs on multiple occasions, and he claimed women were bad comedians. Being easy to work with might be important for being a role model. It seems weird to say, "Jerry was a great role model for me, but I couldn't work with him." Unlike a mentor, we don't have to work closely with a role model, but it would seem that the potential should be present. Also, the little evils do add up and perhaps Lewis didn't change with the times.

Then again, no one's perfect. Chappelle has frequently called transgender people "trannies" and joked about transgender females tricking men into sex. A "woke" person today shouldn't harm such vulnerable groups using false and harmful stereotypes. Chappelle using the word "tranny" is as insulting as someone who is not Black using the N-word (a topic Chappelle likes to discuss). Unlike Lewis, Chappelle realized the error, changed his language, and eliminated parts of some jokes. Comedians are risk takers who should recognize moral boundaries and change jokes that unfairly harm the already punished.

What Makes a Good Role Model?

Role models should live a good life, yet how do we determine what a morally good life is? Philosophers have spent a large amount of time discussing this topic. And in Western philosophy it starts back with Plato and Aristotle. They each advocated a type of virtue ethics which holds that morality should be less focused on right and wrong action and more about what makes a person good. Aristotle believed that a virtuous person is morally excellent and moral excellence is required for a happy or flourishing life. Human flourishing or happiness he called *eudaimonia*. It is the ultimate goal and a virtuous character is the necessary means to achieve it. Following the virtues allows us to live up to our full potential as human beings.

How do we become virtuous persons? We should use reason and reflection about what makes a good life and we should imitate virtuous role models such as Socrates, Jesus, Gandhi, or Martin Luther King Jr. Virtue ethics encourages us to be better persons than we are by following those who have exemplary (albeit not perfect) characters. Virtuous persons are like sports stars who do an action and make it look effortless. They live a good life out of habit with less struggle from distracting demons. They have worked hard to develop good habits and continually think deeply about important issues. The result is that making good decisions becomes relatively easy.

The virtuous person has virtues such as honesty, courage, temperance, justice and even wit. These virtues, according to Aristotle, are defined as means between extremes. Courage, for example, is a mean between being a coward and a fool. Humans are rational beings who should know what the appropriate mean is. Plato agrees when he says in the *Laches* that standing firm in battle cannot be courage for it is often foolish to do so. A virtuous person has the wisdom to know when and when not to stand firm. The virtue of temperance is having control when it comes to pleasures. Reason tells us when we should have control and when we shouldn't and then that gets engrained into us through habit. Living our life according to reason and moderation is what makes a good life. A good character allows virtuous persons to be reliable actors in tough situations.

Dave Chappelle in some of his actions has shown a deft ability to be virtuous in difficult situations. He was given the opportunity to earn fifty million dollars to continue his hit show. It was an offer almost anyone would be prone to take. He turned it down due to what it would do to his own flourishing and that of society. He knew the pressure was getting in the way of his performing at a high level. He chose to step away and live a life of temperance rather than decimating himself like comedians John Belushi and Chris Farley who turned to what they thought were performance-enhancing hard drugs to reign as comedic kings. Also, Chappelle believed his humor was being taken wrongly by some people. Some people were laughing at his jokes due to racism. The KKK skits were to mock their awfulness, not cajole them. In an interview with Oprah in 2006 he said, "I was doing sketches that were funny, but morally irresponsible." Finally, he believed that with higher ratings he was being asked more and more to tone down his edgy humor.

Another part of being virtuous is doing actions for the right reasons. The intentions must be good. A virtuous person visits a friend in the hospital because they are in need and the virtuous person cares about them. They don't do it to look good or feel good. Chappelle did his live show *8:46* after the death of George Floyd, tackling some seemingly unfunny issues for the right reasons. He could have made a different type of special that was more leg-slappingly funny than *8:46*. But he wanted to contribute in his own witty and entertaining way to promoting justice when people most needed it.

One criticism of this virtue ethical approach to being a good role model should be considered. Is this conception of a role model a Western, white, male conception that ignores diversity and requires conformity for traditionally marginalized groups to be considered worthy of respect? This criticism is somewhat justified. We should allow diversity in our role models in their style and substance. Marginalized groups have been left out of leadership roles that allow for role models to develop. Chappelle points to some of that history in our superhero role models. Until recently, few major and strong superhero characters were Black, brown, or female. On the other hand, virtues are universal traits that are necessary for any person and culture to thrive. They are found in diverse settings and should be. There can be cultural differences in emphasis or the proper balance of the virtues, but they determine a moral baseline for any culture.

Is It Possible for Comedians to Be Good Role Models?

There are some professions, such as assassin, that prohibit a person from being a good role model due to their being seriously immoral. Is being a comedian one of those professions? Plato thought that laughter and those who produced laughter were to be avoided due to the harm that laughter caused. Plato believed that laughter overrode the rationality that should be in control of our lives. Laughter makes us unable to think clearly. Laughter also causes harm to others. We laugh at people often for their ignorance. They are not as good-looking, as hip, or as wealthy as they think they are. It is wrong to take delight in their immoral or ignorant beliefs and actions. Plato even says in the *Laws* (816e; 935e) that in an ideal state "No composer of comedy, iambic or lyric verse shall be permitted to hold any citizen up to laughter, by word or gesture, with passion or otherwise."

As might be expected, the Stoics agreed that comedy and laughter should be eliminated or tightly controlled. Epictetus, who was said to never have laughed, wrote "Let not your laughter be loud, frequent, or unrestrained." Laughter causes us to be out of control and harms others. Aristotle agreed to an extent. He thinks comedy often expresses scorn and rudeness, and this feeds into people joking too much. He says in the *Nichomachean Ethics* that "Most people enjoy amusement and jesting more than they should." Jesting is a kind of mockery that he says lawmakers should prohibit due to the harm that is caused.

Aristotle did not want to eradicate laughter and comedy. Aristotle saw being a measured comedian as valuable. A ready wit was one of Aristotle's twelve virtues. We enjoy funny people. Comedians are often the life of the party, and a good life should include amusement. Wit also makes conversation better. The cleverness is enjoyed and admired. So, a ready wit may be a necessary condition for being a role model as much as being just. A professional comedian, like Chappelle, then can be a good role model just as a soldier who exemplifies courage. They have one virtue in a very high degree.

Virtues are means between extremes and wit is no exception. Wit is a mean between being a boring dullard at one end and what Aristotle calls a vulgar buffoon at the other extreme. The vulgar buffoon wants humor at all costs and ignores the pain of the object of the laughter. People with wit need to be moral and do no harm. The boring person does not attempt anything laughable and does not find anything funny. The witty person likes to laugh and be funny within boundaries. Consequently, a person with wit rather than the vices of being dull or vulgar will maintain people's attention and communicate better. In today's lingo, a ready wit is a useful soft skill for one's career and in general.

In many ways these two extremes reflect the extremes of our current society or how each side sees the other. The so-called Left sees the Right as buffoons who laugh at people using racist, sexist, or inappropriate jokes. A prime example might be when President Trump mocked Serge Kovaleski in 2016 for asking a question. The rally crowd erupted in laughter when Trump mimicked his contortions. The Left watched in repulsed disbelief. The Right sees the Left as snowflake nervous nellies afraid to laugh and offend anyone. If Epictetus were alive today, he likely would have been a Democrat.

The Virtue of Dave Chappelle

Chappelle does have a ready wit and this is seen in his ability to appeal to both sides of this humor spectrum. Even his critics agree he is not just funny; he is witty due to his creativity and insightfulness in reflecting on society and our place in it. His fans cannot wait to see what comes out of his mouth. It isn't because he is stirring up deep-seated anger like President Trump; it is because his jokes make us think and reflect on our lives. He brings up important and difficult topics cloaking them with laughter. Chappelle's ready wit provokes laughter that is good for society. John Lombardini says that this democratic laughter causes citizens to interact humorously and harmoniously. Joking brings friends, enemies, and strangers together to realize society's faults and inconsistencies, and bonds build on the virtuous ability to make and take a joke.

Let's look at one of Chappelle's stories panned as vulgar. In his *Sticks and Stones* special, Chappelle says he doesn't believe Michael Jackson's accusers' allegations of sexual abuse, but even if their accusations are true, he says, he knows that "more than half the people in this room have been molested in their lives. But it wasn't no goddamn Michael Jackson, was it? This kid got his dick sucked by the King of Pop! All we get is awkward Thanksgivings for the rest of our lives." One criticism of this joke was that it supported Jackson's awful behavior by suggesting it would be an honor to be molested by him. Another was that he shouldn't doubt the accusers. The joke divided people.

The criticism, though, misses the context and subtlety of the story. He sets up the joke by talking about how he is called a victim blamer. For example, if he heard Chris Brown had beaten Brianna, he would ask, "So, what did she do?" For Jackson, he asks, "What were the kids wearing at the time?" His comment is so obviously wrong, that he is clearly using sarcasm to criticize those who would really say such things. When he says he doesn't believe the accusers of Jackson, his critics seem to miss the fact that he is on their side. They don't miss it when he does race-based jokes in a similar form. His sarcasm is clearer since they know he wouldn't be knocking his own team. Chappelle is not excusing Jackson. He is critiquing our love of fame and how it can override the foibles of life. If he is making fun of anything it is our fascination with fame. Fame is so important to people that they are willing to endure horrendous sexual abuse to achieve it.

Chappelle's jokes seem to exemplify the most popular theory of humor called the incongruity theory. Humor takes place because our expectations are violated. The set-up of a joke creates one expectation and then that set-up is violated. For example, Little Johnny jokes are set up with a child doing something and then the dirty adult punchline follows. We expect Chappelle to defend himself against the serious accusations of victim blaming and then he gives examples of himself victim blaming.

Arthur Schopenhauer, not known for his cheery disposition or upbeat philosophy, was a proponent of this theory of humor. He says, "The cause of laughter in every case is simply the sudden perception of the incongruity between a concept and the real objects . . ." There is a discrepancy between our abstract thoughts and reality. A pun such as, "I have a few jokes about unemployed people, but none of them work" is a prime example as well as Schopenhauer's own line, "the person who writes for fools is sure to have a large audience." All humor follows this format for Schopenhauer and the virtue of wit is the ability to recognize and exploit that incongruity. He says a ready wit, "consists entirely in a facility for finding for every object that appears a conception under which it certainly can be thought, though it is very different from all the other objects which come under this conception." The ability to see concepts and ideas differently from how they are normally construed is what makes a ready wit and a great comedian.

Professional comedians, as we have seen, must also have the other virtues as well in order to be moral and a good role model. And it is tougher for comedians like Chappelle who address fundamental and controversial societal issues. Pointing out the inconsistencies in and problematic aspects of societal and individual beliefs can feel offensive and hurtful. Socrates was not a comedian, but he was killed for bringing up problems in people's beliefs. Even though he was killed for being the opposite, Socrates is now widely thought to be an ideal role model due to his good reasoning, honesty, pursuit of truth, and desire to improve society.

Should we look at Chappelle as a contemporary Socrates? In some ways, yes. He is out there exposing the problems of society. His main goal is entertainment, but he is also teaching, challenging, and enlightening us. Perhaps Plato didn't know a comedian with Chappelle's societal insights. Chappelle exemplifies more than wit. He has the other virtues as well. He has justice by exposing poverty, racism, and sexism. Honesty to say what is really occurring and what we are really thinking. Courage to try new material and to be able to get in front of millions to perform. Temperance to not overindulge as many previous comedians have done. Liberality by using his millions for the greater good by donating and raising money for children's causes, arts, healthcare, and even fellow comedians. He also has patience, magnificence, ambition, and friendliness.

He is not perfect; he isn't a superhero. Chappelle action figures are not likely to be produced and he cannot lift a bus like Tyrone Biggums. Chappelle is a real-life hero like Socrates who was at his time venerated and reviled for asking tough questions to improve Athens. Chappelle is making us laugh at the tough issues to entertain and create societal progress. He exposes discrepancies in our own thinking that makes us think more deeply and laugh at our faults, fears, and biases. Most importantly he makes us better people when we follow and act like him. He probably drinks and smokes too much, but parents should still judiciously be willing to say, "behave like Dave."

3
How Old Is Fifteen, Really?

DAVE LYREWOOD

> All our stars, all our stars, man . . . R. Kelly pissed on his victim. I know it was rough, but I mean, again, I can't even judge R. Kelly. First of all, we don't know if these allegations are true or not. Even if they are true, if you want to know how I feel about it, honestly . . . if a man cannot pee on his fans . . . I don't wanna be in show business anymore! Because, well, that's why I got in the game baby, I got dreams, too! You guys are confusing the issue. While you guys are busy worrying about if R. Kelly even peed on this girl or not, you're not asking yourself the real question that America needs to decide once and for all. And that question is: "How old is fifteen, really?"

This is how Dave Chappelle, in his 2004 standup special *For What It's Worth*, kicks off the roughly six-minute-long monologue most commonly known simply as "How old is fifteen, really?"

The bit has grown to be immensely popular, and a YouTube clip containing it has over ten million views to date. In one of the most striking standup bits of his career, Chappelle zooms in the microscope to dissect our views on the vulnerability, capability, and agency of persons in their mid-teens. In doing so, he taps into a long history of unresolved legal, philosophical, and ethical debates, which remain very much alive until this day. But hidden within Chappelle's blunt question—"How old is fifteen, really?"—are at least three separate questions, which he gradually unpacks throughout the bit.

First, there is the question of the cognitive capacities of adolescents: to what degree is the teenage mind developed, in comparison to that of an adult, or that of a younger child? This is mainly a question for researchers in developmental neuroscience and psychology, and plenty of research has been done on the topic in both fields. The neurological maturation process of the human brain begins well before we are born, and typically ends only roughly around the age of twenty-four.

While there are many mysteries remaining around brain development, what is abundantly clear, is that fifteen is an age at which cognitive capabilities and maturity differs *vastly* between individuals, and that development of such traits often is incredibly rapid. One of the reasons why we're "confusing the issue," as Chappelle puts it, is probably that fifteen-year-olds are not a homogenous group in pretty much any relevant category in the first place.

Perhaps there's some common general trait in that fifteen-year-old people are *generally* in the midst of a more or less chaotic period of self-development. And it is this trait that makes the case of a fifteen-year-old person's agency such a conundrum. If the age group is so diverse, dynamic, and difficult to categorize from a neuroscientific and psychological perspective, what do we make of their right to make decisions, and their ability to take responsibility for those decisions?

Getting Pissed on Was the Least of My Worries

Having looked at the cognitive capacities of adolescents, and how they may or may not differ from that of children and adults, the next question we need to ask ourselves is: how should we think about the moral agency and the responsibilities of young people, and what should we expect from them?

As Chappelle asks the question "How old is fifteen, really?" in his now legendary special, the audience moans. Sure, the topic is in itself taboo, but in addition Chappelle set the question up by first discussing the allegations of sexual assault directed towards Michael Jackson. And so, the audience is already on the ropes as Chappelle stands ready with the follow-up:

> No, that's a good question! That's a good question. I'm not saying that a person is as smart as they're going to be at fifteen. That's not what I'm saying, man! But I am saying . . . fifteen to me is old enough to decide whether or not you want to be pissed on. I mean, that's me. If you can't make a decision like that by the time you're fifteen, then just give up, motherfucker, because life is waaay harder than that! I make tougher decisions all the time. If you don't want to get pissed on, just get the fuck out of the way—it's not even a decision! If I start peeing on the front row they won't have to calculate and think "How do I feel about this? Am I okay with it?" They just move! You can do that at fif-

teen. I could have. I've been fifteen. When I was fifteen, I was doing stand-up in nightclubs. I smoked reefer from time to time. My friends were selling crack. I was trying to finger-fuck people. I knew what was happening around me to some degree. Getting pissed on was the least of my worries at fifteen, trust me. But it keeps coming up.

Chappelle argues that, given your cognitive abilities at age fifteen—"knowing what's happening around you to some degree"—you should be able to make decisions and take responsibility for your own life, at least on some basic level. You exercise a certain degree of autonomous agency. But what does "agency" and "autonomy" even mean in this context?

The *Stanford Encyclopedia of Philosophy* defines "agency" in the following way: "an agent is a being with the capacity to act, and 'agency' denotes the exercise or manifestation of this capacity." In a somewhat more detailed manner, the political and legal philosopher Joel Feinberg (1926–2004) distinguished between four ways in which we may understand "autonomy" as a concept.

First, autonomy can be understood as a kind of basic cognitive threshold *capacity* for rational decision-making. We generally hold most adult humans to normally possess this competence, while "a genuinely incompetent being, below the threshold, is incapable of making even foolish, unwise, reckless, or perverse choices. Jellyfish, magnolia trees, rocks, newborn infants, lunatics, and irrevocably comatose former 'persons', if granted the right to make their own decisions, would be incapable of making even 'stupid' choices" (*Harm to Self*, pp. 28–30).

The *second* kind of autonomy Feinberg identified, was that of autonomy as a *de facto* condition: even if a person possesses a competency and cognitive capacity well above the threshold, she might be coerced, incarcerated, temporarily severely ill, or otherwise incapacitated from expressing her autonomy.

The *third* kind of autonomy we sometimes refer to is that of autonomy as a *right* to self-determination and sovereignty. Much as we believe a country has sovereignty to rule itself, we imagine that people have a right to some level of individual freedom and to decide what's best for themselves.

Fourthly and finally, there's autonomy as an *ideal* to strive for—the virtue of being self-made in some sense, and not blindly following what others do or think we should do.

All of these ways in which we can think of autonomy—and perhaps more—feed into how we conceive of adolescent agency. We've already seen the disparate ways in which the fundamental capacity for autonomous decision-making develops throughout childhood and adolescence. Chappelle, in his bit, argues that fifteen-year-olds typically possess the basic capacity to make the relevant kinds of decisions—or "stupid choices," in Feinberg's terminology. And few would dispute that teenagers can make, and indeed do make, stupid choices from time to time.

So why are we, and the crowd present at Chappelle's show, pulling back, hesitating to agree, when he makes his case? Perhaps there is something fishy about the *condition* in which the young people in Chappelle's case studies find themselves. Indeed, it appears that a situation can be coercive, intimidating, or manipulative to a point where it seems that our choices are not completely free, and where we are not entirely accountable for our actions—or omissions. Particularly in situations where unequal power relations are at play—be they caused by age difference, fame, physical strength, or career related implications—we tend to think that victims of harming actions are not responsible, or at the very least less responsible, than others might have been in a similar situation.

In the case of the R. Kelly scandal, and other examples depicted by Chappelle, including the kidnapping of young girls, unequal power relations are clearly heavily in play, removing any potential accountability from the victims. Hearing the moans of the audience, Chappelle concedes that his case is not watertight, and admits that he might "sound mean." But he has brought more ammunition.

Send The Rock to Arrest Him!

I know I sound mean. And I know what the people are thinking when I'm saying this—"Dave, she's only fifteen"—Alright, but that's the discrepancy, because when you talk about a "little girl" (like Elizabeth Smart) then the country feels like fifteen is so young and so innocent. On the flip side, here comes "fifteen" again. Now we're talking about a fifteen-year-old Black kid in Florida. This Black kid accidentally killed his neighbor when he was practicing wrestling moves that he saw on TV. Now, was he a "kid"? No! They gave him life. They always try our fifteen-year-olds as adults: "This n****r knew what he was doing. He's a goddamn pile driver. . . . This kid gets on the ropes, there's no stopping him. We'd have to send The Rock to arrest him!" And they gave a fifteen-year-old boy life in jail . . . If you think that it's okay to give him life in jail, it should be legal to pee on him. That's all I'm saying.

With this, Chappelle hammers home his point, and the third question we need to ask ourselves is: cognitive and moral abilities, and social pressures and temporary autonomy reductions all taken into consideration, to what extent can we—and should we—hold adolescents accountable for their own actions, decisions, and omissions?

In many countries, for instance, medical procedures require the consent of caregivers if the patient is younger than eighteen—not the consent of the patient. Similarly, the age at which a person may legally make the decision to move from one state to another without or against the will of her caregivers, is also usually eighteen. Although the establishing of this threshold—the "age of majority"—at eighteen years of age has been criticized as being arbitrary, and religiously or politically driven rather than based on psychological and neuroscientific research, it remains the line drawn by more than half of the countries on Earth today. Nonetheless, there are many other thresholds decided by age, which affect young people. The absolute majority of countries around the world, including the UK, the US, Canada and Australia, ascribe criminal responsibility to children significantly younger than eighteen, almost always encompassing the age of fifteen. Sometimes with reduced penalty scales, sometimes not. To varying degrees, these thresholds are set by a general appreciation of when a person is morally and cognitively mature enough to take responsibility—and to be held accountable for her own actions. However, the age at which these abilities are deemed to generally set in ranges all the way from seven to twenty-one, depending on where in the world we turn, and on what kind of crime has been committed.

At age fifteen, as Chappelle points out, there seems to be a strange discrepancy at play, where society on the one hand holds adolescents accountable for their actions, while at the same time prohibiting them from making decisions requiring similar levels of cognitive abilities. In 2018, researchers from the US and the UK compared age and maturity related factors in medical decision-making, to those of criminal accountability, in different countries. They found that the two domains required largely the same capacities, connected to the fundamental ability to process factual and moral information, and to weigh pros and cons in a rational manner. So why are we judging adolescents so differently in these domains? And is it right and just to do so?

The Chappellean Discrepancy

These questions relate to what Feinberg referred to as "autonomy as Sovereignty"—the right to self-government. More explicitly, Feinberg describes it as "the right to make choices and decisions—what to put into my body, what contacts with my body to permit, where and how to move my body through public space, how to use my chattels and physical property, what personal information to disclose to others, what information to conceal," and, more fundamentally, "the right to decide how one is to live one's life, in particular how to make the critical life decisions" (*Harm to Self*, p 54).

The respect for this basic right to autonomy, sovereignty, and self-governance, is inherently relational: we cannot make sovereign choices for ourselves if others do not respect our right to do so, or do not allow our autonomy to be exercised. And this is where the problem with the "Chappellean Discrepancy" becomes clear. If we agree that a fifteen-year-old, in general, has the *fundamental capacity* to make rational decisions, and is in a *condition* to do so (insofar as not being coerced, threatened, manipulated, enslaved, or beyond her wits for any external reason) to a point where she can be held accountable for criminal actions, then it follows that she also has a right to sovereign self-government—a right which is clearly infringed when the same person wishes to make a medical decision, or to leave the country, and is prohibited from doing so.

The example of having a right to leave the country, or state for that matter, is of particular interest, as it pushes the issue to its edge. According to prominent streams of political philosophy and social theory, citizens choosing to stay and participate in any given society implicitly sign a "social contract" specific to that society, to which they agree to adhere. To undo the signing of such a contract, they would need to either revolt, or leave the society in question, to live stateless or to adhere to the contract of a different state. Similarly, to be held in a society where you cannot leave or potentially contract, is to be incarcerated. As French philosopher Jean-Jacques Rousseau famously put it: "Man is born free; and everywhere he is in chains."

The crux of adolescent agency is that fifteen-year-olds, in most places in the world, are held accountable to violations of a social contract they have not signed, and cannot legally opt out of: they are of age to be held criminally accountable, but not of age to vote, nor to legally leave the country by their own choice. In this way, adolescents under the age of eighteen are being held by systems in which they have no political representation, no power to speak of in terms of policy or economy, and no legal way out. Yet, those very systems will impose oftentimes cruel and harsh punishments on the same individuals.

You Can't Hold Me Prisoner around Shit I Recognize—I'll Break Away!

And so, almost twenty years after Chappelle's stand-up special, and despite centuries of philosophical debates, international treaties, and civil rights movements, the Chappellean Discrepancy—the gap between domains in responsibility, accountability, and rights of children and adolescents—remains an ethical conundrum. We still haven't figured out how to conceive of the gradual emergence of autonomy and agency; how to understand the development of accountability and responsibility; how to distinguish between childhood, adolescence, and adulthood. And it's having devastating effects on those young people whose life choices are not respected, and whose protests and demands are ignored by systems which do not recognize them as citizens.

It really is quite remarkable that more has not been done to address this problem, when we consider the force of nature that adolescent agency *can* be: from the Extinction Rebellion to the BLM protests, to the revolt in Hong Kong, young people across the globe have been taking action to combat systems which are not only unjust and oppressive, but violent and lethal. Clearly there are enormous amounts of willpower and well-informed agency packed within these movements. Yet, many of their constituents are continuously and consistently deemed incapable of deciding who to vote for, what medical procedures to go through with, or whether or not they would like to stay in their current state of residence.

As Chappelle wraps his bit up and moves on in his standup special, the questions raised about the peculiar age of fifteen remain unanswered. As so many times with Chappelle's comedy, the point is not so much to make a moral statement, as it is to look through the lens of absurdity and make the audience see that we need to think for ourselves. Because, although Chappelle dresses the bit up as an argument about the hypocrisy of our stances concerning the autonomy and accountability of young people, underneath, he is empathizing with the difficulty of the topic. By unpacking and analyzing the underlying issues of adolescent agency—from the cognitive capacities of teenagers, to their level and ability of moral reasoning and responsibility-taking, to the ways in which we should hold them accountable for their actions or make decisions for them—we're tricked into wrestling with the complexities of developing moral agency.

The sheer depth of this unpacking makes the final joke of the bit all the more brilliant: after riling up the audience, having us tumble between contemplation, laughter, and moral outrage, Chappelle closes with pretending that the question is just as simple as before he started rummaging around in it:

> You've got to make up your mind across the board how old fifteen actually is. That's all I'm saying.

4

Who Is John Galt? Dave Chappelle!

ROGER HUNT

Dave Chappelle is misogynistic, obscene and a terrible influence on youth; but he has also won prestigious awards, been hailed by many as the voice of his generation, and was even invited for a deep exploration of his career, with Maya Angelou among others. If anyone could be called a master of toeing the line, it's Dave Chappelle.

Ayn Rand, on the other hand, was not so graceful. While she also created without boundaries, she failed to achieve quite the broad appeal of Dave Chappelle, and instead settled into a cultish, closed community. While this community has been wildly influential, she never achieved the same kind of acceptance as Dave.

Ayn Rand was a mid-twentieth-century writer whose novels feature moral, political, and individualist themes. Former Federal Reserve Chair Alan Greenspan was in her tight circle and former Speaker of the House of Representatives Paul Ryan, Senator Rand Paul, and Washington insider Grover Norquist have claimed her as among their greatest influences. She has many detractors, however, who not only refuse to label her work "philosophy," but also reject her ideology as defending greed, avoiding social responsibility and encouraging anti-intellectual, destructive instincts. To capture her "philosophy" in a nutshell: things are what they are and you bear full responsibility for what happens to you.

The Backstory on Galt

Atlas Shrugged, the second commercial success by Ayn Rand, was published in 1957. While writing *Atlas* and after having achieved financial security from her first novel, *The*

Fountainhead, Rand was living in Los Angeles where she held a loosely organized weekend philosophical forum to discuss the economic ideas of Ludwig Von Mises—a towering critic of socialism and US foreign military intervention—and ethical theories which would eventually become a moral defense of "rational self-interest" she called Objectivism.

To detractors, Objectivism is a "Do whatever you want whenever you want and damn those who try to stop you" ethic. For others, it's a beacon of clarity and respect for the individual in an increasingly globalized world. *Atlas Shrugged* is the *magnum opus* of this point of view. Sixty of the almost one thousand pages are dedicated to a long, long defense and explanation of "rational self-interest" as the proper moral stance for the future. These sixty pages are written as a speech delivered by John Galt after he hacked into the radio broadcasting system (the novel is set around 1957).

Naturally, we might wonder: who is John Galt? This question serves as an important plot device throughout the novel as we only meet Galt near the end. For reference, *The Wizard of Oz* works the same way. A group of people going off to find this mysterious wizard; "we're off to see the wizard" is the same thing as "Who is John Galt," but with a twist, as some characters in the novel ask this question in the same way people today might say, "Who knows?" or "C'est la vie" or "It is what it is."

We come to learn that John Galt was a promising philosophy student, then a brilliant engineer, then a social activist against Socialism, then he disappeared. The key event occurs while he is working as an engineer and the company implements a series of policies which distribute the profits equally amongst the workers. Galt not only doesn't think this is fair since the better workers should get a bigger share, but more importantly he argues that this policy will result in the collapse of the company. Unable to convince the group, he retreats to a secret location. While in hiding, he hatches a plan to prove to the world that they cannot exploit the talents of exceptional people to benefit the less talented. The plan—and the prevailing thought experiment subsuming the philosophical argument of the novel—is to remove all the talented people from society, as he states the iconic line, "I will stop the motor of the world." The theory is that *if* all the talented people leave, *then* society will fall apart. *Therefore*, society should value and reward the talented people more than everyone else.

You might think "Well, don't we already do that?"

Galt argues that we do not. For while we have been following an ethic of altruism and helping others, evil people who exploit the system have come into power. In order to maintain power, they equalize the talented—who would otherwise take power from them—with the untalented—who are then grateful to the bad people for giving them things they would otherwise be unable to achieve on their own. So, *if* all the talented people went on strike, *then* those people balancing and exploiting this exchange would have no way to make sure the lights stay on, literally. (Spoiler alert: at the end of the book the lights in New York go off and Galt and the talented people return to pick up the pieces and implement a new world order). To put it another way: we need to stop people who exploit those with talent.

The Backstory on Chappelle

Perhaps you can already see the parallel to Chappelle's life. He was an extremely talented standup comic, successful actor, and innovative variety show producer; then got fed up with the system and turned down a fifty-million-dollar contract on principle; disappeared to South Africa for a few weeks, then stayed home to raise his family; and now he's back!

John Galt stopped the motor of the world on purpose and came back to clean everything up. Chappelle certainly didn't think everything was going to stop when he left, but he recognized the same thing Galt did: there is severe injustice in the world. While Galt took on the responsibility of hatching a grand plan to change the world, Chappelle lives in the real world and does what you're supposed to when you feel powerless: take a beat and think. The two ultimately came to the same conclusion: to change the world you must first take individual responsibility.

For those of us growing up in the 2000s, we probably didn't see Chappelle's pensive side. Re-watching old HBO specials, however, you can see many of the same themes and issues he talks about now—still in between filthy jokes, but these days he highlights social themes rather than sex and drugs. I remember watching *Chappelle's Show* when it first aired and thinking: "This guy is deep . . . wait, the guy from *Half-Baked*!!??" Little did we know at the time, not only was he deep, he was also seething with anger at the system. He was angry at the networks for exploiting him, society for dismissing him as only being the jokes he told, and himself for playing into it.

The irony is that laced within those seemingly goofy sketches and dick jokes are important social and cultural critiques. Whether or not you see them depends on how you see Dave Chappelle. Thus, by choosing to step back, travel to South Africa, mourn the loss of his father, and raise his children, he allows that commentary to come to the surface. Sometimes the best way to get your point across is to be quiet . . . sometimes.

The Moment

John Galt becomes John Galt when he stands up at the company meeting and declares that management's decision to distribute the company's profits equally, rather than according to the value of each individual employee, would destroy the company. Dave Chappelle became the Dave Chappelle we know today when he abruptly quit *Chappelle's Show* because he felt exploited by Comedy Central.

We can easily imagine a devotee of Ayn Rand thinking Chappelle was *not* acting according to rational self-interest because he gave up fifty million dollars. I submit Dave Chappelle and John Galt are indeed fighting for the same thing: the ability to *"live as a heroic being, with his own happiness as the moral purpose of his life, with productive achievement as his noblest activity, and reason as his only absolute"* (From the "about the author" section of *Atlas Shrugged*). This is as clear as Rand can be; Galt surely believes it as well. But does Chappelle?

The first objection might be that Chappelle isn't greedy enough to be an Objectivist. There are two issues with this claim, however.

First, even though Chappelle walked away from fifty million dollars, he is outspoken about protecting what's his. He makes a concerted effort to exert respect for the individual, especially oneself. At the end of the day, the only one who can protect you is you. When he moves to Ohio and a white guy walks across his lawn, does Dave call the cops? No: "I see a white dude walking across my property, entitled, like he's supposed to be there. He had a rifle over his shoulder, too. Ain't that a bitch? I said, 'What the fuck is this guy doing on my property?' I was mad as shit, but I was unarmed. So, I ended up just waving to this motherfucker like a bitch. I was just, like . . . And as soon as he got far enough away, I ran to my car and sped to Kmart" (*Sticks and Stones*).

Second, Objectivism doesn't glorify greed in that seven deadly sins sense. It's not wanting to "get all the money" greed, but rather greed for your self. Galt's primary concern is about whether the structure as a whole can survive an ethic which redistributes wealth. That is, it isn't necessarily his own rational self-interest he is protecting, but rather ensuring the conditions which allow acting in accordance with rational self-interest. If the plant owners redistribute the wealth, then he will no longer be able to exercise rational self-interest and thus will remain enslaved to a system which he cannot control. The solution to that problem is to attack the arbiters of it. Galt believes that the plant owners are implementing these policies so that they can control the workers. Furthermore, they need to control the workers this way because as managers they are weak and talentless. No one would follow them because of who they are, so they need to structure their system to maintain power. Give people a little undeserved income and they will be grateful, devote themselves to you, and give up their power to act in accordance with their own interests. Meanwhile, the people with talent are also forced to give up their power. Not only is it unfair for those with talent to sacrifice what they deserve, but the system will necessarily devolve and eventually collapse.

Galt is unable to convince the workers to resist management, so he runs off. While out and about he comes up with the experiment: in order to prove that society should reward those with talent, Galt asks all those with talent to go on strike. Lo and behold, he succeeds. All the talented people leave the world to live with Galt in a little off-grid community, the world comes crashing down, and Galt leads them back to pick up the pieces and rebuild.

The key factor here is Galt's rejection of a power structure managed by those who leverage the weak to control the talented and thus maintain their own power. Dave Chappelle resists the very same power dynamic when he decides to bail on *Chappelle's Show*. He is not being greedy regarding the money, but rather greedy regarding himself. He wants himself to himself.

Ownership over one's self is *the* theme of the new Dave Chappelle. Whether he is discussing race, religion, money, or celebrity, he's concerned with ensuring that the (his?) self is exalted. This is also the key feature of Objectivism. Although shrouded in ideas of money, greed, and anti-Communist rhetoric, Objectivism is about having complete ownership over yourself and resisting the forces that try to take control over yourself away from you. In his discussion with Maya Angelou, Maya says, "There is a line beyond which you will not go when lots of money is dangled before people's eyes" (*Iconoclasts*, 2006), and this raises the question: who is more greedy?

The person who takes the money or the person who takes themselves? I'd suggest it's the latter, and I think Galt and Chappelle would agree.

But Not That Kind of Greed!

There's not caring about yourself at all and then there's only caring about yourself. And both methods fail. Instead, you need to be the right amount of greedy. So what is the right amount of greed? Well for Dave and John, it depends on who you are: there are those of us in this world—bless their hearts—who even if they wanted to help and do good things, they simply couldn't. We lack the skills, knowledge, or determination to do much of anything. Then there are others who would succeed no matter what they do! *Some people are better than others.*

 Now, the problem is: how do we organize a world where some people are better than others!? There are two extremes: A. let everyone fight it out and may the best win; Z. give everyone the same amount no matter what. I don't think anyone seriously believes either option is a good idea, but those who lean towards one side love to cast those who lean towards the other as only representing the extreme; and perhaps no one is more guilty of this miscasting than Ayn Rand herself. She wrote in a letter that Z people (as I call them!), "deprive 'those favored by nature' (the talented, the intelligent, the creative) of the right to the rewards they produce (the right to life)—and grant to the incompetent, the stupid, the slothful, a right to the effortless enjoyment of the rewards they could not produce, could not imagine, and would not know what to do with" (*Philosophy: Who Needs It?*). Much like our tribal culture today, she groups anyone even slightly to left of her position as an outright violent, Stalinist Communist; but even though Ayn Rand wrote John Galt's words, I think he holds a slightly different view, and those differences make him not only more interesting intellectually, but also similar to Dave.

In his manifesto speech in *Atlas Shrugged*, Galt, clearly channeling Rand, waxes and wanes in a relatively sophomoric way about free will, rationality, and morality. While his results may not be that interesting, the problem he is responding to is very important. Galt rallied against his employers who wanted to distribute company profits equally to all employees, and after that failed, he disappeared and started convincing other powerful people to go on strike. If all the important people went on strike, then the *engine of the world would stop turning.* He says, "We are on strike against self-immolation. We are on strike against the creed of unearned rewards and unrewarded duties. We are on strike against the dogma that the pursuit of one's happiness is evil. We are on strike against the doctrine that life is guilt" (*Atlas Shrugged*). When in fact the "engine" does stop, he returns to the chaos and delivers his speech after hijacking a local radio station. He not only explains why he did what he did, but also what people need to do to move forward. The key insight is that the world does not only consist of producers and non-producers, but also managers. And the managers cause the problems. Producers are happy to employ and support non-producers in so far as they contribute their time and energy to projects, but producers shouldn't be expected to support non-producers because of what Galt calls a "false morality of guilt." Where does that morality of guilt come from? The managers. That's their tool. The managers take a cut for implementing and sustaining the false morality. Galt set the producers on strike against the managers, not necessarily the non-producers.

In a similar vein, Dave tells a gut wrenching story about Iceberg Slim, a manager of escorts c. 1940 and the author of *Pimp*. In this wonderful moment of dark truth and self-expression, Dave delivers a transparent vision of what he thinks is wrong with the world. He introduces the Iceberg Slim story with, "We should take care of each other . . . We should forgive the ones of us that are weaker and support the ones of us that are stronger. And then we can beat the thing. If you guys keep going after individuals, the system is going to stay intact" (*The Bird Revelation*). What system is he talking about? I think it's the same system John Galt is talking about. Some people are better than others, and we could live together and help each other out if it weren't for these managers, networks, and pimps hustling out their cut for doing nothing.

In the story about Iceberg, Dave notes the pimp's skills: being able to tell a prostitute's mileage (how many tricks she could turn before she loses her mind); how to control a prostitute; and, his most important skill, how to get more out of someone than he originally thought he could, or how to extend the prostitute's mileage. Slim doesn't produce anything, he just keeps the bitch in line and takes his cut. Dave marvels at "the coldest capitalist concepts I've ever heard in my life. He describes in detail how these men break women so that they will give them the money that they make with their own bodies" (*The Bird Revelation*). This is exactly what John Galt's revolt is about: non-producers exploiting the work of the producers. Pimps exploiting hoes. Managers exploiting workers. Dave doesn't shy away from the obvious analogy: "Why the fuck you think most of us work from nine to five? 'Cause nine to six might kill a bitch" (*The Bird Revelation*).

So what does self-determination require? How do you know if you're a producer? And what can you do to make sure you don't exploit others? For Dave and John that means understanding your value: "You will never get your fucking money back. Fuck that. I'm like Evel Knievel: I get paid for the attempt" (*The Age of Spin*).

Perhaps Too far?

So, how does someone come to an understanding of their value? Luckily—just before I submitted the final version of this chapter—Dave posted *Unforgiven* on Instagram, in which he explains his view on how to do this! For what it's worth, I don't agree with Dave, but what is a philosophy essay without a little critique?!

There are two potential errors one could make: first, you need to make sure you aren't undervaluing yourself, since if people undervalue themselves, then those who understand the system will take advantage of that surplus; second, you cannot overvalue yourself, or the system will simply reject you. I think Dave's provocation is an important step towards opening people's minds to the fact that they are undervalued by the system and need to advocate for themselves. Unfortunately, he doesn't sufficiently warn people about the dangers of overvaluing.

In the *Unforgiven* taping, Dave tells three stories. First, him watching a three-card monte racket. Second, his contract signing with Comedy Central for *Chappelle's Show*. Third, his demands that Netflix stop streaming *Chappelle's Show* until he is properly compensated for his work. Across these three experiences, Dave makes three critical errors as a result of improperly valuing himself, but he only recognizes one of them. Because he doesn't acknowledge the other two lessons, he takes a suboptimal course of action to get what he deserves, and perhaps importantly he sacrifices opportunity to affect the system itself.

While it may work out for him (Netflix did in fact stop streaming *Chappelle's Show* as of my finishing this chapter), taking such a risk is not recommended for those in similar situations. Instead, those who would otherwise follow his lead should heed not only the first lesson, but the other two as well.

Lesson One: Never Get between a Man and His Meal (Three-card Monte)

The most obvious challenge when valuing yourself is negotiating the fact that everyone else is valuing themselves as well! If you value yourself in a way that completely disrupts your counterparts' valuing, then you won't make a deal. At worst, you'll get beat up, or killed . . . Sidenote: my favorite line from *Upload*: "You threatened a six-billion-dollar industry and nobody murdered you, right . . . nobody murders anyone anymore."

Dave relies on this principle a lot. It's the basis of his criticism of the #MeToo movement. You can't call bullshit on the system, and expect the system to magically conform to your critique. Instead, you need to understand not only what you think your value is, but also how the system values you. And if there is a mismatch, you need to position yourself to negotiate with the system to either achieve an acceptable valuation OR create the opportunity for revolution. If you strike too soon, you'll lose. Strike too late, and you'll have to accept your fate.

There is the micro-tactical lesson about how to gain power, and then there's the macro lesson about what to do when you have the power. This raises an important distinction between Dave and Ayn Rand, in fact. Dave learned that if you are lucky enough to have won from the minority position, then you have to set your sights on bigger fish. Ayn Rand, on the other hand, continued to attack the same group after she found success. She continued to fight for herself even after she had won. The effect is that she devalued herself by fighting down, and lost the respect of those she originally sought to impact.

Lesson Two: Set the Right Expectations for Yourself (Signing the Comedy Central Deal)

Dave transitions from the three-card monte mishap to signing the deal with Comedy Central. He recognized the same dynamic: a bunch of people who know each other chewing up the greenie. Rather than getting beat up, he accepts what he considers a raw deal. In this case, however, Dave makes a mistake. He assumes that the board room is the same dynamic, and that he should understand this scenario as reifying the previous lesson. Instead, there is another lesson: in any given scenario you need to not only understand your value, but also set the right expectation.

It's a rare scenario that you will ever receive value equivalent to your value. Normally, you'll have to accept some kind of discount. However, you can mitigate the harm from taking the discount by factoring in your situation when you enter the negotiation. If you have nothing to begin with, then you need to set the expectation for your return commensurate to your needs. You might be worth one hundred million dollars, but you have very little leverage to start so you have to make sure you get what you need from the transaction rather than holding out for what you think you deserve. That is, if you overvalue what you think you should get, you will likely end up getting nothing. And, of course, this is what happened to Dave.

Unfortunately, he doesn't learn this lesson. Instead, he falsely equivocates it to the three-card monte scam. But it isn't the same hustle. The network wasn't simply grifting him. They were factoring the risk of developing his show and the fifty other shows they were piloting at the time. Their return on one success has to cover the loss on the other forty-nine. Forking away from this realization and understanding the network to function like a three-card monte scam sends him down a dangerous route . . . the route Ayn Rand took. I think Dave is striking too soon, and the revolution will fail. BUT, we are still watching this play out and I could very well be wrong.

Lesson Three: Your Value Determines Your Future, Not Your Past (What to Do with Chappelle's Show?)

Because Dave fails to learn Lesson #2, he makes what I think is the gravest error, and the error has nothing to do with his scuffle with Comedy Central or networks in general. The mistake is to Monday morning QB and attempt to rectify systemic injustice. The biggest problem with this is that he KNOWS this lesson. It's the same lesson he teaches to the #MeToo movement. If you try to change the system, it will rebound on you threefold. That is, once you've won, you need to look to the future.

The success was in recognizing the failures and attempting to rebuild the system moving forward, not looking for reparations from the past. Should the networks compensate Dave? Sure. They probably should write him a check. But will that change anything? No. Dave just gets a bunch of money. Whoopie. But that won't change anything except get him a bigger house! And if his gripe for reparations fails, then he is in an even weaker position to enact systemic change. He's picking a fight for a phantom payoff at the cost of the mission.

Dave has a choice. He knows his value now. Project that value into the future to create a new system. Don't make the same mistake as Ayn Rand and hold a grudge against the old one. And he touches on it: Yes, do a new *Chappelle's Show*! Own that show. Move on and create even better stuff, rather than trying to collect on the current value of old stuff.

Closing the Set

Ayn Rand is a tricky person to evaluate philosophically. Objectivism is loose, naive thinking. But there is something important to recognize: understand your own value. Every philosopher and revolutionary understands this, so pointing it out is typically unnecessary; unless you're speaking to people who haven't spent time to explore and evaluate these questions, which unfortunately describes many people!

I don't think Dave is a megaphone for Rand. But he does tease out and give new life to her core insight.

II

Going Hard
in the Paint

5

A Master of Comedic Irony

RAYMOND PERRIER

Imagine that you're in the audience at one of Dave Chappelle's comedy shows. He's already walked out onto the stage and he starts telling you a story.

It seems like a fairly innocuous story at first, but he starts adding characters to it and uses different voices to indicate who is talking at different moments. His mannerisms draw you in, and his tone of voice changes to increase or decrease tension. Maybe he even uses the microphone for an added sound effect (thump!). About two minutes in he gets to a punchline and the story starts to come together. Before this punchline, you and the crowd were already wound up with comedic tension. You may have caught yourself smiling just in anticipation or as a result of Chappelle's calm, relaxed, but intensely playful demeanor on stage. At some point, the final piece of the joke lands and everyone starts to roar with laughter. Even Chappelle starts to laugh a little and smacks the microphone on his knee as he tries to keep his composure.

That's what the comedic moment feels like from our perspective: anticipation, tension and build up, with a tinge of exhilaration. But let's imagine what it's like to be Chappelle in that moment. He's telling a story and acting out a skit that he made up. Or maybe he's recounting a story from an experience in his past, one that he personally had. This is not the first time he has told the story, and he has likely gone through several rewrites of it. He even knows the end of the joke; he knows when it's coming even though the audience doesn't. The audience doesn't even know where it's going or what subverted idea is going to turn the whole narrative on its head.

This imbalance of knowing is what makes the whole experience deeply ironic. The comedian knows something that we don't know, which gives them more control over the outcome. This fundamental sense of irony gives each and every comedian leverage to execute the first goal of all comedy: to make us laugh. But with a comedian like Chappelle there's a second goal, which is more subversive and ironic. The second goal comes from a desire to leverage our perspective against us. It is his goal to deceive us into a new truth or perspective that compels us to share some fundamental truth that Chappelle thinks is important. This second goal is one aspect of many that make Dave Chappelle a master of comedic irony.

Irony is a Common form of Communication

Everyone who has heard a joke experiences a common feeling of irony—not knowing what is going to be said next, not knowing the ending, the punchline. The ignorance at the outset of the joke creates intrigue, tension, and the anticipation that lends to a good dose of humorous shock. A good comedian can design and deliver a joke where the revelation of a punchline releases comedic tension, ideally, through laughter. The comedian knows the ending, but you don't. The comedian knows where it begins, ends, and everything in between, but you don't.

This is a common experience that is one essential feature of why comedy seems to work so well on human beings, but it is also so common and basic to human interactions that it's almost not worth mentioning in philosophical conversations. So, what makes it important here? Quite simply, it's important because it rests at the core of the human experience. It is a universal experience that shows what humans have in common with one another. What's more is that irony is a common human phenomenon that incidentally exposes hidden truths about who we are, sometimes the experience of irony can completely disrupt or change our perspective about the world. This ironic mechanism—the ability to expose hidden truths—is one feature of Chappelle's comedy that is essential to his success. He knows how the joke ends, but before that he knows why the joke is important. He knows that there is some interesting truth about being human that is revealed through the humor contained within the joke.

In philosophical terms the idea of irony goes back a long way. One of the more recent historical examples is seen in the works of Søren Kierkegaard, who lived in Denmark during the 1800s. Irony has always been a powerful tool for communicating ideas or understanding how we communicate ideas in different settings, whether the setting is created in a theater or in the pages of a book, but Kierkegaard believed that irony was especially useful for deceiving someone into a truth they had never conceived of before. For example, a sophisticated use of irony can trick a reader, viewer, or audience member into sympathizing with someone who stands in direct contradiction with their values. Writers from a TV series might create sympathy for the "bad guy" by giving personal details of their past that ultimately humanize them or by creating situations where you can glimpse a moment of compassion. It deceives the viewer on some level by pointing out that even "bad guys" are still humans with pasts and feelings and personal struggles—just like you and me. They use familiarity, commonality, to create sympathy and interest in the "bad guy."

Comedic irony can have equally complex layers of communication that attempt to bring the audience to a different perception of truth, or at least a very simple and different way of seeing the world around them. But it usually takes on a different tone from TV shows and movies since its intention is to facilitate this deception, or transformation of perspective, through laughter and humor.

Calling Chappelle a master of irony means that he understands it's not enough to know something, to understand that something is true. What's more important is knowing how to communicate the realities of truth. And in the end even if you are an excellent storyteller, playwright, or comedian, it's not enough to communicate all truths directly. Some audiences are not ready, are not mentally prepared, emotionally prepared, culturally prepared, or intellectually prepared to follow the logic of the comedian's revelation—assuming it is logical.

So, when I say that Dave Chappelle is a master of comedic irony, I mean that he uses comedy to engage his audience in a very specific way. He utilizes an indirect form of communication, and as a consequence his comedic irony often acts like a kind of deception or trick. He takes truth and wraps it up in such a way that it deceives his audience into some deeper and more fundamental truth about being human. He does this in different ways but some of the more subversive ways are represented in his jokes that reveal white ignorance within American society. Chappelle frequently uses his famous "white person voice" in his standup and, in *Chappelle's Show* he has several skits on Black masculinity, both of which are means of subverting Hollywood stereotypes. His use of irony is not the only way that Chappelle communicates with his audience, but it is one of the more sophisticated methods he utilizes in his comedy.

Chappelle's White Voice Subverts Hollywood Stereotypes

In his first HBO comedy special *Killin' Them Softly*, Dave Chappelle introduces his audience to a whirlwind of iconic characters and voices that reveal certain realities of race relations in America. Take Chappelle's "white man" voice as a prime example of his comedic irony. This voice is ostensibly funny because a Black comedian uses a special voice to indicate when he is playing a white man. It's hard to pin down why it's funny; no single reason can ever be given why something is funny, but on one level the laughter emerges through a moment of self-awareness. The audience comes to an awareness that stereotypical voices are not objectively truthful since no single individual sounds exactly like any other individual. And yet we all recognize the tone and timbre of this general white man voice when Chappelle uses it. Ironically, we know that no voice is exactly like any other and yet it's funny because it is recognizably "white sounding." The impact of this irony on the audience is heightened more because the stereotype comes from the perspective of a non-white person. Chappelle is using the voice ironically to lean into and highlight the pervasiveness of stereotypes in American culture.

The voice, in a deeper sense, is also subversive. The targets of this irony are Hollywood cultural motifs. First, it subverts the common stereotype perpetuated by Hollywood that only Black men speak in a stereotypical way. Second, it subverts Hollywood because the voice is created by a Black man whose culture is largely excluded from Hollywood or misrepresented by it. The execution of Chappelle's "white voice" is hilarious, and it's ironic because it allows Chappelle to ease his audience into a different perspective: the way white people talk is funny too. This small revelation to the audience (or confirmation for those who needed no convincing of Chappelle's point of view) shows how irony can reveal the cultural perception that whiteness = normal. The "white voice" is a simple but highly effective deception that eases his audience into more complex narratives of white ignorance.

Chip and the Problem of White Ignorance

White cultural normativity is part of what perpetuates white ignorance in America, and de-scaffolding white ignorance can be accomplished more easily by highlighting the fallacy of white cultural normativity. During his same HBO comedy special, Chappelle introduces us to a more complex normative white male character named Chip, who is a friend that Chappelle alludes to several times in this comedy special. Chappelle's introduction of Chip goes well beyond the irony of stereotypical voices. The prominent theme is Chip's ignorance of Black fear in America, specifically fear of police. Chappelle is fearful and concerned that each of his police experiences will end in brutality or death, while his friend Chip is quite ignorant of these fears. Of course, Chappelle wraps this entire series into a hilarious web of stereotypes by, again, falling back on his use of voices for each character of the story. There is his white friend Chip, a cartoonish sounding police officer, and Chappelle's personal narration of this experience.

Irony plays extremely well with the audience as Chapelle explains his experience with Chip. Apparently, Chip and Chapelle are both highly intoxicated from smoking marijuana when they happen to encounter a police officer on the street. Chappelle begins to explain the differences between how he approaches the police and how Chip does. Chappelle says that even though Chip is "high as shit" he did not hesitate to go up to the officer. Chip is so nonchalant that he is completely ignorant of Chappelle's warnings. Chip comes up behind the officer and begins to poke and touch him to get his attention, all the while Chappelle is voicing his concern and confusion—"a Black man would never dream of speaking to the police high." In the end, Chip got directions from the police officer and they went on with life without the slightest issue.

While talking about his experiences with Chip, the audience is taken in by the irony of his presentation. A single person plays three characters: a Black man, a white man, and a police officer. The entire display is hilarious and invites the audience into the story—it's like you are there with him and his friend Chip. But the subtle irony of this skit isn't just that Chappelle is playing three people including a person who is white. Still the irony goes deeper than just the stereotype of the "white man's voice." Throughout this entire skit Chappelle never directly offers up a way of seeing this situation for what it "really is," and he isn't giving an opinion about how one should relate to the police themselves. Indirectly, however, he tricks the audience into at least considering the perspective from his shoes, as a Black man who fears the police.

The irony allows Chappelle to expose one version of truth at the heart of this situation. Chip, a white man, is naive and volunteers to talk to the police officer even while high on a drug that has been used to systemically imprison Black men across America. Despite this heavy reality the comedic moment remains present—the hilarious use of voices and the juxtaposition between Chappelle's and Chip's experiences—lead the audience to see things from a Black man's perspective, to sympathize with the reality that white people and Black people have very different experiences of our society's "peace officers." The humor lets the guard down from the audience and allows them to remain more open to considering their own ignorance of the Black experience in America. It is an incredible display of how white ignorance is pervasive in the year 2000, and the point is to bring this ignorance to the fore for all to see. Anyone who watches this skit, especially back in 2000, will at least be made aware of the fact that Black people, Black men, do not have the same experiences with the police as everyone else does.

White Ignorance and Black Masculinity Through the Lens of Tyrone Biggums

Chapelle visits the topic of Black masculinity frequently in his comedy. He jokes about the treatment and perception of icons like Michael Jackson, Kevin Hart, O.J. Simpson, and many more. And his portrayal of Black masculinity is starkly opposed to the standard ideal of masculinity in America that is represented by white male actors. Perhaps the most well-known and important figure to mention here is a fictional character named Tyrone Biggums that Chappelle created himself. Biggums, a friendly neighborhood crackhead, represents Chappelle's attempt to critique predominant motifs of masculinity, while ironically pointing at some of the tragic images of Black masculinity in American culture. If you want to see Biggums in action, then look him up in *Chappelle's Show*.

Masculinity in America is primarily defined through images and themes of white masculinity, one which is predominantly an image of violent white masculinity. Think of iconic white celebrities like John Wayne, Clint Eastwood, Bruce Willis, Chuck Norris, Sylvester Stallone, Tom Cruise, Jason Statham, Chris Hemsworth, Chris Evans, and many, many more. These actors primarily play violent characters, who are intended to be heroic, images of masculinity, and it's hard to deny that they are central representations of masculinity in America today. Yet, they are all *white* and *male* images that are known for their leading roles as violent action adventure characters. There are other images of white masculinity as well that aren't violent and heroic, but these are definitely some of the most widespread images of masculinity in America.

Now, Tyrone Biggums is far from being a standard hero though he gets cast ironically as one. In Season One, Episode 2 of *Chappelle's Show*, Tyrone Biggums gets invited to talk to elementary school kids for an anti-drug talk. His appearance is that of a homeless person, who inadvertently teaches the kids more about how to get drugs and what drugs to use than how and why they should avoid drugs. The kids quickly take notes about how to get drugs, where to go, and which ones are best. He says hilarious but ridiculous things like "You know what dog food tastes like? It taste like it smells . . . delicious!" At the end he ends up scaring the white lady teacher with a small display of violence. But the comedic irony is obvious: this "role model" is somehow representative of how Americans view Black men—as drug addicted, homeless, and not worth taking seriously.

In another episode with Tyrone Biggums ("Tyrone Biggums's Red Balls Energy Drink"; Season Two, Episode 5), we learn that the crack drink "Red Balls" gives Biggums superpowers. His senses are heightened, and he has super strength and speed, but each time he uses these powers things take an unexpected turn. One time he hears a far-off woman cry out because her baby is locked in the car, but when Tyrone gets to the scene he breaks open the window and steals the radio. Another time Tyrone sees a bus run over a coin and he speeds over to lift the bus so he can retrieve the nickel. In an episode where he wins the show *Fear Factor* with Joe Rogan, we learn that Biggums feels no pain and fears nothing. His standards are low and he is even willing to eat raw animal penises and sleep in a vat of live worms overnight, well after the show is done for the day. In each case, the humor emerges because Biggums subverts our expectations.

What Tyrone Biggums represents are negative stereotypes of Black masculinity. The episodes make us laugh, of course, and it would almost be impossible not to laugh in my opinion. But when Chappelle puts Biggums in these situations where white male figures would normally "shine"—Captain America (Chris Evans) talking to elementary school children, or the super heroic efforts of Ethan Hunt (Tom Cruise) when he saves the world from yet another nuclear holocaust—it makes you wonder why we don't see more Black men in these roles. The irony of this Black man (Tyrone Biggums) points to the absence of these Black heroic characters in media. Not because there aren't Black heroes in media and in real life, but because Hollywood would rather them be cast as poor, homeless, and drug addicted than as Superman or James Bond.

The goal of Chappelle's comedic irony is to subvert the "normal" way of seeing and thinking about things. He uses humor and comedic storytelling to subvert our enculturated under-standing of racial norms in American society. In a way he deceives us into a truth he is trying to communicate about America's image of Black culture by playing into and commit-ting so completely to the humor of stereotypes that he reveals some underlying absurdity in our way of conceiving of race and ignorance. Yet, at the same time, he shines a light on the truth that underlies so much of his comedy: humans take themselves too seriously.

6

Dave Chappelle
Knows Better than That

MIA WOOD

2020. Dave Chappelle's posture was bereft. Exhausted legs hauled his burly body up the short flight of stairs to the small stage, as if barely completing an arduous climb up a steep mountain. Words left his mouth slowly, as if hesitant to enter the place where they become real. Heavily muscled shoulders slumped underneath a tight-fitting shirt, as if weighted down by boulders. Chappelle sat—sat!—on a stool, rather than striding nimbly across the stage, which so often serves as an invisible gallery of places, faces, and actions for the audience to picture. "It's hard to figure out what to say about George Floyd, so I'm not gonna say it yet," he said in a smoky voice at the opening of *8:46*. Then, looking down at the open page of a notebook he'd brought with him, Chappelle chuckled ruefully. "But I'll say something." The alternative is too horrible.

2000. Dave Chappelle's posture was relaxed. Lanky legs strode onto the large stage at D.C.'s Lincoln Theater, lithely holding up an equally long body. Slender arms spilled out of a baggy shirt, as raised fists pumped in triumph and a broad smile spread across his youthful face. Walking to the front of the stage, Chappelle reached out to touch eager fans. He grabbed a mic off the stand. Not a stool in sight. "Thank you! Thank you!" he called out to the cheering crowd. "All right." All right, indeed. *Killin' Them Softly* was Chappelle's homecoming and first HBO comedy special.

Twenty years have passed since that special, but for many, nothing has changed. Indeed, since 1619, Black lives in America have largely been lived in an alternate—and terrifying—universe. Consider Chappelle's bit from *Killin' Them Softly*, in which he talks about the difference between Black and white experiences with police:

> That's that whole brutality thing. That's common knowledge, man. There was a time when only minorities knew about that. I won't say whites wouldn't believe us. But they were a little skeptical. A little skeptical. I mean I don't blame you. Even Newsweek printed it. It was Newsweek. White people were like, "Oh my God! Honey, did you see this? Apparently the police have been beating up negroes like hot cakes. It's in the May issue." I mean really how could you know about that? How could anyone else know?

The irony, of course, is that we all could know. Brutalizing Black people has gone on for hundreds of years (and isn't limited to police). From lynching party postcards to Emmett Till's open casket to the video of Rodney King being beaten by a group of Los Angeles police officers, being Black in the United States means something different from what it means to be white—and that meaning has been almost exclusively defined by the latter. It's a dastardly mind that makes it all but impossible to live your life alongside fellow citizens, and then says you're lazy or you're dangerous or you're not intelligent.

White people's slow awakening to the problem is complicated, if for no other reason than by complicity. In other words, to realize the history of subjugating and marginalizing an entire group of people requires realizing also your own contribution to the system built on it. This, as we will see, is at the core of Chappelle's subversion of all oppression—and so it includes misogyny and discrimination of members of the LGBTQ+ community.

Fast forward to 2020. Chappelle sits heavily on the stool, paging through his notebook. It seems clear that he does not believe comedy is required in this moment. After all, comedy can function as a sort of indirect communication, where what the author wants their audience to understand is not straightforwardly asserted. Chappelle's use of direct communication in *8:46* reflects the fact that there can no longer be any excuse for not knowing. The facts of racism are indisputable. They have been from the beginning, but here we are, all of us living now, and we cannot look away.

Does Chappelle Know Better?

Dave Chappelle has long mined profound moral problems for fundamental truths, generating arguments that, at their core, seem to aim for change at an existential level. With subject matters such as racism, sexism, and homophobia, you might think Chappelle would have an academic career in sociology, political science, psychology, or philosophy. Instead, he is a stand-up comedian. In fact, substance is arguably inextricable from Chappelle's comedy, in which he is a racism connoisseur, a misogyny provocateur, a homophobia saboteur.

To claim that the content of Chappelle's routines is intertwined with its presentation implies a particular demand made on the audience. Chappelle is funny, but his funny is not mere entertainment; the delivery of the vast majority of his jokes forces attention on the content in a way that sets each member of the audience back on themselves. Consider another example of entanglement. The sixth-century Greek philosopher Heraclitus was often called "the riddler" for his oracular aphorisms. What he had to say was arguably inextricable from the way he said it. Paradoxical claims such as, "The road up and the road down are one and the same," challenge us to disentangle the apparent contradiction. Indeed, part of Heraclitus's implicit point—implicit because of the style in which he wrote—is that you must do your thinking for yourself.

A similar mechanism occurs in Chappelle's work, a sort of indirect communication, which forces the issue of thinking for oneself. So, yes, Dave Chappelle could write academic essays on moral issues; he could write investigative reports on systemic racism, misogyny, and homophobia. There is, however, something distinctive about comedy that, when leveraged by an intellect such as Chappelle's, invites his audience into a discussion and then throws them off balance—only to gently (or not so gently) reach out a steadying hand.

He conducts all this through an orchestra of word play, deliberate pauses, intonation, facial expressions, gestures, postures, and gaits. Through-lines that serve as reversals and reminders. All these and more are constituents of Chappelle's comedy. What we want to know is why they result in laughter, rather than tears. We want to know why the laughter is sometimes that of realization, recognition, or even responsibility. We want to know why Chappelle's comedy is insightful critique, rather than mean-spiritedness. These are big asks. After all, Chappelle has been criticized for effectively parroting dehumanizing beliefs and attitudes.

But Is It Funny?

If some people find Chappelle's routines offensive, rather than funny, perhaps Plato is correct when he rejects humor, and more specifically laughter, as what we would now think of in terms of dehumanizing both ourselves and others. Laughter precipitated by humor is, he argues, malicious, in that it reflects the delight we take at scorning another (*Philebus*). More specifically, we take "evil pleasure" in another's ignorance (particularly of their own situation). We laugh, for example, when someone does not realize their own incompetence, but instead thinks themselves quite excellent—and we often think such persons deserve our contempt. For Plato, however, ignorance is no laughing matter. It is a vice. Knowledge, by contrast, is virtue. To enjoy ignorance is vicious because it has a corrupting effect on one's character. Think about how cruel it is—and what that cruelty says about you—to laugh at someone unaware they have toilet paper on the heel of their shoe as they walk across a restaurant from the bathroom.

Plato wasn't the only thinker to take a dim view of laughter associated with certain types of humor. Aristotle asserts that "jest is a kind of mockery" (*Nicomachean Ethics*), while Thomas Hobbes associates laughter with the good feeling of superiority. After all, Hobbes views the life outside society as "solitary, poor, nasty, brutish, and short" (*Leviathan*). Similarly, René Descartes homes in on the laughter of one who takes joy in another's (supposedly deserved) evil condition (*Passions of the Soul*). Curiously enough, all four of these thinkers have rather disparate views on a number of important philosophical areas, but in their characterization of a certain type of laughter, they all agree.

According to this view, comedy as we know it today is relative to the perceiver. There's what's funny to the intended audience, and then there's the one who is laughed at. In the process, the one laughed at becomes (or is already assumed to be) inferior and, effectively, less human than the one laughing. It is not surprising then, when you've been dismissed, demeaned, and denigrated entirely because of your identity as non-white, as a woman, as LGBTQ+, a joke at your expense—a joke intended to get the audience to laugh *at* you—is entirely unwelcome. To be devalued in this way is surely *not* funny. It might even be particularly galling that a Black man would deploy this style of humor, given the United States' historical and contemporary racism. Chappelle, one is inclined to say, should know better.

Or suppose you are the victim of sexual assault or abuse. The emotional trauma is so intense, laughing about it or at it just *can't* be funny. The fact that Chappelle himself tosses off ignorant, victim-blaming retorts like, 'Well, what was she wearing?' in response to hearing a woman was sexually assaulted is understandably hurtful. Here again, one is inclined to say that Chappelle should know better.

Yes, Dave Chappelle Knows Better than That

In fact, he does. Dave Chappelle likely knows a lot of things aren't good to do, but does them anyway. Now, as then, Dave Chappelle smokes. Dave Chappelle drinks. Dave Chappelle swears. Dave Chappelle says what most would be afraid to even think, which is, arguably, partly why he says it—but exactly why a lot of people think he shouldn't. To paraphrase Chappelle in 2017's *The Bird Revelation*, however, "I'm not saying it to be mean, I'm saying it because it's funny. And everything is funny. Until it happens to you." There is a significant argument packed into these sentences, one which sums up what Chappelle might really be after when he tells jokes about Michael Jackson's accusers, sexual assault victims, and LGBTQ+. Chappelle's humor does not aim to engender feelings of superiority over those about whom the jokes are made—it's not schadenfreude. Instead, the structure of the routine is directed toward the audience's moral improvement.

Take, for example, 2019's *Sticks and Stones*, which some found horrifying because of Chappelle's apparent cruelty. At one point, Chappelle says, "I am what's known on the streets as a victim blamer. You know what I mean? If somebody come up to me like, 'Dave, Dave, Chris Brown just beat up Rihanna.' I'll be like, 'Well, what did she do?' 'Dave, Michael Jackson was molesting children!' 'Well, what were those kids wearing at the time?'"

The implicit callback to "Well, what was she wearing?" forces the audience to ask if that was the wrong response, after all. Chappelle puts himself forward as a version of each of us who overtly or implicitly engages in victim blaming, for example, and then, when we're all on that path together, he swerves—and swerves hard. Sometimes, it's a complete reversal, a form of indirect communication that operates similarly to metaphor.

Consider Ralph Ellison's *Invisible Man*. The nameless Black man is not literally invisible, yet he is not seen. Metaphors work at the level of cognitive collisions between literal and imaginative thought. They require the capacity to toggle, as it were, between standpoints. From the standpoint of the literal, or denotation, "invisible" means "cannot be seen by the organ of sense called the eye." From the standpoint of respect for persons, "invisible" means "is not respected as a person." Complicating matters further, this invisibility is a matter of convenience for the one who does not "see." After all, the invisible man is, nonetheless, seen enough to be criminalized, shut out of educational and professional opportunities, and generally viewed negatively.

Similarly, a certain type of comedy relies on the incongruity of concepts, and the argument that structures a routine enlists a reversal that yields the desired conclusion. One way this works is by setting up a joke going in one direction, only to veer off in another. This happens, for example, through word play, or logical or conceptual absurdity. The audience is left to draw the relevant inference. For this reason, there's an important intellectual component to this sort of humor, which is often combined with the familiarity of shared lived experiences.

In Chappelle's case, the incongruities that make us laugh are constructed not just from the quality of the writing—the jokes, skits, and stories. The quality of the intellect choosing the topic, the words, the structure, and the pace of the work is also essential. We can unpack Chappelle's work to find theories of knowledge, social criticism, and so forth in a way that's similar to an analysis of a philosophical text. Much goes into the development and production of the work; the result invites the viewer or listener to do the work it takes to understand what he is after, and to grasp how and why it's funny.

The general structure of a Dave Chappelle argument runs something like this: He begins with a premise that invites you in as a member of some unnamed club. Of course, you may feel offended by the premise, you may feel you are the one targeted, the one who is going to bear the brunt of the joke. Take, for example, the bit on Louis C.K. from *The Bird Revelation*. There are those who nod in agreement when Chappelle says, "Them women sounding like . . . I hate to say it, y'all, they sound weak." Then there are those who think Chappelle should know better than to say something like that. Initially, he justifies his claim by appealing to his own condition, to which, again, some people nod in agreement, while those offended are set back:

> Don't forget who I am. Don't forget what I am. I am a Black dude. And don't ever forget how I got here. My ancestors were kidnapped. I don't even know where the fuck I'm from. They were put on the bottom of boats. They sailed them across the Atlantic. Many of them died. Only the strongest survived. And once they got here, they beat the humanity out of my people. They turned us into beasts of burden. They made us do their work, and the irony is, hundreds of years later they're calling us lazy. We fought in the Civil War. We damn near freed ourselves. Then, with Reconstruction, Black people did great. My great-grandfather was a very wealthy man. But then the Black Codes came, Jim

Crow came, and it was a hundred years of unspeakable oppression again. Lynchings, all kinds of terroristic acts to keep us in the margins of society. Yet, we still fought. And Dr. King was born. And then, things got better. Twenty years after Dr. King was assassinated, Michael Jackson was moonwalking on television. Something, something, something. Barack Obama. [laughing] Donald Trump and . . . Now here we all are. Four-hundred-year nightmare.

He continues on in this vein for a bit more, and then transitions to a story about his earliest years as a comic:

I used to do shows for drug dealers that wanted to clean their money up. One time I did a real good set, and these motherfuckers called me in the back room. They gave me $25,000 in cash. I was probably eighteen, nineteen years old. I was scared. I thanked them profusely, I put that money in my backpack, I jumped on the subway and started heading towards Brooklyn at one in the morning. Never been that terrified in my life. Because I'd never in my life had something that somebody else would want. I thought to myself, "Jesus Christ, if these motherfuckers knew how much money I had in this backpack, they'd kill me for it."

Just when the entire audience is wondering where he's going next, he makes the reversal:

Then I thought, "Holy shit. What if I had a pussy on me all the time?" That's what women are dealing with. I'm going to tell you right now. It's real talk. If them same drug dealers gave me a pussy and said, "Put this in your backpack and take it to Brooklyn," I'd be like, "Nigga, I can't accept this."

The audience—regardless of their beliefs and attitudes—is forced back upon themselves. In this instance, it's Chappelle himself who puts himself in a position to learn, bringing everyone along with him. The inference we make is that treating people poorly because we can, because they're different, because we're ignorant—whatever the reason—is unacceptable. Toward the end of his *Sticks and Stones* routine (remember, the one that many found offensive) he says, "If you're in a group that I made fun of, then just know that I probably will only make fun of you if I see myself in you." What Chappelle realizes, and what the brand of comedy he employs requires, is that the audience has to get to these "aha" moments ourselves. Crafting routines that ultimately structure moral arguments make Dave Chappelle "a good dude."

A Good Dude

In remarks at Antioch College, where his father was a dean and faculty member, Dave Chappelle said, "You shouldn't really worry too much about what happens outside of yourself, because what's happening inside of yourself is oftentimes more important—to yourself." This, he said, was one of his father's "main pillars." A consistent moral through-line in Chappelle's routines, skits, and jokes is the existential weight of thinking for oneself, bearing the responsibility of that thought, and recognizing the universal in it. In other words, each individual is, in a moral reckoning, anyone—"I" am universal.

Discriminating against, abusing, and murdering people is immoral precisely because no human being has any greater claim to value than any other. According to this view, one person does not determine the moral worth of another, as such. In other words, we evaluate each other's character and actions as morally praiseworthy or blameworthy, but such evaluation does not thereby render one person more deserving of dignity than another. But, when we do not agree that this is so, or we do not realize that our attitudes and beliefs devalue others, merely being told about our error is typically not effective. Instead, conditions for realization are key. For someone like Dave Chappelle, those conditions involve a complicated comedic jazz.

None of this definitively or exhaustively explains why what Chappelle says is as funny as it is true. As mentioned earlier, he could have written serious essays or exposés. Moreover, it's not entirely clear that the nature of what's funny, in general, is always distinguishable by the sort of viciousness described by Plato and other philosophers. Laughter can be prompted by silliness or innocuous word play, just as it can be prompted by the joy of seeing one's child take their first steps or in celebration of one's beloved achieving a goal. In addition, the dissonance or incongruity built into a joke that makes us laugh can also work in a serious context, as well. So, it too is not a defining feature of what makes us laugh. Nevertheless, "This is the last stronghold of civil discourse," Chapelle says in closing *8:46*. "After this, it's just rat-a-tat-tat."

7
Introduction to White Stupidity: Philosophy 101

Mukasa Mubirumusoke

Professors and students of western philosophy alike are at least intuitively aware that stupidity plays an important and powerful role in the touted intellectual history of the West—which may explain why I was drawn to a class that bore the title "Stupidity" by Professor Elmer Griffin my last semester of college.

Enter Socrates: the former soldier turned moral gadfly was sentenced to death via hemlock spritzer in the name of knowledge and justice. For ages people have gleefully imbibed the sage wisdom to "know thyself." But, lest we forget, in his famous defense, or apologia, the only knowledge Socrates claimed to have was that no man knew the true knowledge of the gods. He then took it upon himself to prove this to the citizens of Athens, much to their chagrin, and often made them look, for lack of a better word, stupid. In a way, then, it was Socrates's own professed ignorance and the way he was able to unveil this ignorance in even the most confident Athenians that catalyzed the story of the pursuit of knowledge.

At this point you may anticipate that I am here to introduce Dave Chappelle—and perhaps the figure of the comedian in general, Chappelle being an example par excellence—as a modern-day descendent of Socrates: imbuing wisdom through a court jester–like dressing down of America the Emperor, and unveiling in shameful nudity its idiosyncratic hypocrisies.

However, before turning to Chappelle, I would like to ask the reader a seemingly innocuous question: just a moment ago, while describing with Spark Notes efficiency the story of the great sage Socrates, when you envisioned him, what race was he? Was he a white man?

For the majority, if not all of you, I imagine that indeed he was. If not merely physically—perhaps accompanied with beard, toga, and a predecessor to Birkenstocks—but also intellectually. The history of Western philosophy is also the history of white philosophy, is it not? If my intuition about your idea of Socrates is correct, it is at the very least curious since the idea of the white race as a distinct category of the human species has had a limited intellectual shelf life, only spanning from around the age of Enlightenment to the mid to late twentieth century. Intellectual consensus has come to tell us that indeed the argument of distinct races based on skin color falls short of any measurable biological, anatomical, or intellectual metric. Instead it is now commonplace to speak of a "socially constructed" concept of race. This conception of race has real effects on human experience and is grounded in historically contingent norms, behaviors, and prejudices. But only anachronistically could 'race' be applicable to the most likely olive-toned and culturally Greek Socrates.

This is all to say that for us contemporary readers, lurking behind the common understanding of Socrates's humility as the wisest Greek, we still perceive him with our own ignorance. And how do we perceive him? As a singular white sage who is the forefather of the most recognizable and legitimate pursuit of human knowledge. What I have hoped to have shown in this short digression is not only how there was a pedagogical role for a concept of stupidity in the methodology of philosophy's patron saint, but also that our very own conceptualization of this saint may fall victim to another form of stupidity, that is, accepting whiteness unconsciously as a neutral transhistorical standard.

Knowledge + Whiteness = Stupidity

The ignorant reduction of whiteness to humanity has been recognized as belonging to a branch on the tree of knowledge by philosopher Charles W. Mills. He calls this the epistemology of ignorance. Epistemology is a branch of philosophy that concerns the study of knowledge. The epistemology of ignorance is a specific kind of knowledge study and acquisition employed by whites that purposely ignores or creates inaccurate knowledge claims about themselves or non-whites in order to justify a racial hierarchy and practices of subordination.

In the example of Socrates, attributing a concept of whiteness to him works to a certain advantage for whiteness; the same may be said of a white Jesus. What advantage? Well it places him within and helps fortify the lauded, revered, and standardized history of western philosophy as being composed of a lineage of white men with non-whites at the margin or excluded. Now while it may be white supremacy that compels us to believe that western philosophy is the only real philosophy and therefore it's kind of stupid to call Socrates a white man since it falls under the aforementioned racist standard of epistemological ignorance; this chapter will look past Socrates and show how there is a phenomenon of white stupidity that animates some of Dave Chappelle's most memorable jokes.

In Chappelle's comedy, white stupidity is not just a seemingly naive observation or punchline based on misdirection, but a powerful performance of white superiority where the crux of its power is revealed in unbelievable and humorous fashion.

For Chappelle, we find with greater clarity and humor how white stupidity functions less as a matter of willful or passive ignorance and more as a brazen expression of the power of whiteness to shape reality. Time and time again we see white characters in Chappelle's jokes reject common sense—for example, asking a police officer for directions while high or lying about knowing driving rules while drunk in the HBO special, *Killin' Them Softly*—not merely from a position of not knowing better, but more explicitly from a position of power that goes beyond the distinction between rational or irrational choices based on good or bad knowledge. To "stupidly" ask a police officer for directions while high is not willful or sincere ignorance, it is an expression of power in an entire epistemology of ignorance that is more than just "knowing better."

Getting Smart Acting Stupid

Philosophical reflections on stupidity are not abundant nor are they absent. As said above, one may very well attribute a certain method of stupidity to Socrates. In *The Encyclopedia of Stupidity,* Matthijs van Boxsel leans on the Socratic method of human ignorance and true wisdom by suggesting that stupidity is a sort of productive double to intelligence. He writes, "intelligence is nothing but the result of a series of more or less unsuccessful attempts to come to grips with stupidity," and a bit further along he states explicitly, "the main premise of the book, that culture is the result of a series of more or less unsuccessful attempts to come to terms with stupidity" (*Encyclopedia of Stupidity*, p. 25).

By this I take him to mean that the content of our cultures and what we contend to be intelligent or successful are achieved through mistakes or stumbled upon through contradictions and the need to create new paths. On a micro scale, think of the way you learn a new skill or craft. You often make stupid mistakes in order to hone skills and reach the desired end, for example learning to play an instrument. This sort of process allows Boxsel to say, "Stupidity recognized is an additional bit of wisdom" (p. 29). You recognize your mistakes and missteps in a process towards certain types of wisdom, where and how to put your fingers for a barre chord on a guitar broadens and fortifies your wisdom of guitar playing and maybe even brings about something totally new. The innovations of DJ Grand Wizard Theodore, who stumbled upon scratching as he held his record while his mother was calling him, also comes to mind.

For comedy, stupidity commonly serves as a humorous, counter-intuitive, enlightening of some aspect of culture or society. We laugh at Kramer in Seinfeld, for instance, in the different ways his half-baked, absurd, and sometimes stupid observations and claims reveal some unexpected wisdom about human relations or the functions of society—most memorably with the help of Black attorney Jacky Chiles, but that relationship is for another book. Chappelle's own brand of observational humor also uses this type of stupidity to solicit laughs, although the racial dynamics of our society are all the more glaring; in fact, they often are the punch line of the joke.

Chip, No! Don't Do It!

In the hopes of tracing the connection of white stupidity to wisdom or the wisdom of white stupidity, I have in mind a joke from an early Chappelle special where he highlights how white stupidity, when recognized, is indeed an additional bit of wisdom. Specifically, a sort of wisdom about the structure of white supremacy. In *Killin' Them Softly*, Chappelle offers a politically poignant performance of white stupidity through his friend Chip, this time in the context of those often all too funny police interactions.

The history of Black people's outright hostile relationship to police in America is well documented: from the slave patrols of the antebellum era, to Bull Connor and Jim Crow, and the more recent phenomenon of police executions caught on camera. With this history in mind, Chappelle's bit on the police starts with a very simple, but powerful observation. "Black people are afraid of the police. It doesn't matter how rich you are, how old you are, we're just afraid of them. We have every reason to be afraid of them" (*Killin' Them Softly*). The power of this statement speaks not only to the hostility of police towards Black people, but the indiscriminate nature of race beyond other mitigating factors such as age—dismissing the young thug stereotype—or financial security—good luck not being a menace to society in your Kia or your Maserati.

As the joke develops, he makes a number of different observations between white people's interaction with the police and Blacks, but the stupidity of his friend Chip comes to the fore when they are smoking marijuana and are lost in a city. Dave's white friend grabs his attention, saying, "Dave. Dave! It's the goddamn cops," followed by a pregnant pause. The anticipated horror of a dalliance with the law is humorously exacerbated when his friend continues with confidence, "I'm going to ask them for directions." Chappelle, placing himself in the situation, is aghast, yelling "Chip, no! Don't do it!" and then with resignation, "It was too late, this man was high as shit." What then transpires is even more shocking to Chappelle. Chip is not only confident in his approach but brazen upon his interaction, touching the police officer and confessing to his illegally achieved altered state, that is to say, he was high.

We need to take just a moment to admire this stupidity. This is not a possible slip of the mind—or slip of the finger as in the Grand Wizard Theodore example. We must be fairly confident that Chip has a pretty good knowledge of the police and their role as enforcers of laws. Chip simply disregards the most intuitive knowledge of the primary function of the police and embraces the more authoritative understanding of his power as a white man. Ignoring his intuitive knowledge of the police is stupid; enacting and fortifying his exempt status as a white man, however, is wise beyond his age.

What Does Chip Know?

Let's be honest, the police are not out in New York to give directions, not even the traffic cops who would strip search you for thinking about jaywalking rather than tell you where you are, at least for a Black person. But for Chip to ask for directions while high unveils a level and condition of knowing that betrays all common sense. What we see with Chip's behavior— and the behavior of the cop who reluctantly capitulates to Chip's request, responding to his question of 'Where is Third Street?' with the answer that he is on Third Street—is that whiteness is not about knowing better, but about power. By this I mean, Chip should know all the better that his actions are not how you interact with the police, especially when accompanied by a Black friend. Yet, he does not feel beholden to the norms of respect or laws against drug use since his whiteness, whether it is conscious to him or not, is the most important

mitigating factor in his relation to society and the laws that
govern it. Chip not only accepts that he does not need to fear
breaking the rules of society, but his whiteness shows how he
is also the creator and enforcer. Therefore, exceptions can be
made even when he knowingly and willfully contradicts society's accepted norms. In other words, Chip shows white is right
or will make it right if necessary, even if he doesn't really know
it (consciously). Chappelle knows it though and he becomes a
little wiser.

Chip shows us that the arrangements in society that secure
justice and success are not grounded in having and using more
accurate knowledge of the world in any objective sense, but
rather they are in knowing your role in society that is estab-
lished first and foremost by power. The stupidity of soliciting a
police officer's advice while breaking the law shows that white
is right, no matter the contradiction in terms or disregard of
common sense. Chip's stupidity is white in one of its purest
forms not simply because he is white in a world predominated
by whiteness, but because it unveils that one can act stupidly
in what would intuitively be a hostile situation, without fear of
the most feared consequences because his whiteness outweighs
the rules that mediate the situation.

Rules Are Meant to Be Broken

—Chip's Ancestors

This is brought into undeniable relief as the joke continues and
a now drunk Chip challenges another driver—unbeknownst to
the driver—to a race. Chip's reckless driving gets himself and
a high Chappelle pulled over. As Chip blasts on the stereo defi-
antly Twisted Sister's "We're Not Gonna Take It," he tells the
police officer, Chappelle reports, "He didn't know he couldn't do
that." Once the officer lets them off with, "Now you know. Just
get out of here!" Chip addresses Chappelle's understandable
befuddlement with the acknowledgment, "That was good
wasn't it, because I did know I couldn't do that."

Chip's whiteness trumps all in bold and fantastic fashion,
where even when in this instance he knows what he did was
wrong, he cannot even imagine that what he did should be
enforced as wrong. There is no knowledge claim that needs to
be respected aside from the officer knowing he is white. As
stated above, these ostensibly stupid actions by Chip are actually a bit of wisdom in that they lay out and reinforce for
Chappelle the lay of the land. The wisdom, of course, is not that

the law or knowing the law is right, but that white is right and that is all Chappelle needs to know and it would actually be stupid of Dave to think otherwise.

Wisdom Born of Ignorance

What Chip knows, does not know, pretends not to know, and the authority he is given qua his whiteness, can also be understood using Charles Mills's idea of the epistemology of ignorance that he develops in his renowned book, *The Racial Contract*. In this book Mills recontextualizes western political philosophy with a spin on the social contract, a once popular philosophical device. The social contract is an imaginary contract that is used to describe the terms that rational humans would agree upon to create a government and social order. It is often conceptualized as a quid pro quo, whereby it is rational for individuals to sacrifice their ability or desires to pursue their own ends without regulations in order to enter in a social arrangement or form of governance that, while limiting one's absolute freedom, will ultimately protect them from many of the desires and whims of other people.

Mills contends that our current world takes for granted a real social contract that is tacitly agreed upon and exclusive to the constituents of the white world, people like Chip and the police officer. The racial contract divides the socio-political world between consenting humans and non-consenting sub-humans, whereby the former (white people) rule over the latter (non-white people). Essentially, Mills argues that in our world there is a de facto agreement amongst the white people to enjoy more extended political rights, have a higher moral standing, and have better knowledge than non-whites. We observe how this agreement plays out through the racial hierarchy of the western world. Mills' epistemology of ignorance is one tool to secure this hierarchy and can explain why Chip's feigned ignorance and stupid actions are in fact consistent with a larger picture of white wisdom.

Mills insists there is an epistemology, a way of knowing, employed by whites that purposely ignores or creates inaccurate knowledge claims about non-whites in order to justify practices of subordination. I think it's safe to say we are taught that true objective knowledge of the world will help not only in social advancement, but in determining good from bad knowledge and behavior. However, since our current school curricula insist that the white man's knowledge is true and good, while non-white knowledge is backwards and bad, there is reason to be suspicious and concerned.

In fact, the agreement that white knowledge is good knowledge amongst the racial contract signatories is in all reality a cognitive dysfunction, or as Mills says, "to a significant extent . . . white signatories will live in an invented delusional world, a racial fantasyland . . . One could say then, as a general rule, that white misunderstanding, misrepresentation, evasion, and self-deception on matters related to race are among the most pervasive mental phenomena of the past few hundred years" (p. 19). This "white misunderstanding, misrepresentation, evasion, and self-deception" is the epistemology of ignorance, or a knowledge born of purposeful ignorance. We then can extrapolate from this description a pervasive and active process of interpreting the world in a way that justifies the violent political agenda of the racial contract.

The most standard example is the discovery of the Americas. A world inhabited by a people is not really "discovered," but it's clear how the narrative many of us learned while sitting cross-legged in elementary school was just an echo of the unfurled flapping American flag we pledged allegiance to earlier that morning. This epistemology of white might and right contends that anything worthy of knowing must pass a simple test: does it make white people seem superior or non-white people seem inferior or threatening and thus deserving of their plight or destruction? If so, then yes, it must be true.

In the case of Chip, the stupidity of his actions shines forth from and through the backdrop of the epistemology of ignorance. Framing Chip's interaction with the police, there is an accepted knowledge, similar to the idea that Columbus gallantly—as opposed to murderously—'discovered' the Americas, namely that the police are neutral and forgiving arbiters of the law. Holding up this frame, however, there is a more objective wisdom secured by power. This is similar to the fact that the Americas already had people, but power insists that Columbus discovered it. This white wisdom necessitates that the police are not neutral arbiters of the law when it comes to their particular circumstances, but are there to serve white interests first and foremost, and the execution of the law is far more arbitrary and often in favor of keeping the safety and superiority of white people intact. The former is the epistemology of ignorance and when Chip displays its parameters explicitly with his bold interactions with the police it is on the one hand an act of stupidity, but also an additional bit of intelligence that tells both Chip and Chappelle, at least implicitly, that white people may not know more but they subconsciously do know better and that's funny.

George Washington, Run!

Speaking of skewed American history, Chappelle himself does not shy away from the broad history of the epistemology of ignorance in America and the white stupidity that may arise when it is confronted. The title of this section is one of a few punchlines to a joke from his 2004 special *For What It's Worth*. The joke follows from a digression on money; transitioning from a joke about Disney World and "Disney Bucks" to the sincere pride felt when Saddam Hussein was removed from Iraqi money. He observes the political and affective significance of this removal, noting, "it's a subtle nuanced form of oppression having a dictator on your money" (*For What It's Worth*); this allows him to contemplate aloud about the presidents and folk heroes that adorn American currency. We unabashedly admire and revere these "baseball cards of slave owners" and so it's curious that the same sense of revulsion that was attributed to Hussein is not common when looking at our own money.

Chappelle, of course, is bringing into relief a certain formulation of the epistemology of ignorance discussed above, this time smuggled through white American exceptionalism and nationalism. At the level of a historical national narrative, it's commonplace for the dark history of America's moral and political transgressions against Blacks to go underappreciated, ignored, or to be completely whitewashed. We are taught in classrooms to simply accept indubitably the political ingenuity, military prowess, and moral fortitude of those "founding fathers" and to set aside as a minor misstep the original sin of chattel slavery.

In this context, it comes as a humorous surprise when Chappelle declares George Washington "the worst of the worst" (*For What It's Worth*). The "mythologization" of Washington is stupid at least if we consider how he supported slavery. And this specific context of (white) American stupidity really rears its head when he offers a simple thought experiment. "If I go back in time with a white person" he proposes, "and we saw George Washington walking in front of our time machine, my white friend would probably be like 'Oh my God, Dave, look there's George Washington. It's the father of this great nation. I'm going to go shake his hand.' I'd be on the other side, like, 'Run n*****r, it's George Washington!" Time travel absurdity aside, we know what's funny and it's the white friend's stupidity. The friend presumes a warm welcome from the President with his Black friend, despite the unhidden, yet easily negligible fact, that George Washington was an unrepentant slave owner. The epistemology of ignorance that foregrounds the mythologization of America's history as great for all is what allows the white friend to act so stupidly, that is putting at risk Chappelle's life to admire the greatness of George Washington.

As the joke continues, Chappelle further contextualized the epistemological framework that leads to his friend's stupidity. With resignation he admits, "And we'd both be right. We like him because he wrote the Declaration of Independence and all that shit. 'We hold these truths to be self-evident, all men are created equal—go get me a sandwich n****r or I'll kill you'—liberty, justice for all . . ." (*For What It's Worth*). Here, again, he highlights the contradiction in terms and sentiments that we recognize at the foundation of the American ethos that could do nothing but demand his friend's stupidity. Interestingly enough, however, Chappelle's own confusion and conflation—it's not clear if it's intentional—of Thomas Jefferson who wrote the Declaration of Independence and George Washington, the first American president, actually only further highlights the ubiquity of those racist anti-Black sentiments during the nation's founding years.

Conclusion or Considerations of Black Stupidity

Predating his eventual departure from Comedy Central's *Chappelle's Show*—which was instigated in part by an incident where a white member of his staff laughed a little too hard and he decided to rethink what indeed people were laughing at on his show—Chappelle broke from his set at a comedy club in Sacramento, California in 2004. The audience members interrupted his set by yelling out 'I'm Rick James, bitch!' and this audience's inability to respect him as a comic, as a human doing his job, sat with him the wrong way—it sat with him like a kind of white "manspreading," if you will. He was served a dose of his own bitter medicine through an ironic performance of white stupidity, so he reasoned aloud to them, "You know why my show is good? Because the network officials say you're not smart enough to get what I'm doing, and every day I fight for you. I tell them how smart you are. Turns out, I was wrong. You people are stupid" (Jim Carnes in the *Sacramento Bee*).

In that moment, it's as if Chappelle realized he would never simply be a comic performing on his own terms; he had stood by his own Black stupidity of giving his white audience credit for years and it ricocheted right back at him, sharpened by the sometimes imperceptible and yet also suffocating atmosphere atop the mountain of white supremacy. He wasn't meant for those elevations. Chappelle stood on that stage stark and wooden like a puppet, a stupid puppet, without the same political capital afforded to the enlightening and enriching stupidity of the white kind. The success of *Chappelle's Show* obscured the racial contract from those heights, and he began lying to himself; however, the nose of Chappelle, the Black Pinocchio, was not getting longer, it was getting wider; he was "breathing all the white man's air" (Season One, Episode 1).

Chappelle's aptitude to find the humor in white stupidity is undeniable, although we see it is clearly risky business precisely because stupidity tends to be so unwieldy. Nevertheless, in this chapter he exposes the dexterity of this white stupidity, compelling his audience to notice the different ways it not only shields white people from understanding the full reality of their position of power, but also perpetuate it in seemingly innocuous and also fantastic situations—all foregrounded by an epistemology of ignorance. As we learned above, the term implies its own contradiction, whereby the vaunted position of knowledge in the West has achieved its prestige at the expense of systematically and strategically blinding itself to much greater landscapes of knowledge, which includes its own unbecoming morality. This way of knowing is stupid undoubtedly and Chappelle leaves our eyes open and mouths agape to unveil with Black wisdom how white stupidity is just another side of an insidious white intelligence.

However, while our laughs still faintly echo in the valleys below the mountain of white supremacy, Chappelle has also showed us how stupidity and laughter are not always the formula to address the very difficult issue of anti-Blackness in America. In his latest special, *8:46*, the humor of white stupidity has gone completely AWOL. The dour performance is in response to yet another extra-legal police execution of an unarmed Black person and its eerie and somber mood is set by an Ohioan audience arranged to comply with protocols for the COVID-19 pandemic. He recalls the video of a police officer who decided that kneeling with his full weight on the neck of George Floyd while being recorded—perhaps even because he was being recorded—for eight minutes and forty-six seconds was an act of justice. He then recalls another incident where John Crawford III in his own hometown in Ohio was shot in a Walmart while checking out a bb-gun by the same police officer that had pulled him over earlier that evening.

Is that fortune? Serendipity? Happenstance? Stupidity? Perhaps all of the above, and we should thank Chappelle for these types of provocations and the undoubted challenge to the epistemology of ignorance and the supremacy of whiteness found in so much of his productions, even those where laughter and stupidity are sold separately.

8
Dave Chappelle's Positive Propaganda

Chris A. Kramer

Americans are told in a multitude of ways, from a variety of sources, from a very young age, that the United States of America is the land of freedom and opportunity—it's the greatest. If you work hard, you can make it because everyone is treated equally and therefore has the same opportunities in our schools, granted equal concern in our hospitals, equal access to our free markets, and is equally respected under the law. We should therefore be perplexed to hear stories like this about Dave Chappelle and his white friend Chip encountering the police, while high:

> My white buddy, he was smoking a joint. [*Chappelle as Chip shouts*] "Dave! It's the goddamn cops, [*Chip takes a long comfortable drag on a joint*] I'm gonna ask him for directions." I said "Chip, no! Chip, don't do it!" It was too late. He was walking over there. This man was high as shit. "Excuse me. Excuse me, sir. Excuse me!!! I need some information." He starts confessing things he shouldn't confess. "I'm a little high. All I wanna know . . . which way is Third Street?" The cop is like, "Hey, take it easy. You're on Third Street. You better be careful. Go ahead. Move it. Move it." [*Chappelle in his own voice*] That's all that happened, that's the end of the story. Now, I know that's not Black fellas here, that shit is fucking incredible. (*Killin' Them Softly*)

Chappelle is not describing anything new, especially for Black folks, and it *should not* be news for white people either, but largely due to what Jason Stanley refers to as undermining, demagogic, negative propaganda, the reality of situations like this has not filtered through, certainly not in 2000 when this was performed, even with decades of forceful argument and direct protests highlighting police brutality against Black citizens. But through his comedic performance, we're encouraged to take another (or a first) look at something that has always been right in front of us, here expressed in a manner that can evoke the desire to listen empathically to another person's point of view and experience. One message here: white and Black people have *very* different interactions with the police.

He then imagines what might have happened if Chip were Black: "A Black man would never dream of talking to the police high. That's a waste of weed. Seriously. I'm scared to talk to the police when I'm sleepy. Fuck around and get the wrong idea or something. [*Acts out being struck by a cop*] "Oo-oh! Oh my God! That n****r was on PCP, Johnson. I had to use necessary force. You saw him. No, no paperwork. Just sprinkle some crack on him. Let's get out of here" (*Killin' Them Softly*).

Chappelle was not beaten by cops who then framed him by planting drugs on him, and I have not been able to determine if he even has a white friend named "Chip," so this story is likely not entirely true. But it would be an odd requirement of humor that it must completely track the truth in order to be compelling or funny. Chappelle's performances are both and it's helpful to view much of his work as positive propaganda that counters the negative that has been dominant for so much of US history.

Dangerous Propaganda in a Liberal Democracy

Joseph Goebbels, *Reich Minister of Propaganda* (and that was its public name!) in Nazi Germany, used his government agency to propagate anti-Semitism explicitly with the publicly professed ideals of that nation. They openly scapegoated Jewish people for the ills facing the country, slowly building up a "justification" for their "final solution." *That* is likely what immediately comes to mind when we hear the word "propaganda" today—it's all negative, perpetrated by the worst fascist regimes in history.

We can see elements of this in authoritarian nations like Putin's Russia, Assad's Syria, Xi Jinping's China, or Erdoğan's Turkey. But we rarely consider the role that propaganda might play in democratic countries that explicitly extol liberal ideals such as freedom, equality, or civil rights. According to Jason Stanley in *How Propaganda Works*, even these open societies can be fertile grounds for the rise of *demagoguery*, the sort of propaganda that obstructs empathic recognition of others and undermines reasonable debate among citizens regarding policies that affect the justice system, welfare, inequality, and race, for example.

This is hard to see because "the distinctive danger propaganda poses in liberal democracies is that it is *not recognized as propaganda*" (*How Propaganda Works*, p. 47). Instead, it remains cloaked in the language of freedom, saying one thing, while causing the opposite. For example, we are told we need to cut taxes in order to foster economic liberty, while a consequence of this "tax reform," "revenue enhancement," and other euphemistic phrases denoting the same act, is increased inequality and reduced opportunity for impoverished citizens. We can't raise the minimum wage, we're told, as that would harm the very workers it presumes to help. Meanwhile, minimum-wage workers require more than a single job to survive; the "gig" economy is the newest manifestation of this.

President Trump literally hugs the American flag (often grabbing its pussy), standing for those who have fought for all it symbolizes, namely, Americans' right to free expression, but he does so in the act of denouncing athletes, like Colin Kaepernick, as "sons-a-bitches" who kneel during the national anthem in protest against police brutality. Trump's explicit words and deeds touting freedom actually undermine freedom. It should be extraordinary, not that socially conscious Black athletes might protest during the national anthem, but that so many white people are morally outraged by this act of political freedom: "Took us four hundred years to figure out as a people that white people's weakness the whole time was kneeling during the national anthem. That's a brittle spirit" (*The Bird Revelation*). Granted, this is part of an analogy with the brittle spirit he sees in the female comedians who were confronted by a masturbating Louis C.K. Chappelle seems at times understanding and claiming to be an ally (an imperfect one), and at others, mocking those who are oppressed in what might be called a "reckless" manner.

Administrations advocate for "law and order" as an ideal to protect the people, while the policies enacted behind that phrase, for one example, push hundred to one harsher sentences for crack-cocaine use, found predominantly in Black neighborhoods, over purer powder cocaine, used in proportionately similar numbers, but in white areas. Disparate treatment in the justice system is ubiquitous. This is what makes propaganda in liberal democracies so insidious—it's in our faces all the time, but it's driven by a flawed ideology, a mistaken belief-set about our institutions, which obscures the contradictions in the under-mining-propaganda.

This is harmful propaganda that pretends to embody universal ideals, but in fact diminishes them. The absurd levels of mass incarceration of Black and brown people today has a direct lineage to the executive propagandistic actions of President Reagan and before him, Nixon, who said the darndest things, and recorded almost all of them: "You have to face the fact," Nixon muses, "that the whole problem is really the Blacks . . . The key is to devise a system that recognizes this while not appearing to" (*How Fascism Works*, p. 25). From here we have an explicit and systematic social and political agenda promulgated from the very top, but deviously in a manner difficult to directly confront or even expose without appearing to be hyperbolic in the extreme; to accuse the government, and importantly, the supporters of these "freedom-enhancing" policies, of propaganda would sound silly, even anti-American.

The tactic with all of the above examples is to cultivate a flawed ideology among the very people who are harmed by the propaganda that helps push policies anathema to actual American ideals: "What, you're against law and order?" "You don't think *all lives matter*? "You're against economic liberty, political free speech, the flag and all our soldiers who died for your right to protest?" and so forth. This sort of propaganda fosters ideological beliefs that, like cultural stereotypes, are largely immune to argument and are highly resistant to rational revision because they are not presented logically or directly: "It's hard to advance a policy that will harm a large group of people in straightforward terms . . . Political propaganda uses the language of virtuous ideals to unite people behind otherwise objectionable ends" (p. 25). Since this is so difficult to counter with traditional means of discourse, even protest, something more creative is needed in order to get citizens to see from a non-dominant perspective. This is why W.E.B. Du Bois suggests an alternative approach; he "recognizes that . . . an indirect method is required to stir White interest, one that appeals 'to white folk,' yet will somehow call attention to the Black perspective. Du Bois is calling for a certain kind of undermining propaganda" (*How Propaganda Works*, p. 64). He will do this through the medium of art, a means adopted by Chappelle in his performances.

All Art Is Propaganda

Du Bois writes this in "Criteria of Negro Art" (1926): Beauty is essential to art, but, "I do not care a damn for any art that is not used for propaganda. But I do care when propaganda is confined to one side while the other is stripped and silent" (p. 22). The "one side" is that which appears to cultivate American ideals, but in reality undermines them, perpetuating the subordinate status of Black citizens. Replace "beauty" with "humor" and we see striking parallels between Chappelle's socio-political performances and Du Bois' call for positive propaganda, each of which constitute "civic rhetoric" broadly construed.

Melvin Rogers's analysis of Du Bois' *Souls of Black Folk* and *Criteria for Negro Art* offers a clear conception of civic rhetoric: "persuading white Americans to embrace an expanded view of themselves and the political community. The relational and binding quality that Souls [of Black Folk] seeks to forge follows from making the reader a *coparticipant* in the arrival of a truth hitherto unavailable" (p. 198). Chappelle's civic rhetoric "is a different kind of propaganda" (*How Propaganda Works*, p. 5) that is *anti*-demagogic. Like Du Bois, it appeals to emotion, in particular white audiences' sympathy for the lived experiences of Black folk, but also a bit of shame, with the recognition of white America's failure "to live up to a standard with which they identify," namely, freedom for all. These truths have always been "available," but due to negative propaganda, they've been hidden.

Du Bois focuses on essays, books, poetry, photography, paintings, and film. Chappelle's humor most closely resembles a mixture of short story or narratives, with poetry. I don't mean his comedy amounts to spitting poems on stage, but the artistic mediums are remarkably similar: both provide unique perspectives on ordinary events making them extraordinary, and both rely heavily on economy and precision of language, as every word counts and too many can diminish the impact. This means cooperation with an audience is essential to the art. When we read a poem, in contrast to a syllogism, we must participate with the poet to find meaning in an ambiguity or subtle metaphor. Comedy requires even greater participation from listeners, in fact it might be the most collaborative of all the arts, as well-formed jokes and humorous stories, in almost every case, succeed in part with their brevity and purposeful omission of content that must be filled in by audiences; we are "*coparticipants*" to use Rogers's term.

We no longer live in Du Bois's America of systematic *explicit* denial of rights. In many ways our situation is worse; the mechanisms of exclusion are implicit, difficult to dislodge, because they are driven by invisible propaganda. Chappelle's comedic art draws attention to subtle demagogic propaganda that has been normalized in our liberal democracy, transforming it through his counter-propaganda into the spectacle that it *should* be: ubiquitous democracy-denying propaganda that is extraordinary. Here is the rest of the Du Bois quotation: "Thus all Art is propaganda and ever must be, despite the wailing of the purists. I stand in utter shamelessness and say that whatever art I have for writing has been used always for propaganda for gaining the right of Black folk to love and enjoy" (p. 22). We don't have to be purists to differ with his strong view on this, for his onception of "propaganda" is so broad as to render it useless: Chappelle's narrative about Chip's interaction with the cops can be deemed positive propaganda, but not so with his "So I kicked her in the pussy" bit (*Equanimity*). But there are plenty of examples from Chappelle that fit Du Bois's constructive sense of propaganda.

Not All Propaganda Is Created Equal

This is morally difficult terrain because a positive aspect of propaganda would need to be resurrected from one of its earliest usages in the Catholic Church when Pope Gregory XV in 1622 deployed it as a missionizing weapon to spread the good news, presumably, the Truth. "Propaganda" in this context connoted persuasive preaching and teaching, typically positive, unless you happened to be one of the "heathens" who was not interested in that particular gospel, or the forced assimilation.

But it is used again with great dexterity by Martin Luther King Jr. in his "Propagandizing Christianity" sermon, 1954. He prodded his congregants to become "propaganda agents" for the cause of Jesus: "If Hitler could do all of this with an evil idea it seems that we could rock the world with the truth of the saving power of the gospel. If the advertisers can convince men that they can't do without their products, we ought to be able to convince men of the productive power of God in Christ" (p. 185). For what cause does Chappelle's propaganda fight? Hint: it's not Jesus.

Chappelle understands the power of his comedic art, and, significantly, the influence of those positioned to market ideas:

> That's why I don't have a sneaker deal, 'cause if you say something that people don't like, they'll take your fucking shoes off. If Martin Luther King had a sneaker deal, we'd still be on the back of the bus. It's true. The Nike exec would come up—"Hi, Martin. Uh . . . we need you to tone down the talk of civil rights and Blacks being humans. It's

upsetting our Southern distributors." "But I don't understand. I thought that's why I had a sneaker deal in the first place." "Not quite. Really, it's a walking shoe. And we like the marching, but . . . Try to understand." Fuck that shit. (*The Age of Spin*)

Even extremely popular figures can have their messages derailed if they "cross a line," especially if they feel beholden to behemoths like Nike that have their own political-economic agenda that has been at odds with their publicly professed ideals: "Just do it" could have been a phrase yelled at Nike's child laborers in Pakistan or China. Melding Du Bois with MLK, Chappelle is often (not always) a positive "propaganda agent" who knows how to market positive ideals on behalf of the marginalized.

Chappelle's Counter-Propaganda

You dumb motherfucker. You are poor. He's fighting for me.

— *Equanimity*

While standing in line to vote for the 2016 Presidential Election, Chappelle paid attention to the many Trump supporters in Ohio: "I listened to them say naive poor white people things. 'Man, Donald Trump's gonna go to Washington, and he's gonna fight for us'" (*Equanimity*).

They said these things, and continue to, because the demagogic propaganda has succeeded. The language of concern for the welfare of the "forgotten Americans" resonates, yet these voters seem unaware that they are acting in a manner contrary to their own ends when they continue to support, even adulate, Trump, largely because they are not cognizant that the administration employs anti-democratic propaganda that adversely affects them; unless they are billionaires like former President Trump, who we know is one, because he tells us, often.

This is evident where there is significant inequality which can lead to flawed belief systems that are used to perpetuate an unjust status quo. Those with wealth and access must continue to hold onto the myth of meritocracy to justify gross and growing inequalities. Poor whites glom onto this myth as they sense the possibility of upward mobility as the norm, and at least they're not Black: "Not to sound fucked up, but I felt sorry for them. I know the game there. I know that rich white people call poor white people trash. And the only reason I know that is because I made so much money last year, the rich Whites told me; they said it at a cocktail party. And I'm not with that shit" (*Equanimity*). Chappelle does confess that the "poor Whites are my least favorites," but that does not interfere with his accurate understanding of history, recognized by others like Du Bois, that stoking racial animus among poor whites almost always succeeds in stifling a collective voice among impoverished people from all races.

Yes, in the performance Chappelle refers to his fellow Ohioans who support Trump as "dumb motherfuckers," which sounds less than sympathetic. But like *some* of his first-person accounts with people who are gay or transgender, he is expressing both critique and at least a little care, rather than applying blanket epithets: "I stood with them in line, like all of us Americans are required to do in a democracy, nobody skips the line to vote, and *I listened to them*" (*Equanimity*). Equal access to voting is likely *the* most important aspect of citizenship, and, as Chappelle is keenly aware, one of the best means to make real and lasting change, even with socially divisive issues such as voting rights (of course), police reform, or the Second Amendment.

Only a Good Guy with Propaganda Can Stop a Bad Guy with Propaganda

The NRA gun lobby adamantly supports the citizens' right to bear arms, but that freedom has been infringed when the gun-toters happen to be Black. This was evident with the propaganda and counter-intelligence attacks by the FBI and police departments against the Black Panthers, who *legally* armed themselves for protection in the late 1960s. For a current contrast, consider the white, heavily armed, visibly enraged, protestors in the capitol building in Michigan— screaming inches from the faces of police who remained calm and motionless—demanding government officials open up all businesses even as COVID-19 continued to ravage the city. Compare that with police response to unarmed, peaceful protestors in the wake of George Floyd's murder by police— tear gas, flash grenades, and swinging batons. This is not new, but it has become, like our expectations of another mass shooting by a white male, *normal*. Such normalization, making what should be extraordinary seem ordinary, requires successful anti-democratic propaganda.

How to respond? "I don't see any peaceful way to disarm America's Whites," Chappelle says, in reference to school shootings, transitioning into elections. "There's only one thing that's going to save this country from itself . . . Listen, no matter what they say or how they make you feel, remember, this is your country, too . . . And you know what we have to do. This is a fuckin' election year." We can see where he's going with this and applaud his highlighting the importance of everyone's civic duties. He continues, "Every able-bodied African American, must register for a legal firearm. That's the only way they'll change the law [gun control]" (*Sticks and Stones*). Ah, we have been misled, rhetorically *disarmed* but joyfully so, and not without some insight.

Chappelle's socio-political humor, especially the acts that counter a flawed ideology, constitute "*Supporting Propaganda*: A contribution to public discourse that is presented as an embodiment of certain ideals, yet is of a kind that tends to increase the realization of those very ideals by either emotional or other nonrational means" (*How Propaganda Works*, pp. 53–54). His humor appeals to emotion—it can be sensational, exaggerated, or understated, as with his Chip and the police story, and it can be haranguing and cajoling, to use Du Bois's terms for positive propaganda. Positive propaganda propagated through humor is a unique mode of resistance as it both appeals to emotion and reason, if only indirectly.

Regarding two descriptors from Du Bois on positive propaganda, "cajoling" and "haranguing," Chappelle's comedic "lectures" are seductive. These terms seem mutually exclusive, but they are not in this context. A lecture typically connotes something dry, straightforward, logical, factual, while "seduction" implies persuasion through pure emotion and even manipulation, and maybe sex. These two distinct mechanisms combine in Chappelle's "civic rhetoric" which is nondemagogic propaganda, the sort that works towards achieving the social or political ideal it represents, in this case, equal protection under the law, and more generally, empathic recognition of the perspectives of all citizens. This can be found in his latest "surprise" YouTube special, *8:46*

> What are you signifying that you can kneel on a man's neck for eight minutes and forty-six seconds and feel like you wouldn't get the wrath of God?
>
> —DAVE CHAPPELLE, *8:46*

Chappelle *harangues* the audience with a furious reminder of how long eight minutes and forty-six seconds is, and the agony George Floyd experienced, and the pain of watching this happen on video, over and over. What does the normalization of police brutality against Black bodies mean? Chappelle answers this with his question above: the officers knew they were being recorded, they knew Floyd was not a threat, they knew he was perilously close to death, and, if they were believers, they assumed God was watching, and they didn't give a damn. It takes considerable aggressive ignorance to avoid any uncomfortable dissonance there.

This is not an exculpating ignorance, but it is probably present due to the constant demoralizing propaganda that has for centuries criminalized Black people with the very policies and language that promote "law and order," "public safety," "protect and serve." There is a new one from former President Trump, "free and fair elections," vocalized while explicitly and very publicly working to dismantle the USPS, thereby making vote by mail-in ballot, an otherwise intelligent option during a pandemic, *less* open and extensive. This harms those who are most susceptible to COVID-19 due to underlying medical conditions, African Americans.

Chappelle's *cajoling* comes in the form of a narrative that slowly reveals the intended connection between the protests against police brutality and the reaction of the police in response to the death of "one of their own." The analogy is with Chris Dorner, a Black cop who was removed from the LAPD even though he did "everything right." In response to his dismissal, Dorner murdered fellow officers and their family members. The LAPD reacted: "no less than four hundred police officers showed up and answered the call." It's not hard to understand why they felt such righteous fury, or, for many, even their use of force (they set afire the cabin Dorner was holed up in): "And you know why four hundred cops showed up? Because one of their own was murdered. So how the fuck can't they understand what's going on in these streets? *We saw ourselves like you see yourself*" (8:46). In other words, white folk supporting the police, and the police themselves, DO know why so many Black people are in the streets protesting yet another "death of one of their own."

This is an emotionally-laden piece of persuasion that could be described as "manipulative" in the way so much propaganda is, but his intention is to empathically disclose the perspective of Black folks that has been continually ignored, erased since the time of Du Bois and before. The normal channels of communication about these issues have proven ineffective because the demagogic propaganda, the ubiquitous myth-ologizing has been so successful. So, a novel, even artistic mode, "a kind of propaganda that is politically necessary to use to overcome fundamental obstacles to the realization of democratic ideals . . ." is needed, and it is the sort of propaganda Du Bois fostered, and Chappelle creates, that "induced its audience to recognize their moral obligation to grant equal political participation to a group that had been invisible" (*How Propaganda Works*, p. 111). Chappelle listens to those he disagrees with politically, even those who have historically marginalized people like him. What his positive propaganda seeks, in addition to amusing his audiences, is mutual accountability, respect, and basic recognition.

Motherfucker, you have a responsibility to speak recklessly.

— *Bird Revelation*

Yes, that word again. I take it as an expressive term meant to cajole and harangue more so than a gratuitous slur. Here is the context: "I know there's some comedians in the back. Motherfucker, you have a responsibility to speak recklessly. Otherwise, my kids may never know what reckless talk sounds like. The joys of being wrong. I didn't come here to be right; I just came here to fuck around" (*Bird Revelation*). Chappelle is slippery here, not unlike Nietzsche whose aphorisms can at times appear inconsistent, cajoling us to "live dangerously" while he himself lived more like a "timid deer." The phrase "being wrong" is ambiguous: it could mean inappropriate, irreverent, a violation of social norms, or it could mean being incorrect, stating something false. Or it could mean both. I tend toward the first sense, as the use of "joy" and "fucking around" imply pleasures gained from rule-breaking or bending.

Chappelle's "reckless" talk above is addressing the #*MeToo* movement and revealing his ambivalent attitude toward it, but this bit is relevant to understanding his sort of propaganda in general. He is an ally for women, but admittedly with reservations: "If you guys keep going after individuals, *the system is going to stay intact.* You have to have men on your side. And I'm telling you right now, you're gonna have a lot of imperfect allies" (*Bird Revelation*). Similarly, to connect with racial oppression, the sort he often juxtaposes with injustices related to gender and sexual orientation, racism is *systemic*; it is not going to be adequately addressed if we are only concerned with individual instances of one racist harming one person of color. But, demagogic propaganda has pushed this individualistic account of racism for so long that many Americans will claim there is no institutional oppression against people of color today. And a large subset of that group dumbfoundingly admits they believe white males are currently the ones most oppressed.

Chappelle offers little by way of answers to these issues, but he does provide what good philosophical dialogues can do; leave us somewhat confused, hesitant, unsure, and uncomfortable. These are emotional states necessary, if not sufficient, to begin philosophical work on an issue. He is "fucking around" with social and legal conventions that did not have people like him in mind when they were constructed, other than to exclude him, so in that sense he is "wrong," but in a similar way that civil rights activists were "wrong" in their civil disobedience. There are good reasons for this sort of resistance, even as it might not directly appeal to reason.

Chappelle uses expressive language often, accentuating an idea hyperbolically—a common tool in humor—but that does not make his acts *un*reasonable, as most propaganda is. He surely appeals to emotion, mirth being just that, but his brand of comedy, like Du Bois's conception of propagandistic art, does not preclude reason. If Stanley's definition of "reasonableness" is apt, a "disposition to take the perspective of others in the community in proposing reasons, to be empathetic to them, and to respect their dignity" (p. 121), then Chappelle might be a *reasonable propagandist* who can navigate between different, and at times, adversarial points of view, sometimes out of necessity: "We who are dark can see America in a way that white Americans cannot. And seeing our country thus, are we satisfied with its present goals and ideals?" (*Criteria*, p. 17). His and Chappelle's answer is "No." Otherwise, what need is there for counter-propaganda? Artists like Chappelle dwell on the boundaries between the privileged and the marginalized, the latter often possessing deeper and more accurate insights into the perspectives of those with power. A white person rarely needs to reflect on what it means to be Black *or* white in America; but a Black person's failure to see from different perspectives, to be able to see themselves like others see them, can be lethal.

Chappelle's *explicit* language is not intended to be comforting, we have more than enough of that from demagogic propagandists, as Du Bois reminds us: "We have too often a deliberate attempt so to change the facts of history that the story will make pleasant reading for Americans" (*Reconstruction*, p. 758). Something like that has to be maintained in order to rationalize multiple systems, education, employment, healthcare, and of course, the *justice* system, and most relevant to Chappelle's comedic counter-insurgency, the "copaganda" perpetuating the myths about police benevolence in their purpose "To protect and serve" all people equally.

Positive, counter-propaganda is not revisionist history, or not merely that; it is calling out the errors in historical accounts that have real impacts on society today. It is disclosing by rendering it weird, an unjust status quo. In contrast, "What normalization does is transform the morally extraordinary into the ordinary. It makes us able to tolerate what was once intolerable by making it seem as if this is the way things have always been" (*How Propaganda Works*, p. 126). Chappelle's bit that opened this chapter at first glance appears to present an everyday, normal experience, but he wants us to view it as intolerable. What his propagandistic comedy does, as Shelley says of poetry, is transform what has become morally ordinary, normalized, and accepted, through negative propaganda, into something extraordinary that should compel us to say, "That shit is fucking incredible."

III

Everythings's Funny Until It Happens to You

9
Blouses and Pancakes

Mona Rocha and James Rocha

Charlie Murphy's True Hollywood Stories taught us many things. The Rick James story taught us that Rick James was very aware of what his name was, has a ring for his song "Unity," and that "cocaine's a hell of a drug."

That's already an awful lot, but we learn even more in the Prince story. We learn that Prince has serious basketball skills, makes delicious pancakes, and gender norms are a hell of a limitation on our autonomy and so must be challenged.

Significantly, we also learn a lot about Charlie Murphy. Charlie's inability to truly figure out Prince represents a widespread difficulty, which many of us share, to escape our reliance on socially constructed identities. As Charlie notes, Prince and his friends dress flamboyantly—yet, their socially designated feminine dress style has nothing to do with their ability to excel at basketball. At the same time, Prince then shifts effortlessly from dominance on the court to being a generous host serving late-night breakfast treats.

So what is gender? Gender generally refers to the idea that there are certain things commonly associated with being a woman or being a man, or with femininity or masculinity. Specific traits or behaviors, such as being caring, being emotive, or the color pink are linked to femininity, while being strong, being stoic, or the color blue are supposed to be linked to masculinity. Society propagates and teaches us these gender norms in myriad ways, from the TV we watch to the products that we buy, and even prior to birth. For example, gender-reveal parties associate the colors pink and blue with the girl or boy baby, setting up prescriptive behavior norms even before the child is born!

From an early age, young women are taught that being pretty will help them ensure that they find a mate and that

domesticity is their domain—toys for girls encourage domesticity. Additionally, women on magazine covers are presented as
solely concerned with their appearance or fashion, while
women in movies are depicted as helpless and in need of rescu-
ing. Young boys are taught that they need to hold in their feelings and that they should learn to fight to further their goals;
toys marketed for little boys encourage these traits, with action
figures, and superhero costumes proliferating toy aisles.
Likewise, on film, the action heroes of many blockbusters are
shown to be buff, aggressive, manly men who rescue or protect.
From daily behavior expectations ("Act like a lady!" or "Be a
man's man!") to Bic for Her pens in pastel colors vs. Cottonelle
Dude Wipes, gender norms are inescapable it seems, and
deeply entrenched in the collective consciousness of us all.

As you may have guessed, feminists—individuals who support equality for men and women—criticize gender norms as
arbitrary: why should a little girl play with an Easy Bake oven
and not with action figures? Or why not allow a little boy to
take ballet lessons instead of forcing him into football practice?
Gender norms are deeply entrenched in society, but they
shouldn't be taken unquestioningly and problematically as
markers of identity (as if people couldn't determine their own
identity regardless of the way society sees them). But gender
norms often place formulaic limitations around individuals, so
that they cannot explore the things that make them flourish as
persons.

Feminists hold that gender norms—the adherence to these
socially constructed traits associated with femininity or masculinity—are problematic and limit the authentic self-development of all humans. In other words, feminists support
self-expression for all. In feminist theory, this idea is also encap-
sulated under the heading of autonomy, or the trait of being self-
legislating—everyone should be able to take charge of their own
lives. Feminists believe that supporting the autonomy of others—their choices, life plans, likes or dislikes—and not reducing
them to a repressive gender binary, results in a reduction of
harmful stereotypes and in increasing respect for one another's
humanity. Importantly, it results in people embracing their true
selves. And in a way, that is exactly what the Prince in Charlie
Murphy's True Hollywood Stories is trying to do.

Versus Me and the Revolution

In the Chappelle skit, Charlie Murphy reminisces of a time
"around 1985" when he met Prince. Thus, the skit takes place

after Prince and his band, The Revolution, had released the widely successful album *Purple Rain* (which came out in 1984). Described as a "supernova of a performer who danced as hard as any of his dancers and played every instrument he could get his hands on" (*The Most Beautiful*, Chapter 3). Prince and his crew were gaining fame from their adoring public.

It is against this background that we see Charlie first meeting Prince. On the one hand, Charlie openly (and somewhat jealously) acknowledges that during this time, the guys who presented as "the most androgynous" were "getting all the women"—Charlie also characterizes this happening as "wild" (Season Two, Episode 5). He is also judgmental about it all. As such, Charlie is demonstrating the power of socially constructed gender normativity: male gender norms do not prescribe an androgynous look, but endorse attire that (somehow) communicates masculine traits, such as strength or toughness. Mixing in feminine elements for an androgynous look works against gender normativity and Charlie has been trained by society to disapprove of them.

Interestingly, though, Charlie ends up confessing that even he was adopting an androgynous look to appeal to women. After all, it was paying off in terms of attention from women and was being displayed by the immensely popular Prince. Prince—who embraced flamboyant fashion and make-up while blurring gender markers—was an admired sex symbol. However, it's important to heed a little caveat. Even while Prince (and other famous artists such as Boy George) modeled this gender fluid fashion, and helped normalize it to some extent, it can still be argued that fame and popularity at least somewhat insulated Prince from the various, serious harms that less affluent persons experienced for not fitting in with gender norms: after all, hate crimes proliferated during the 1980s (and similar hate crimes unfortunately continue to this day). Thus, in spite of introducing and popularizing a genderless image that played with identity markers, tension still remained in respect to societally prescribed gender normativity, resulting in various pressures or violence against those individuals who did not fit in with societally accepted identity markers for masculinity or femininity.

The skit illustrates this tension. For while remarking on the androgynous fashion trend and his own adoption of it, Charlie also hypocritically mocks Prince for his physical appearance, with his "big perm" and "drawn on" mustache (Season Two, Episode 5). Charlie further observes that Prince stood out from others in the club because of his generally extravagant look. He recollects that Prince had on "a Zorro type outfit, it had the ruffles that come down the front . . . it looked like something a figure skater would wear" (Season Two, Episode 5). In other words, Prince's image was not in accordance with male gender norms. Prince's image, of course, was intentional: former wife Mayte elaborated on Prince's look by noting that Prince put it together beautifully, with "eyeliner, heels, and ladies' perfume" (*The Most Beautiful*, Chapter 3). Yet, Charlie reacts to Prince's carefully curated appearance adversely, and further disparagingly calls Prince's top a "blouse" (Season Two, Episode 5). Charlie even follows up on his disapproval with another negative judgment: Charlie assumes that Prince is weak and unathletic for wearing this garment and fully expects that they would easily defeat Prince and The Revolution in a game of basketball.

Charlie's attitude perfectly illustrates the problem with gender normativity: oftentimes, a person's self-worth is not evaluated according to who they are, but according to how well they measure up to a gendered ideal. In other words, individuals end up disrespected or devalued for not measuring up to the artificial standards that society expects to see for men and women.

Gender norms problematically hold that young boys are weak or spineless for being emotive or displaying caring behavior (which, in accordance to gender norms, should be traits belonging to people who were assigned "female" at birth). But of course, these traits—being caring or in touch with one's emotions—should not be associated with a particular gender, much less be seen as markers of weakness; rather, being caring and emotional should actually be encouraged for all persons for the sake of everyone's mental health and well-being (and for a slew of other reasons).

Unfortunately, though, not fitting in immediately with prescribed gender norms is seen as a deficiency that provides an opportunity for insult—which Charlie's behavior illustrates when he treats Prince as feeble for wearing a blouse. And Charlie still has this belittling attitude in spite of being star struck and somewhat jealous of Prince. So even the famous and successful are stereotyped and prodded for not fitting within standard gender norms.

Purifying in Lake Minnetonka

Charlie Murphy recalls that Prince invited him and his crew to his place after meeting at the club, and asked them to join in a game of basketball. As a generous host, Prince even provided workout clothes to his guests; in fact, Prince was known in real life to go "to great lengths to see that guests were comfortable and well cared for" (*The Most Beautiful*, Chapter 4). Unfortunately, Charlie repaid this welcoming attitude and kindness with rudeness in that his reaction was homophobic or transphobic. As Charlie recalls, he burst out laughing when Prince invited them to a game of basketball, exclaiming in disbelief: "This n****r must be joking man . . . I don't know where he's going with this shit" (Season Two, Episode 5). The belief that someone who would wear a feminine shirt must be unskilled at basketball is so strong for Charlie that it results in his outright derision of his host; he ends up calling the game "the shirts against the blouses" and is assured of his upcoming victory (Season Two, Episode 5).

The skit illustrates an important lesson against judging people negatively for not fitting in with prescribed gender norms. Not only is that offensive, it's also wrong, as gender and identity markers do not entail the presence or absence of any skills. As Charlie explains further of the basketball game, "And when I said that, this look came on Prince's face. He ice grilled me" (Season Two, Episode 5). Charlie still defends his insults: "You know where you got that shirt and it damn sure wasn't from the men's department" (Season Two, Episode 5). He is so deeply entrenched in the societally accepted narrative that gender normativity dictates identity that he just keeps going down the wrong path.

But, as it turned out, Prince had serious basketball skills. Prince and his crew—even playing in their club clothes and without the benefit of athletic gear—decisively beat "the shirts." Charlie wonderingly acknowledges that Prince was "getting rebounds like Charles Barkley" and setting up intricate plays like "Computer Blue" or "Darling Pinky" (Season Two, Episode 5). As Prince's friends recall of the artist, "he was an excellent basketball player" even at five feet two, and had started playing in junior high and avidly played basketball with friends, lovers, and roadies alike throughout his life (*The Most Beautiful*, Chapters 1, 3, and 5). It comes as no surprise that he would dominate over Charlie's team. Prince possessed athletic prowess, in sharp contrast to the fictitious image of Prince imprinted in Charlie's mind.

As Charlie discovers in the skit, a dress style that is socially designated as feminine is nevertheless consistent with Prince excelling at basketball. That is because gender norms and gender normativity do not translate to who an individual really is. But even as he recognizes that Prince is like "ice" on the court,

Charlie Murphy still engages in demeaning and homophobic commentary, problematically describing the plays Prince successfully sets up as "fruity" and indicating that their play was somehow sexually deviant (Season Two, Episode 5). This mix of attitudes—on one hand recognizing Prince's skill, on the other hand putting him and his friends down—illustrates not only the deep entrenchment of gender norms, but also Charlie's inability to understand Prince's authentically chosen identity traits, and a widespread difficulty to escape our reliance on socially constructed identities.

Prince's landslide basketball victory is immediately followed with him serving everyone pancakes—thus showing that Prince is shifting without trouble from dominance on the court to the role of generous host serving late night breakfast treats. The skit seems to come close to real life yet again. In real life, friends and companions recall that Prince enjoyed cooking, often preparing scrambled eggs and pancakes for guests from scratch; his former wife Mayte recollects many happy occasions when Prince cooked for them (*The Most Beautiful*, Chapter 5).

What comes across, then, is a Prince who is comfortable with domesticity, and dons it because it is meaningful to him in some way—perhaps practically (hey, it's better if you know how to cook since you need to eat) or because it's associated with a special bond between him and a loved one (Mayte saw their happy breakfasts as a way for Prince to recast a joyful childhood, since he was deprived of such happy moments growing up) (Chapter 5). or simply because feeding others fits under the duties of a host. In any case, Prince is actively resisting gender norms being imposed on him, and is effortlessly shifting between them in accordance to what he wants to do and what he wants to accomplish in the moment. To Charlie though, none of this makes sense, as he bewilderedly asks, "Who the fuck can make up that shit?" (Season Two, Episode 5).

This fluidity resists the binary categorization artificially imposed by society and goes back to underline the importance of autonomy. As Prince explained once in a letter, life was about making choices and being true to ones' self: "sometimes freedom moves in mysterious ways and in the end it's 'whatever peanut butters your jelly'" (Chapter 7). Prince's attitude here, of embracing, accepting, and celebrating "whatever peanut butters your jelly" is all about respecting the autonomous choices others make, and not boxing in others based on artificial, preconceived gender norms—which matches the feminist project discussed earlier.

The tension between societal expectation and authenticity nevertheless carries a cost. As Prince said, "you can't look at yourself through other people's eyes . . . if you don't act like they expect you to, then you're the bad one" (Chapter 4). In other words, most people remain socially conditioned to see the world through the lens of gender stereotypes. Prince challenges this confused viewpoint through his very existence: Prince unapologetically defies our social expectations for gender while also capturing the wider public's admiration and approval.

Charlie Murphy's experiences with Prince thus show the danger of unreflectively categorizing people based on our pre-conceived notions of their identity traits. And for a tiny bit, Charlie Murphy seems to get that lesson, but to him, in the end, it's all so bizarre that he ends up insisting that he is not making any of it up. Of course he's not making it up: people are varied and so are their choices. And it sure would be a much more of a beautiful world if we all practiced a "whatever peanut butters your jelly attitude" and folks were accepted for who they are.

In the end, Dave Chappelle has provided a skit that challenges gender roles at the most fundamental level, while also illustrating the need to restructure our society for the better, which ultimately allows us to conclude: "Game: Blouses."

10
Upsetting the Alphabet People

Zoe Walker

In his Netflix special *Sticks and Stones*, Dave Chappelle lets his audience in on an "unwritten and unspoken rule of show business," a rule that ended Kevin Hart's Oscar-hosting dreams and has plagued Chappelle's own career too: "You are never ever allowed to upset the alphabet people."

Ominous words indeed. And just who are these tyrannical overlords of showbiz, whom all comedians ought to fear? They are of course "them L's and them B's and them G's and them T's," or, if we dare speak their true name aloud, the LGBTQ+ community.

Considering his usually on-the-money observations about politics and society, Chappelle's characterisation of the LGBTQ+ community as the gatekeepers of popular culture is a little odd. The near-absence of any stories in popular culture that prominently feature any of those L's, G's, B's or T's is pretty upsetting for many alphabet people, yet that doesn't seem to have got in the way of anyone's showbiz career. And even when comedy overtly makes fun of LGBTQ+ people—as do Chappelle and Hart and other successful comedians like Ricky Gervais—the repercussions are hardly severe. Chappelle continues to win Emmys and Grammys for his Netflix specials. Hart voluntarily chose to step down as Oscar host rather than apologize for his jokes, and his show *Seriously Funny*, in which one of the offending jokes appears, is still available on Netflix.

Gervais received online backlash for his jokes about Caitlyn Jenner at the 2016 Golden Globes, but that didn't stop him from getting invited back for the same gig a few years later, or from having a Netflix special—*Humanity*—in which he discusses and adds to those jokes. So it's not hard to be skeptical about Chappelle's view of the LGBTQ+ community as all-powerful rulers of comedy.

But let's forget about all that for the time being, and assume that Chappelle is right: making jokes about the LGBTQ+ community is risky business. Is that a bad thing? How wrong is it for comedians to receive serious backlash for making fun of LGBTQ+ people? The title *Sticks and Stones* suggests that Chappelle thinks that what he says should not be policed, because, as the saying goes, sticks and stones may break your bones, but words will never hurt you. His critics, on the other hand, seem to think that his words are capable of more damage than he realizes. So let's take a look at some of the ways Chappelle has upset the alphabet people, and see whether they have good reason to be upset.

Slurring Words

- CONTENT WARNING: Discussion of homophobic and racist slurs.

One way that Chappelle is likely to have upset a few alphabet people is in his frequent use of homophobic slurs—particularly "f****t" but also "d*ke." Indeed, this is one of the things Chappelle tells us has got him into trouble before: in *Sticks and Stones*, he recounts a story from the days of *Chappelle's Show*, when a woman from the Department of Standards and Practices—Renée—told him that he couldn't use the word "f****t" in the show. In response to this criticism, he asked why it was that he couldn't use that slur, but he was allowed to say "n****r" with impunity. He was told "you are not gay," to which he pithily responded, "I'm not a n****r either."

This exchange touches on two philosophical questions about slurs. Chappelle's claim—"I'm not a n****r"—is a view about the meaning of slurs: what does it actually mean when you use a slur in a sentence? Renée's claim—that Chappelle can't say "f****t" because he's not gay—is a view about the "reclamation" or "appropriation" of slurs: can slur words be used in a way that no longer has the force of a slur, and if so, who can use them in this way? Thinking about these questions will help us determine what Chappelle's view of slurs is, and whether it's okay for him to use homophobic slurs in his comedy.

Let's start with the question of what slurs actually mean. Clearly, a slur targets someone because of their membership of a particular social group: because they're gay, for example, or because they're Black. But when you address or describe someone with a slur, you're not just neutrally addressing or describing them as being a member of that social group. You're also doing something derogatory towards people in that social group—hence why using slurs is (usually) viewed as wrong. The puzzle is about that derogatory bit of a slur: is it part of the meaning of the word or not? Does "you are a f****t" mean something like "you are a gay man, and gay men are inferior"? Or does it just mean "you are a gay man," but gets used in a way that conjures up a set of pernicious beliefs and attitudes about gay people?

Chappelle suggests both of these views at different times. On the one hand, as we've seen, he says "I'm not a n****r." If all that word means is 'Black person,' then he must be saying "I'm not a Black person," which can't be right. But on the other hand, he uses the word 'n****r' very frequently himself, and if it means something like "a Black person, and Black people are inferior," then he's constantly saying that Black people are inferior, which can't be right either.

One way to resolve this puzzle is to suggest that a slur isn't saying something is inferior about all members of a group, but only about a specific subset of that group. This seems to be how Chris Rock uses the racist slur in his infamous routine "N***as vs. Black People": for him "n****r" refers to a particular sort of black person with negative characteristics, to be distinguished from most Black people, who aren't like that.

Understanding Chappelle's use of the slur in this way makes sense of his claim that "I'm not a n****r" and would also make it possible for him to be using the slur all the time without claiming that all Black people are inferior. However, when Chappelle uses the slur, he doesn't seem to mean anything negative about anyone, and if anything uses it in an affectionate way. So I don't think this can be what Chappelle takes the word to mean.

A second way to resolve the puzzle is to suggest that when Chappelle uses "n****r" it has a different meaning to the meaning it has when racist people use it. When racists use it, they mean something like "Black person, and Black people are inferior." But when Chappelle uses it, he means something like "Black person, and Black people are equal to white people," or "Black person, and I approve of Black people." If this is right, then his word n****r" is really a different word than the racists' word "n****r" a homophone that's just spelt the same—like how "ruler" as in "person in charge of a country" and "ruler" as in "measuring implement" are two different words with different meanings that are spelt the same. This homophone interpretation is backed up by the fact that Chappelle actually often uses the word to describe some-one who isn't even Black—for example, when talking about Louis C.K., he says that women "ruined this n****r's life." This suggests that his use of the word really is entirely different from the racist's use.

If this is right, then we might understand Chappelle to be defending his use of "f****t" by claiming that he means some-thing different by it from what homophobic people mean, just as he means something different from what racists mean when he uses the other slur. What a relief: Dave Chappelle is not homophobic after all, but merely homophonic.

But I don't think this way of understanding Chappelle is going to cut it. Chappelle is asking why it's okay for him to use "n****r" with impunity when he's "not a n****r." Surely, then, these two occurrences of that word are not just homophones: he is talking about the same word. Otherwise, this response he gives would be irrelevant—like bringing up measuring implements in a conver-sation about people in charge of countries. Instead, it looks as though he is using the same word with the same meaning in both cases, and it's just the derogatory force of the word that differs.

If we're going to understand Chappelle as thinking that derogatory force is separate from the meaning of the word—let's call it the "outside force" view—then we'll have to explain away two bits of data that supported our homophone view. First, we need to explain why Chappelle says "I'm not a n****r," because of course we don't want to claim that he was saying "I'm not a Black person." Now, according to the homophone view, Chappelle must have been using the racist version of the word here rather than his own non-racist version, so what he was denying was "I'm a Black person and Black people are infe-rior." The outside force view can say something similar. When Chappelle says "I'm not a n****r," he's saying the slurring word with the derogatory force that a racist would say it with, and it's this derogatory force that he's rejecting when he makes this claim.

The other thing we need to explain is why Chappelle uses the slurring word to talk about people who aren't Black, like Louis C.K., if it only ever has one meaning, and that meaning is "Black person." To explain this, we'll need to think about who is targeted by derogatory uses of slurring words. Are slurs that target a particular group only ever directed at members of that group? I think not. There have surely been occasions when someone has said of a straight man, for example, that "he's not gay, but he's still a f****t." What someone means when they say this is that the man is like a gay man in some relevant way—and are derogating the man for that reason. We can imagine a similar thing for racial slurs too, or gender-based slurs. So it looks as though even in the derogatory case, we need to expand the meaning of a slur: "f****t" means not just "gay man," but "gay man or someone who is like a gay man in a relevant way."

How does this help us with the Louis C.K. problem? Well, similarly, we are now saying that "n****r" means (in both derogatory and non-derogatory contexts) "Black person or person who is like a Black person in a relevant way." From the mouth of a racist, describing Louis C.K. as being like a Black person would come with a derogatory force, but from Dave Chappelle's mouth, the force it carries is affectionate, suggesting friendliness or sympathy.

It looks, then, as though we can defend our "outside force" view of slurs. But how is it that Chappelle can change the force of a slurring word like this, to make it affectionate rather than derogatory? This brings us onto our second puzzle about slurs: the puzzle of reclamation. As we saw, Renée from the Department of Standards and Practices thought that whether or not someone could reclaim a slur had to do with whether or not they belonged to the group targeted by the slur—she thought Chappelle couldn't use "f****t" because he's not gay. This looks like a pretty common-sense view, in line with what people tend to think about who can reclaim slurs. But it would be handy if we had some kind of explanation to back this intuition up.

To answer this, we need to think about what exactly the "derogatory force" of slurring is. Sure, when a homophobe uses a homophobic slur, they're derogating gay people, but how exactly does that derogating work? So far, all I've really said is that slurs conjure up a set of pernicious beliefs and attitudes about the target group. But it's not just that slurs bring to mind those beliefs and attitudes—if that was all they did, they'd be no worse than a history lesson about racism, or homophobia, or whatever relevant form of discrimination. Instead, what they do is licence those beliefs and attitudes in the here and now. When someone uses a racist slur, they're signalling to anyone listening that they think the associated racist beliefs and attitudes are a-okay, and suggesting that it's appropriate for other people to share them, and act on them. When you use a racist slur, you're not just saying a word—you're performing the action of altering what's appropriate in that context, so that it includes racist thinking and behaviour.

So why is it that when Dave Chappelle uses a racist slur, we don't take him to be licencing racist thinking and behavior? Well, because we know that he doesn't think racist thinking and behaviour are appropriate. Not only is he himself Black, but he also regularly criticizes and mocks racism in his comedy, which makes it really obvious that he doesn't intend his use of the word to have a derogatory, racism-licencing force. And because it's so obvious that he isn't intending this force, he doesn't have this force.

Now things are starting to look a little clearer. Whether or not a slur has a derogatory, discrimination-licencing force behind it will depend on whether or not we as hearers take it to have that force. The default is that it does have this force—after all, that was what the slur was developed for in the first place. But sometimes people mean to use the slur in a different way—to reclaim the word—and when we as hearers have enough evidence to conclude that they're reclaiming the word rather than using it with its original force, the force changes. It's a joint effort, between speaker and hearers.

Finally, then, we can answer the question we started with: is it okay for Dave Chappelle to use the word "f****t"? That depends on whether his use of it is derogatory and discrimination-licencing, and that in turn depends on whether he's given us any evidence to think that he's reclaiming the word, rather than using it with its typical homophobic force. Chappelle is not gay, so that's one potential piece of evidence—perhaps the most convincing—out of the window. But maybe if everything else he said was really obviously anti-homophobic, that would suffice.

The trouble is, it isn't. Chappelle implies that he's quite literally afraid of LGBTQ+ people, suggesting that they have the ability to ruin his career if he upsets them. He also makes a lot of jokes at the expense of gay and trans people, and defends other comedians who do too. So, even if we're being generous, it's at least unclear whether Dave Chappelle is homophobic, meaning he has not done enough to cancel the derogatory, discrimination-licencing force of the word "f****t." And that means the alphabet people are licenced to be upset.

Trans-gressions

Slurs are not the only place that Dave Chappelle has fallen foul of the LGBTQ+ community. In *Sticks and Stones*, he tells us that "the T's hate my fucking guts," the T's of course being the transgender community. And Chappelle initially appears to take responsibility for this: "I don't blame them. It's not their fault, it's mine. I can't stop telling jokes about these n****rs. I don't wanna write these jokes, but I just can't stop!"

Great—here's an instance of Chappelle recognising that he's done the LGBTQ+ community dirty, and offering something like an apology. But wait—what's this? A mere six minutes later, and he's already changing his tune: "I feel bad for T's. But they're so confusing. And it's not all my fault, I feel like they need to take some responsibility for my jokes." Oh well. It was nice while it lasted.

What Chappelle is suggesting here is that transgender people have brought his jokes on themselves, by being so confusing, and, as he goes on to say, comical. "I didn't come up with this idea on my own," he tells us, "this idea that someone can be born in the wrong body. But they have to admit that's a fucking hilarious predicament."

Once again, Chappelle's LGBTQ+-themed comedy prompts some interesting philosophical questions. First off, do transgender people have to admit that theirs is a fucking hilarious predicament? And second, whether or not there are good grounds for finding transgender people funny, is Chappelle doing anything particularly objectionable by making jokes about them, or is he just having a harmless laugh?

To start tackling these questions, let's think a bit about what makes things funny. There are a few competing theories in the philosophy of humour, but the most widely accepted one is incongruity theory: the view that what makes something funny is the presence of an incongruity—something unusual and surprising that shocks us into laughter. It looks pretty likely that this is the sort of thing Chappelle finds funny about the experience of transgender people. Being, as he puts it, "born in the wrong body," or in other words being a different gender to the one you were assigned at birth, is unusual and surprising to most people, and comedy about transgender people tends to play off that fact.

But incongruity isn't all it takes for something to be funny. Sometimes surprise and shock and confusion aren't funny but scary. Horror movies make heavy use of this, with jump scares that startle and frighten us, or with characters slowly going insane whose increasingly strange behaviour makes us more and more scared. These strange, surprising things could easily be funny if we felt less tense and threatened—which is sometimes what happens when a horror movie with bad acting or effects fails to make us tense, so we start finding it funny rather than scary. This lack of tension or threat appears to make the difference between whether we find a surprise funny or scary. Think also of when someone says "boo" to a baby—whether the baby laughs or cries will depend on whether it feels threatened.

So for something to be funny, it needs to be surprising, but in a context where we don't feel under threat. For someone to find the transgender experience funny, then, they need to find it surprising and unusual, but in a non-threatening way. This tells us a lot about Chappelle's view of transgender people: he's not very used to seeing or hearing about transgender people, so still finds it incongruous, but he doesn't feel threatened by transgender people, so finds them funny rather than scary.

Should we expect transgender people to be in a similar position, and to find their own predicament "fucking hilarious"? For some transgender people, who've grown up with more exposure to the LGBTQ+ community, being transgender will not be as unusual or surprising as Chappelle finds it. But for many, it will be just as confusing and hard to wrap their head around as it is for Chappelle. The difference is, though, that when you are transgender yourself, it's not just some hypothetical and non-threatening concept. It's actively dangerous to be transgender, with transgender people facing a huge amount of discrimination and harm. It's pretty unlikely, then, that a transgender person would find their predicament both confusing and non-threatening—extremely unlikely that they'd find it "fucking hilarious."

This is a lesson that Chappelle knew once, but seems to have forgotten. In his 2017 show *The Bird Revelation*, he makes a very similar joke about transgender people being born in the wrong body, and how funny that is. But that time, he admits: "it's funny when it's not happening to you."

So transgender people are unlikely to find Chappelle's jokes about them funny. But this alone wouldn't make his jokes morally bad. So is he doing anything worse to the transgender community than just telling jokes they wouldn't find funny?

One good thing about Chappelle's comedy, that we've already seen, is that he's painting transgender people as non-threatening. A major reason why transgender people have been denied rights in the past is that people have felt threatened by them—in particular, some cisgender women have felt threatened by the idea of allowing trans women into women's spaces. If Chappelle can change cisgender people's view of the transgender community so they view them as non-threatening, and stop being afraid to allow them to live as a different gender from the one they were assigned at birth, this could help remove some of the obstacles to the progress of trans rights.

On the other hand, being viewed not just as non-threatening but as comical is a barrier to acceptance. If people are encouraged to find your existence absurd and ridiculous, then they're unlikely to treat you with respect and dignity, and accept you for who you are. We can explain what Chappelle's doing here in relation to the incongruity theory. When Chappelle makes lots of jokes about how funny being transgender is, he's saying that transgender people are non-threatening, but he's also saying that they're incongruous: unusual and strange. Now incongruity is not some objective fact about the world—something is incongruous in relation to a particular norm, a particular set of expectations about how people ought to be.

If you keep painting transgender people as incongruous, then what you're really doing is insisting that people ought to be cisgender, that this is the normal way to be, so that whatever differs is incongruous. And clearly this is damaging for transgender people—much as using a homophobic slur is damaging for gay people, or using a racist slur is damaging for Black people, by suggesting that certain derogatory ways of thinking about them are appropriate and licensed.

That's not to say that there's no room for comedy about being transgender. There are many trans comedians with plenty of funny incongruities to point out about their experiences. For example, consider this joke from trans comedian Jeffrey Jay, making fun of transphobia amongst gay men: "When I tell a gay guy I'm trans he says, "Awww, sweetie, I like real boys." What am I, Pinocchio?" The difference is that jokes like these are pointing out incongruities in the status quo, and laughing at those, rather than insisting on the status quo by laughing at people who fall outside of it.

Why Upset the Alphabet People?

When Dave Chappelle uses homophobic slurs, or makes jokes about trans people, he is insisting on an anti-LGBTQ+ way of seeing the world. Perhaps this isn't always intentionally malicious, but there's no denying that he feels he has a serious bone to pick with the LGBTQ+ community. He never misses the opportunity to crack a joke about gay men, or trans women, and, as we saw, he rather bizarrely thinks "them Ls and them Gs and them Bs and them Ts" wield an undue amount of power in show business. So where does this vendetta come from? There are clues to this in *Sticks and Stones*, but for a better understanding of why Chappelle is so keen to upset the alphabet people, it will help to look back to some of his earlier Netflix specials.

In *The Age of Spin*, he talks about his reaction to Caitlyn Jenner coming out as trans (misgendering her as he does):

> And when I heard he was gonna do it, I was scared. I didn't think the public was ready. I didn't think the media was ready. And you know what? I was wrong. Not only did the public embrace him, but the media was nice. I'd never seen anything like it. "Welcome to the world, Caitlyn. So long, Bruce. Hello Caitlyn."

Chappelle expected the public and the media to tear Jenner down, and was shocked when they didn't. And as an American, he tells us, he was pleased for his country. But as a Black American, he was "a little jealous." Neatly referring back to an earlier joke about Jenner beating Africans in the Olympics when she was an athlete, he recounts:

> I was like, "How the fuck are transgender people beating Black people in the discrimination Olympics?" If the police shot half as many transgenders as they did n****rs last year, there'd be a fucking war in L.A. I know Black dudes in Brooklyn—hard street motherfuckers—that wear heels just to feel safe.

As Chappelle sees it, while systemic racism and racially motivated police brutality and murder are still a huge and largely unaddressed problem in the US, transgender people like Caitlyn Jenner are able to find immediate acceptance and stop facing discrimination with relative speed and ease. From Chappelle's point of view, in the "discrimination Olympics," trans rights, and LGBTQ+ rights more generally, are progressing a lot faster than Black rights. No wonder then that he feels such frustration towards the LGBTQ+ community.

In *Equanimity*, he offers us a diagnosis of the situation:

> I cannot shake this awful suspicion that the only reason everybody is talking about transgenders is because white men want to do it . . . It reeks of white privilege. You never asked yourself why it was easier for Bruce Jenner to change his gender than it was for Cassius Clay to change his fucking name?

Chappelle's observation is that gay rights and trans rights have gained a lot more traction than Black rights because the former are advocated for by people who already have some kind of social power, as a result of being white and (viewed as) male. The comparison he draws between Caitlyn Jenner and Muhammad Ali is especially stark as an illustration of this. Now, I don't think Chappelle is right about everything here, but he definitely has a powerful point.

Where I think Chappelle goes wrong is in taking Caitlyn Jenner to have a typical transgender experience. She is about the most socially powerful it is possible for a trans woman to be. She is white, to begin with, but that's not all she has going for her: she is extremely rich, and also already had social capital as a celebrity. Even amongst the white trans community, this is not the typical experience, and most would have a far harder time gaining acceptance and avoiding discrimination and abuse than Jenner has. And importantly, there are also many Black trans people, who are possibly the most vulnerable demographic there is, with Black trans women being routinely attacked and even murdered.

So while certain members of the LGBTQ+ community have benefited from being white or rich, many haven't, yet they suffer just as much from anti-LGBTQ+ jokes—indeed, given that they're more vulnerable, they probably suffer more. Viewing discrimination as a competition is unhelpful, and distracts us from who's really in power, and really to blame. I am skeptical that a Black man would be safer on the streets of New York if he pretended to be a trans woman, but the main thing is that even if he were safer, he certainly wouldn't be safe.

On the flipside, here's where Chappelle is right. While it's good whenever the public and the media are able to accept some gay and trans people, it is certainly really insulting to Black people that they by contrast have been denied rights, power, and freedom from discrimination and police brutality for so long. Mocking the LGBTQ+ community isn't the way to redress this injustice, but you can see why Dave Chappelle is so angry.

---

[1] This chapter was informed by work on slurs by Luvell Anderson and Ernie Lepore ("Slurring Words"), Quill Kukla ("Slurs, Interpellation, and Ideology"), and Cassie Herbert ("Precarious Projects: The Performative Structure of Reclamation"), and work on the philosophy of humor by Noël Carroll ("Horror and Humour").

11

Is Dave Chappelle a Feminist?

CHRISTOPHER M. INNES

I've considered Dave Chappelle the man's comedian for years. His view is that women's femininity ought to stay, in contrast with his view of men's masculinity. He once told Oprah that he refused to wear a dress in a movie sketch, believing it was not something he'd do and feel comfortable with. (They told him that all good comedians have worn a dress at least once.) I'm not talking about their not having his size; it's to do with his individualism and strong masculine identity. But one evening, watching an old 1998 HBO *Comedy Half Hour* episode, I heard him say, "Women have made a lot of progress in a short amount of time." That struck me as funny, but not in an amusing way.

Being in favor of equality between men and women would not be a surprise from a man in the comedy limelight. Not supporting women in their fight to gain equal rewards for their work and skills is not only bad for business (they do make up a large part of his audience—or at least so the frequent chorus of boos and howls at some of his risqué jokes tells me), but it isn't funny. In *Killin' Them Softly*, he makes fun of women for living a complex double standard—of wanting equality with men but also wanting to be seen as sexually desirable to men.

> You can see it. You ever have this happen? This is how confusing it is . . . Like a guy will be out . . . this happens a lot, guys . . . you see a girl. You might try to talk to her. It just might not come out right . . . The girl gets mad at you. "Oh, uh-uhh. Oh, wait a minute. Wait a minute! Just because I'm dressed this way, does NOT . . . make me a whore." Which is true. gentlemen, that is true. Just because they dress a certain way doesn't mean they are a certain way. Don't ever forget it. But, ladies, you must understand that that is fucking confusing.

This is a joke at a cost to men as well as women. But making fun of women's and men's complex roles does indicate awareness of a liberal feminist position where there is a demand for equality. Perhaps Chappelle is showing sympathy for this demand by being funny about its absurd application in real life circumstances where there seems to be more conservative observance to traditional gender roles. Chappelle says this is confusing to men. But this is confusing to me because I am trying to figure out his position on feminism. Is Chappelle sympathetic to liberal feminism or is he in favor of a more conservative line of thinking?

What Is the American Liberal Feminist Line of Thinking Anyway?

American Liberal Feminism is largely a movement for legal equality between the sexes. It asks mostly for legal change as the solution to anything that is preventing women from gaining equal rights. As a call for liberation of women, it expects that women and men should benefit equally from their hard work and talents. To have men benefit more from their efforts is seen as unjust. Spotting this injustice is the start. The next stage is to address this disparity. For liberals, it's straight forward: you change the laws and regulations that have hitherto hindered women. For the modern feminist, this will certainly include laws on employment.

For mainstream American Liberal Feminism, the solutions are pretty clear: legislation such as the Kennedy 1963 Equal Pay Act. Or, more fundamentally, change to the US Constitution such as the Nineteenth Amendment giving women the vote in 1920. Ratification of the Equal Rights Amendment (ERA) is a continuous goal.

The First Wave of feminism in the nineteenth and early twentieth centuries saw Susan B. Anthony and Elizabeth Cady Stanton fighting for equal voting rights after being inspired by the writings of women like Harriet Taylor Mill. The Second Wave in the 1970s also called for equality in social, and family life which would affect ways women are expected to act. Betty Friedan's *Feminine Mystique* inspired major players such as Gloria Steinem. Her magazine, *Ms.*, agitated for women to have the right to an abortion as central to the struggle for women's liberation. The Supreme Court's 1973 *Roe v. Wade* decision made abortion legal. This is a legal right. Legal justice is not radical, and legal justice aims to create justice by extending the Law, as it exists, to include women. It's only with the Third

Wave that feminism becomes less legalistic, with strands such as eco-feminism where women like Greta Thunberg later play a major part. The Fourth Wave is more to do with #MeToo and the revival of pressure groups in getting the ERA ratified. But wait, the Equal Rights Amendment has been hanging around for decades and still isn't ratified? What happened?

HBO's *Mrs. America* dramatically shows the 1970s second wave of feminism as the struggle for the ratification of the ERA. In the docudrama series, Phyllis Schlafly, the leader of the "No-ERA" movement is an anti-feminist. She says the "libbers" want to take away the rights women already have. These rights are the everyday courtesies such as women having the door opened for them, and more serious privileges such as not having to fight in wars. No longer expecting women to be obliged to stay at home, not to mention having them go to war, will result in the corrosion of what it is to be a woman. To lose these privileges is to give up women's real rights. Schlafly's *slippery-slope* rhetorical style argues that if women are given equal rights, they are, by a natural process in the distribution of equal rights, given the right to be drafted into the armed forces. If drafted into the armed forces, they will be fighting in fox holes. If they fight in fox holes, then they will die. One part of the argument slips down the slope, uncontrollably, to the next. This is a bad argument dressed up to look convincing— convincing enough that Schlafly and her followers effectively tabled the Equal Rights Amendment.

Is Dave Chappelle Mrs. America?

Like Schlafly, Chappelle often gives the impression of not being sympathetic to feminism. We can compare Schlafly's positions with Chappelle's routines and his saying that "Chivalry is dead, and it's women who killed it."

> Chivalry got killed by the feminist movement on all them magazines that got women going crazy, because women got too much advice about men from other women. And they don't know what the fuck they're talking about. (*Killin' Them Softly*)

Later in this piece, however, we see that he's very much sympathetic with the plight of women. He says that the feminists influence the magazines which then trick women and pick at their self-esteem by making them feel fat. He seems to sympathize with *women* while criticizing the feminist movement. We see Schlafly openly declaring that she is a conservative and not a feminist. Is Chappelle a conservative without any feminist sympathies, or do we have to look closer to see if he holds the view that conservatism and feminism are in some way compatible?

In a 1998 HBO *Comedy Half Hour* (Season Four, Episode 1) routine, Chappelle tells of his three-o'clock-in-the-afternoon trip to a strip joint. He admits he's going to see some topless women, a confession of sorts, but one where you know he's going to do it again. A strip joint worker asks one of the patrons to take off his baseball cap because it's disrespectful to the "ladies"—the strippers. He describes that strip joint as having a "weird morality," which is explained with vivid imagery showing the absurdity of being allowed to slip a $20 bill to one of the strippers, but he'd better not be wearing a hat while he does it. Chappelle, here, is walking a tightrope between women's rights and preserving the masculine and feminine divide. Is the tightrope walk one that provides a sound balance of conservatism and feminism, with Chappelle's ideals tilting toward feminism?

Where Do Black Sisters Come into This Picture?

Many Black feminists such as Margaret Sloan-Hunter saw that Black women were not being represented in the wide mainstream feminist movement. She attempted to correct that. But feminist interests based on the presumption that white feminists represent Black feminists, created policies that were largely only in the interest of white women. As seen in Friedan's *Feminine Mystique,* such interests largely ignored the issues of Black women. This led Margaret Sloan-Hunter to create the National Black Feminist Organization.

The Black feminist outlook has more to do with a woman's experience as a social, political, and sexual being whose role is subverted in a patriarchal hierarchy where men subject women to their needs at the cost of women's needs. It's born of many different types of oppression that white feminism fails to understand. Black women are taught from an early age to be subservient to white people and Black men. This is a double disadvantage. This subversion might be seen more as oppression than the simple liberal view of disadvantage. Overall, Black feminism wants to express what it is to be a Black woman and not be perceived through a "token" perspective perpetuated by the general media. Simply being included in broad feminism to give the appearance of diversity is not good enough. It's this tokenism that reduces the Black woman's experience to being viewed in a shallow way, reducing its significance.

Black feminism, though, includes many aspects of disadvantage not acknowledged or experienced by white feminists. To be a Black woman means that you are more likely to live in poverty than a white woman. The National Women's Law Center, in its October 2019 fact sheet, gives statistics showing twenty percent of Black women in poverty compared to nine percent of white women. It is more difficult for Black women than it is for average middle-class white women to get access to education and welfare provisions. Sexism and class are often entwined and inseparable making a single gender equality strategy impossible.

This might be a good place to note that Chappelle is well aware that the Black working class is disadvantaged. In his 2004 special in San Francisco he talks about a bridge being a race divider, which tells us that he sees "the surreal nature of racism" (*Killin' Them Softly*). He raises the issue of justice-system disadvantage when he depicts Black people's having a surprisingly high level of knowledge of the judicial penal sentencing by knowing what crime gets what sentence. This is in contrast to a white person's reply to a cop, "I didn't know I couldn't do that." And not to forget Chappelle's routine about why every Black group of friends has at least two white dudes. It's so they can negotiate with the police.

Returning to Black feminism, Black women's sexist experience is different from that experienced by white women. It's difficult for Black feminism to confront Black male attitudes. There is a fear of disproportionality where Black males will be dealt with more severely than whites. Black males are often blamed for being more sexist than are white males.

Gary L. Lemons says that Black men are often trapped in the "othered" space. "It is the racist sexual masculine myth" that Black men are this unreachable gender. bell hooks speaks of the "Blaxploitation" TV shows and movies such as *Shaft* and to a lesser extent Huggy Bear in *Starsky and Hutch* who are these super masculine Black men. They with the "dick-clutching" hip-hop artists are an echo of the racist past where Black identity is removed and super masculine sexuality forced in its place.

Chappelle's sketch about *Roots* and Kunta Kinte being whipped until he accepts the name given by his new master shows a glimpse of the United States' racist past. This was a form of social control. Myisha Cherry of University of California at Riverside, talks of the burdensome nature of this masculinity as a virtue forced on Black men and femininity forced upon Black women: ambition for women is vice and for men is a virtue. A Black woman's being ambitious is nasty and a man's being caring is unmanly. Chappelle is in a tricky situation where he might want to make progress on feminist issues but is held back by being super-masculine.

This is where we see the rise of Black feminism and where we see Chappelle placed as a Black man. He is a Black comedian making jokes and writing skits about women's political and sexual liberation. Are we to expect him to have the same attitude as a white male? It's in this situation where it's necessary to ask: What type of feminist is Dave Chappelle? It's not likely to return a straightforward answer. I have to keep in mind the possibility that he's not one at all.

Being a Liberal Feminist Is Easy

We might draw a hasty conclusion that Chappelle is a liberal feminist in support of equality of the sexes. Showbiz types are notorious for jumping on the feminist "bandwagon," but we like Chappelle for not being the type of comedian that does things just because others do them. Chappelle's feminist sympathies are not likely to be the normal showbiz liberal "bandwagon" type we have learned to expect from others.

With Chappelle, we often see him making jokes about feminists getting it wrong. There is the *Killin' Them Softly* comment about feminists pressuring the women's magazines and as a result women being given the wrong sexual advice. I'm not sure if the pressure was really to give women sex advice. Chappelle's somewhat overgeneralized interpretation of feminist influence is nonetheless a display of his concern that feminism in a general way is guiding women in the direction that he doesn't agree with. In one of his *Sticks and Stones* bits he portrays women as being worse off because of new expectations and laws. He talks of abortion as a right, but he also says men have a right to abandon a baby if they so choose. I get the feeling that Chappelle thinks the scales of justice have been tilted too far in favor of women at the cost of men.

Chappelle has many routines and sketches that highlight men's scanty understanding of women's liberation demands. Could he be making a connection with Black feminism in *Chappelle's Show*, Season One, Episode 12, in a segment called "Trading Spouses"? There is an interracial marriage swap where couples split and live with the other's spouse for a month. Chappelle's rather belligerent character, Leonard, is not ready for what might be a more liberated woman, Katie. He finds what he thinks is a vibrating mini-lightsaber in her side of the bed's headboard cabinet. Her sexual liberation becomes a bit much for Leonard who makes it clear to her in bed that he does not go "south of the border." He is not comfortable with sexual needs being fulfilled for her and sees lovemaking as something that happens "from time to time." We might say the other husband, Todd, also played by Chappelle, is not much more liberated, but he does cater to Sharon's needs, somewhat, and he cooks dinner—cauliflower, corned-beef hash, and parsnips, while Leonard refuses to even clean the dishes after dinner.

> **KATIE:** Just so you know, Todd would usually do the dishes after dinner.
>
> **LEONARD:** Well, just so you know, his ass will be back April 13th. Go on and do your thing, girl.

Chappelle clearly addresses feminism and women's needs with Leonard's not appreciating Katie's sexual needs. We get the impression, as indicated in the history of Black feminism and male participation being limited, that he has trouble keeping up. We are not saying that he should keep up with the Black feminist movement, or that it is possible to do so. To maintain an equal standing with feminism as a man is difficult, if not impossible. To do it as a Black man is much more of a task, which we might say is doubly impossible.

In *Killin' Them Softly,* Chappelle shows he has a strong sense of individual responsibility that suggests that individuals should be attentive of their own conduct.

> We're sitting there; we're watching Pepé Le Pew. And I say to my nephew, I said "Now pay attention to this guy cause he's funny. I used to watch him when I was little." And we're watching Pepé Le Pew and I'm old now . . . My nephew was sitting there cracking up: "Hehehe. See? Sometimes you gotta take the pussy, like Pepé" You're like "No! Nooo!" I had to turn the channel real quick."

He encourages the boy not to see the misrepresented skunk's sexual harassment of female cats as acceptable. There is no mention of Tarana Burke, the Black woman who founded the #MeToo Movement, or Anita Hill and her 1991 complaint against Supreme Court nominee Clarence Thomas, for sexual harassment, both of which might increase Chappell's feminist credentials.

Being a role model and showing his respect for women, most of the time, does not make Chappelle a feminist. As we've discussed already, Black feminism is not the same as broadly accepted white feminism. Chappelle's feminist outlook is also complicated by his being a man. So being considered as credibly sympathetic to liberal feminism will be difficult. It's not like making wisecracks at a comedy club and getting an easy laugh; with feminism you have to prove your credentials.

How Can Philosophical Thinking Come to the Rescue?

There is a term used in philosophy called "feminist epistemology." This term will either clear a room of men or make most of them inflamed, with rage! (Both conservative and liberal men will react in the same way.) The problem is that men don't have experience in what it is to be a woman. Men appreciate their general view of the world as THE view of the world. They get angry when challenged, and they get furious when accused of being biased and in favor of a masculine outlook. For them there is only one outlook.

Feminist epistemology states that there are many views of the world and that the traditional male view is only one of them. This is what men don't accept. Australian sociologist R.W. Connell of the University of Sydney talks of "masculine hegemony," where male-dominated thinking perpetuates our culture. In Alice Walker's novel *The Color Purple*, also made into a 1995 movie, Shug dominates Celie by not allowing her to have her own sexuality. Connell says that both women and men lose out because of this arrangement, and she is possibly more qualified than most to make such a remark because she has transitioned from a man to a woman.

Now, Connell may qualify as someone who is knowledgeable to say what it takes to satisfy women's demands, which isn't to be said of Chappelle. There is little hint of female disposition, and his jokes about his wife in stirrups getting her annual cervical examination with his pushing the doctor out of way to take over is not a sign that he is giving up his "hegemonic masculine" vantage point . . . which is when men's dominant position over women in society is made to look natural and acceptable . . . with its "masculine dividend" . . . which is the benefits you get for being a man . . . paying off all types of advantages at a cost to women.

It's this "self-assuredness" of the masculine character that is held in doubt by feminists; men tend to hold their views as indisputable. In fact, men do not have much in the way of what is known as "transcendent procedure of rational assessment." This is to say that those in power create knowledge for their own benefit. These people are men, and their knowledge is falsely seen by men—and many women like Phillis Schlafly—as true. Thus, men get angry when challenged. Kathleen Lennon, my B.A. dissertation supervisor at university, writes a lot on feminist epistemology. Our meetings would start with our standing in her office and her refusing to sit down before I did. My "residual" chivalry is hardly an example of "masculine toxicity," but it does fall within "masculine hegemony" that liberal feminism wants eradicated.

Do We Have Evidence that Dave Chappelle Is a Feminist?

To accept that Chappelle is a feminist, and that he is not trapped in a super-masculine role, I need to see his sympathy to women's disadvantaged role. He is aware of Black disadvantage and has a thread of feminist sympathy, but not much more. I need to be convinced that a man can be a feminist and be convinced that a Black man can be a feminist. With his being a man, and Black, and wealthy, I see a triple-whammy which will demand proof that he is a feminist. He would need something like an understanding of what Sharon Smith calls "intersectionality" which is much like being one of many witnesses at a car crash at a road intersection with many causal factors. Being Black, female, and, maybe poor are three causal factors making what renowned lawyer and civil rights activist Kimberlé Crenshaw calls a matrix. Making sense of being Black, female, and poor involves understanding all the interplay and influences of many differing types of discrimination not experienced by rich Black men.

We have to ask whether Chappelle has the needed qualities to be a feminist at all, let alone a Black feminist. One case where Chappelle steps in the right direction is his feeling sorry for Monica Lewinsky for wanting to have sexual relations with a powerful man, namely President Bill Clinton:

> That girl was young, and she made a mistake that young girls make. She wanted to fuck a powerful man. Period. That's as far as she thought it through. She wasn't thinking about how powerful the president was. She had no wisdom. (*Killin' Them Softly*)

Lennon says such comments are contextual and down to earth, allowing women to face the dominant masculine view. In this situation we have Chappelle, aware and maybe reluctant to accept full liberal feminism but somewhat progressive. There is what Lennon refers to as the "world traveler" who engages in discussion with opposing forces. They or the other party might feel dejected, but there has been talk!

Chappelle is clearly aware that women are not truly heard. This is a good start. This is made evident in his piece on magazines making women ashamed of their bodies. (*Killin' Them Softly*). Next we would have Chappelle listen to these groups and take their view seriously. We might presume that Chappelle's "masculine hegemonic" viewpoint is restricting his ability to see women as disadvantaged. Chappelle might feel perturbed, but there is hope of change with ideas translating into Chappelle's language and being accepted by him.

Is There a "New Man" on the Block?

I'm not expecting Chappelle to start a new type of masculinity. Being a "new man"—a man who in good faith accepts sexual equality in public and home life—with a whole-hearted sense of equality for women, especially Black women in a white female-dominated movement, will not be taken seriously, and most of all would not be seen as funny. Myisha Cherry suggests that it's more possible and more of a practical concern to "man down" instead of "man up," as many Black men should have more progressive energy instead of surrendering to the "hegemonic masculinity" forced upon them by dominant masculine culture. Cherry suggests a mild type of relaxing of masculinity. The more progressive man attends men's "Groups" where men discuss their sexist attitudes with hope of change. Chappelle would not join such liberal feminist group other than to get some ripe material for one of his routines. The men's magazine *Achilles Heel* (1978–1999) has many anti-sexist articles with the emphasis on equality and men taking their role seriously. Long gone are the days when the likes of Germaine Greer would humiliate men in public for even asking what they could do to progress feminism.

Cherry discusses Quentin Tarantino's 2012 movie *Django Unchained* where property ownership in the Antebellum South is a rite of passage for rights and manhood. Black men can't own land or have full rights. Django "steals" himself by escaping and rejects "hegemonic masculinity," replacing it with an ethic of care. We can add that Chappelle, like Django, can express masculinity in a more caring way.

This is where Alice Walker's "Walkerion" virtues of care and empathy come into action. Walker calls this "Womanism" where men regain their Black bodies, which have been taken by dominant society. As Walker says, "Womanism is to feminism as purple is to lavender." This includes men. Movies like *Waiting to Exhale* (1990) stimulated lots of discussion about male domination. It's this discussion that Chappelle could easily join. After all, there is a history of Black male writers such as W.E.B. Du Bois (1868–1963) who are not anti-feminist, and in fact in favor of women's liberation.

Is There Comedy Without Sexism?

Yes, Chappelle could "man down," but would his comedy be the first casualty? He has made it clear, in *Sticks and Stones,* that the #MeToo movement is giving him a headache. As a comedian, he's in favor of women going to work. He plays on generalities about women's situations, and from this he creates tension. As comedian Hannah Gatsby says in her *Nanette* routine, stand-up comedy is a form of emotional abuse; the comedian builds tension and releases that tension with a punch line.

I have to ask whether the release of tension, in the case of Chappelle, is at a cost to women. His routine describing LGBTQ+ as the alphabet people is at best a "language joke" in the refrain of Jerry Seinfeld, and at worst a "rubbish joke" in the refrain of, well, anyone who tells jokes. Here the joke builds tension by Chappelle likening a vulnerable group with a joke about African Americans wanting to identify as Chinese Americans. His outrageous impersonation got a laugh; it was most likely a nervous laugh, but a laugh nonetheless, and that's his job.

Just as Chappelle denounces and then minimizes and mitigates the offenses committed by men, I feel the laugh is at the cost of any cause which condemns such acts. Is Chappelle siding with women or with the boys? Is Chappelle paralyzed by guilt or fear of being a "feminist snowflake"? We might have sympathy with Chappelle's position. He is more savvy on race issues than most comedians. I might hope that Chappelle is condemning bigotry, but the evidence might be in favor of the argument that he has surrendered to the conservative view that men and women should accept their gender with all the trappings of traditional male and female virtue. Chappelle's being a feminist may be made credible by his attaching himself to the #MeToo movement with his emphasis on the need to focus on structural issues leading to sexual inequality. As he says, in *The Bird Revelation,* to feminist activists:

You got all the bad guys scared, and that's good, but the minute they're not scared anymore, it will get worse than it was before. Fear does not make for a lasting peace.

Maybe Chappelle is the man on the inside passing out notes to the feminist activists. With such a powerful undercover force, it may be possible to create a feminism that embraces both men and women.

12

Why Chappelle Needs to Get Over His #MeToo Headache

Neha Pande

Dave Chappelle is an unforgettable name when it comes to comedy. He has been doing comedy since he was fourteen years old, and in a span of three decades has created a massive amount of work, in spite of taking a long sabbatical in between. A wonderful feature of his comedy is that he vividly illustrates his experiences in the form of jokes on stage. His jokes are performed physically as much as verbally; however, he has certain patterns in his performances.

Once I finished watching the specials by Dave Chappelle namely *Sticks and Stones* (2019), *The Age of Spin* (2017), *Deep in the Heart of Texas* (2017), *Equanimity* (2017), *The Bird Revelation* (2017), *Killing Them Softly* (2000) and *For What It's Worth* (2004), there seemed to protrude a fashion, the pattern in which he conducted his comedy. We can better understand what Chappelle is doing by applying some of the insights of Feminist Standpoint Theory.

Chappelle is, no doubt, very aware about racial discrimination, and understands the politics of race well in America. In fact, he analyzes the society around him like an anthropologist. He not only clearly sees structural and institutional racism but has also developed language to bring it out clearly through comedy. He has frequently talked about the social, cultural, political, and economic marginalization of the African American community, and he describes it using various aspects, from historical events to eating habits.

Throughout his specials, Chappelle brings to light the structural and institutional racism faced by the African American community, and how it affects people of the community in their personal lives on a day-to-day basis. He constantly uses terms commonly employed in the community and uses the shared knowledge and experiences to communicate, but mostly to the men of the community. While he shares episodes of discrimination from the standpoint of an African American man, when it comes to other conventionally marginalized communities, especially, women and the LGBTQ+ community, their standpoints are completely sidelined. Women and people who identify themselves to be a part of the LGBTQ+ community are seen in their stereotypical images. The intersectional identities like class, race, ethnicity, religion, and region are not taken into consideration. They are narrowed down to just being women and LGBTQ+ people, or "alphabet people" as he calls them, and they are talked about in terms of the conventional stereotypes which have been used for years to not only create and reproduce their stereotypical images, but also to oppress them using these images.

Dave Chappelle's Standpoint

In his special *Equanimity*, Chappelle revisits the abusive and violent history of the community in America, telling the story of the violent and cruel murder of Emmett Till, a fourteen-year-old boy who was brutally murdered because he allegedly wolf-whistled at a white woman. This propelled the Civil Rights movement in the country. The incident becomes important because it addresses the collective consciousness of the community in the form of shared history. This shared history over time also created their social position in the country and thus influenced their experiences and their understanding of society in America.

In the context of the audience, they are able to relate to it because these experiences are a part of their consciousness too. They have had many of the same experiences, and these experiences have shaped their racial identities in America. It is also important to emphasize here that a standpoint is not merely a perspective that is occupied simply by belonging to a marginalized position. It is a result of being not only conscious about one's socio-historical position but also through the experience of collective political struggle.

As mentioned, Chappelle frequently addresses the various social, cultural, and political aspects of American society in his jokes to address the collective consciousness of the African American community. In his special *For What It's Worth*, he brings these aspects to life through food. He talks about how many African American people "don't have the privilege of knowing about grape juice" because they get "grape drink," which does not have any of the healthy vitamins that the former has. Here he tries to bring attention to the poverty faced by the majority of African Americans in America due to racial discrimination. In *The Bird Revelation* he jokes about an African American audience member by pointing out that by "just being big and Black with that hairdo," he would always be "under an enormous amount of pressure," as he would be a suspect for everything in America due to racial discrimination and biases.

An essential component of Feminist Standpoint Theory is its sensitivity to the social position to which a person belongs, and its emphasis on the voice of the members of these communities. So, when Dave Chappelle in *Equanimity* talks about the 2008 election scene in Ohio, he explains the feelings of the African Americans as a community about how they were "hugging each other" and "people were singing hymns and spirituals" and that he had never seen them "this happy." These emotions are related to their social position too, and thus, their response to Obama as the Presidential candidate is from the lens of this identity.

Furthermore, in dealing with social position, Feminist Standpoint Theory emphasizes that the knowledge and understandings of people are socially located, and people from different social positions have access to different experiences that shape their understandings. In his special *Killin' Them Softly*, Chappelle talks about how police brutality is a part of institutional racism in the USA and is felt by the African American community as a group. It is ingrained in the system to the extent that the fear it creates in people has become a part of their culture. He further emphasizes that "Black people are very afraid of the police" and that it is a "big part of our culture."

Even the monetary status, class, or age does not make a difference. Chapelle says, "No matter how rich you are. No matter how old you are. We're just afraid of them. We got every reason to be afraid of them." Further he talks about the blatant humiliation which the people from the community have to go through in the wake of this structural racism. He again uses the context of police brutality. He, humorously, brings the humiliating experiences of the people from the African American community under the sun through a conversation between a Black man and a white policeman where the policeman is asking the man to "spread open his cheeks and lift his sack" instead of asking for his driver's license to prove his identity.

He continues the joke and points out how his racial identity exposes him to the consequences which a white man would not be exposed to. He calls it "a Black thing." He jokes about his white friend Chip who was able to get out of the situation with police by smooth talking. However, he, despite being famous, would have faced consequences. He reiterates how he would never have the audacity to do the same, due to his racial identity. He further jokes about how "every Black dude in this room is a qualified paralegal" and everyone is well aware of the law and the penalties which are a part of the defense mechanism. The people of the community have to ensure that they do everything legally correct or else the consequences can be huge.

Feminist Standpoint theory also emphasizes how this difference of social position, in the form of race in these cases, produces different experiences for white and Black people, and thus creates different experiences and understandings of the world around them. Therefore, their racial identities facilitate or hinder their understanding of a situation and create different experiences. In his special *Sticks and Stones*, Chappelle talks about how the white community in America did not accept that the crack crisis was a "health crisis" when the African American community was going through it. It was understood to be a health crisis only when white people started facing it with opioids.

Feminist Standpoint theory further emphasizes that such stereotypes also act as controlling images which are further reproduced and reinforced by everyone including the ones oppressed, and therefore, ways of thinking from the point of view of the dominant becomes normal. This becomes further oppressive as it solidifies the image of the oppressed community.

In all these cases, using the standpoint of his African American identity, Chappelle becomes a knowing subject instead of merely being an object to others. Moreover, the theory strongly emphasizes that these are not mere "perspectives" of Dave Chappelle as a man who belongs to the African American community; instead this is "unique knowledge" that has been produced as a result of his experiences which he has had due to this identity. His racial identity has a history of oppression and political struggles attached to it, and he is well aware of it. His social and cultural experiences of being marginalised due to his racial identity have given him a shared history of oppression and political struggle, and it has become part of his content. During his specials he constantly uses the pronoun "we" while addressing the people belonging to African American community in the audience, and he calls the structural injustice faced by the community in the hands of the police administration "common knowledge."

Dave Chappelle vs Standpoints

While Dave Chappelle is able to put forth the standpoint of an African American man, the sensitivity to understand, or making an attempt to understand the cultural and social marginality, humiliation and exploitation faced by women and LGBTQ+ community is absent in his specials. All these specials are punching down at these communities and groups.

The collective consciousness which is evoked by Chappelle with the crowd of African American men, takes the form of mocking when addressing the solidarity among women and people in the LGBTQ+ community. The #MeToo movement, in which many powerful men were called out by the victims for sexual exploitation, molestation, and even rape, is made to sound like a "witch hunt" of men. The solidarity of women, the courage it takes to call out these men, the safe space created by other women and their allies for them to express, are blatantly mocked.

One of the reasons women have to go through sexual molestation or other crimes of sexual nature is because the social and cultural understanding of a woman's body for a long time was attached to their lower social position and the male gaze, which saw her body as a sexual object. The feminist movement has been continuously problematizing these understandings of women's bodies. In these specials, women are consistently narrowed down to their anatomy and identified through it.

Apart from this, Chappelle also literally narrows down feminist women into a stereotypical image. He discusses with the crowd about a woman being uncomfortable with the use of the word pussy for her, and calls her "definitely a feminist," because she had a "short haircut and plaid shirt." But unfortunately, he does not stop at this. There are sets of jokes where Chappelle is not only insensitive towards women but also blames the victims.

In *The Bird Revelation* while talking about Harvey Weinstein he says that in case someone like Brad Pitt was molesting the women, no one would have "heard a peep." He further emphasizes that Harvey Weinstein could molest and rape women for forty years because "a bitch want a stupid ass part."

Further, he defends Louis C.K. In *The Bird Revelation*, he jokes about the #MeToo movement and implies it to be unnecessary persecution of men by women. He mocks one of the women who called out Louis C.K. for sexually molesting her and puts the complete blame on her. The joke goes,

> I'm not supposed to say that, but one of these ladies was like, "Louis C.K. was masturbating while I was on the phone with him." Bitch, you don't know how to hang up a phone?

He says that these women "sound weak" and normalizes the exploitation of women in show business by making the argument that "show business is just harder than that." He says, "well, then I dare say, Madam, you may have never had a dream . . . That's a brittle spirit . . . You think if Louis C.K. jerked off in front of Dr. King, he'd be like, 'I can't continue this movement. I'm sorry, but the freedom of Black people must be stopped.'"

Here, we need to ask, if these women are weak, then what exactly does being strong mean in that space and time? Do women being forced to be exploited in exchange for an opportunity validate the conduciveness of the show business for this exploitation? Chappelle seems to think that these women had a choice, and it was only a matter of convenience that they still chose to get molested and exploited instead of calling the people out. This argument has been repeatedly made in and by a patriarchal society, and Chappelle just reproduces it.

He further jokes about the molestation cases against Louis C.K., Michael Jackson, and Bill Clinton, but defends them in the very next line. He also defends Kevin Hart on making homophobic statements. Similarly, the LGBTQ+ community is mocked and becomes the "alphabet people." There is no empathy or sensitivity shown towards the political struggle, including the intentional choosing of the nomenclature. In *Deep in the Heart of Texas*, he mocks the queer community by joking about Q in the name LGBTQ+ and calling them "gay dudes that don't really know they're gay." He continues his joke by calling them "prison f*gs" who suck dicks "to pass the time." That this umbrella term is meant to suggest the spectrum of gender and sexuality against the conventional binary understanding of gender and sexuality, and that it is chosen to express solidarity among the members who face social, cultural, political, and economic marginalization and invisibility due to these identities are completely overlooked.

In *Equanimity* Chappelle cracks a joke on gender dysphoria (a conflict between a person's physical or assigned gender and gender with which he/she/they identify). He mocks the transgender people and jokes that the transgender people "need to take some responsibility" for his jokes, as it is a "hilarious predicament" that "a person can be born in the wrong body." He describes transgender people as "n * * * as [who] cut their dicks off."

He then jokes about Caitlyn Jenner contemplating posing nude in an upcoming issue of *Sports Illustrated* and uses the word "yuck" to express his perspective on it.

He continually shows a lack of understanding of their political struggle and the intersectionality of identities of class, ethnicity, race, religion, and region within the LGBTQ+ community. In *Deep in the Heart of Texas* he jokes about the idea of self-image amongst transgender people and the use of pronouns. Again, he misses the point that self-image is an important part of the trans* struggle. Trans* is an umbrella term used by people in the gender and sexuality spectrum, who choose non-binary and gender non-conforming identities, and the asterisk shows the deliberate attempt to not perpetuate the default binary in trans identities. The pronouns are an important part of the identity for the community and have been chosen by them.

According to the Feminist Standpoint Theory, the standpoints emerge when the marginalized become conscious of their social position with respect to socio-political power and oppression, and begin to find a voice. Therefore, the knowledge of being oppressed because of one's gender and sexuality, and the constant struggle to achieve the right to be represented as them is not available to Dave Chappelle in this particular context. The years of marginalization due to socially and culturally conventional understanding of gender and sexuality as binary gives the community the knowledge which the dominant groups would not have. And this is not acknowledged by Dave Chappelle anywhere.

Further in *The Bird Revelation* Chappelle emphasizes that it is the best time for comedians to say these jokes, and be "reckless." He emphasizes this by adding that it is their responsibility. It makes us question the cause for being reckless. Does it mean to continue the circulation of vicious cycles of stereotypes regarding women and the LGBTQ+ community? The argument isn't that no comedian should be allowed to joke about women or the LGBTQ+ community, but does joking about them mean showing them in the same light and using the same narratives which have been used for the longest time to exploit them and constrain their images to only those conventional limits? Do these jokes serve any purpose to prove a point, or do these jokes just elicit some discriminatory laughter?

As the Feminist Standpoint Theory emphasizes on intersectionality, the importance is given to various standpoints, instead of normalizing the dominant one in any context. These standpoints are created due to different social positions of people in the society, and further decide their political and economic positions in the society. Furthermore, not only are these standpoints a result of the consistent political struggle, but the loss of these standpoints of women and LGBTQ+ community would mean the loss of the unique social and cultural understandings, and experiences of these marginalized communities which cannot be attained by majority communities. We also have to understand that these experiences and understandings are a huge part of their identities. And at the same time, it is because of their certain identities that they are able to inculcate those understandings through their lived experiences. And thus, their marginalized identities, experiences and understandings are closely related to each other, and are created and produced simultaneously.

Furthermore these different standpoints help us achieve less partial and less distorted understandings of all of our lives too because we do not continue to understand lives only from the understanding of the dominant communities. They enable a more complete understanding of what the society is for people who are marginalized or oppressed in different ways. It is through these standpoints that any society will be able to understand the changes it needs to bring to create a more inclusive and sensitive society. It is in these ways Dave Chappelle fails to understand and be sensitive towards the understanding of society through the lens of different communities.

IV

Overwhelmed
by the Irony

13

Clayton Bigsby and the Social Construction of the Self

RICHARD BILSKER

I was a little late to pick up on *Chappelle's Show*. Once it was suggested to me, I quickly became a fan. Like the best sketch-comedy shows, it was full of commercial parodies, recurring characters and segments, and musical interludes. The sketch that most struck me is from the very first episode, which aired in January 2003. It was the first of a recurring series of bits, a parody of the PBS show *Frontline*. *Frontline* has aired on PBS since 1983 and has won numerous Emmy and Peabody awards for its journalism.

The first *Chappelle's Show Frontline* sketch was "*Frontline:* Clayton Bigsby." It tells the story of Clayton Bigsby, introduced at the beginning of the sketch as a leading voice in the white supremacy movement, popular but reclusive. When the documentary crew arrives at his house, the crew (and we as audience) see that he's Black. We learn that Bigsby was born blind at an unspecified location in the Southern United States.

After a cutaway, the *Frontline* presenter asks, "How could this have happened?" When staff at The Wexler Home for the Blind are questioned, they tell *Frontline* that they saw no reason to tell him that he was Black. Since he grew up to be a white supremacist and he's blind, he is not aware that he's Black. This sketch is filled with some great comedic moments. Here I'm interested in how this sketch illustrates some important features of the development of identity.

Our Multiple Selves

In 1890 William James published one of the most influential books in the entire history of psychology, *The Principles of*

Psychology. In Chapter X, James wrote that each person has many selves, "as many different social selves as there are distinct groups of persons about whose opinion he cares." We show these selves to these different groups as the situation demands. Later in the same chapter, he notes that how we think our selves are seen by others becomes a part of how we see ourselves. This idea was taken up and transformed by two other writers, George Herbert Mead (1863–1931) and W.E.B. Du Bois (1868–1963). It is the way James's ideas were transformed by Mead and Du Bois that is most relevant to the case of Clayton Bigsby.

Mead focused on the social nature of self. His view has come to be called "The Social Construction of the Self." In Chapter 18 of *Mind, Self, and Society*, Mead tells us that we do not come with fully formed selves. Instead, it "arises in the process of social experience" of the individual "as a result of his relations to that process as a whole and to other individuals within that process." A key element in Mead's view is reflexivity. Reflexivity is the idea that the self can be both subject and object. We can experience ourselves from the standpoint of others, either individuals or a social group. Seeing ourselves from the outside, "the generalized other," becomes a core idea in the sociological perspective called 'symbolic interactionism'. It is through communication that we can address and be addressed by others. Real or imagined, we react to how others think of us. Mead calls the process "the conversation of gestures." He has incorporated James's idea of multiple selves.

According to Mead, "we divide ourselves up in all sorts of different selves with reference to our acquaintances." If you consult your own experiences, you quickly realize you do not act the same way with your friends that you do with your boss, your co-workers, or the parents of your romantic interest. Most of us manage the movement between selves (or role-switching) with little difficulty, or even conscious effort. However, sometimes problems with switching can become pathological, if we forget or "leave out the rest of the self." Ultimately for Mead, "the unity and structure of the complete self reflects the unity and structure of the social process as a whole" and each individual is part of groups which themselves are constructed of the constructed individual members.

Discovering Our Difference

Both Mead and James note that the self corresponds to, but is not identical with, a body. Neither of them explicitly discusses how differences in bodies affect the self or the process noted here. As Bigsby is unaware that he is Black, that has not entered into the way his self is constructed. What's instructive here is the discussion of the self in W.E.B. Du Bois's essay, "Of Our Spiritual Strivings," which can be found in his 1903 book, *The Souls of Black Folk*. Du Bois notes the time that he became aware that he was different ("the shadow swept across me"). His elementary school classmates had decided to exchange visiting-cards. One girl, new to the school, refused his card. He was "different from the others . . . shut out from their world by a vast veil." This notion of a veil that separates, but can still be seen through, is used several times in Du Bois's essay. This leads to the notion of "double-consciousness" which arises from "looking at one's self through the eyes of others." This doubling of being "an American, a Negro; two souls, two thoughts, two unreconciled strivings; two warring ideals in one dark body" is part of African American history. Du Bois makes explicit something that is only implicit in James and Mead, that our embodiment of difference is one of the elements of the social construction of the self.

A similar story to the one Du Bois tells can be found in a 1928 essay by Zora Neale Hurston (1891–1960), "How It Feels to Be Colored Me." In it, she tells us "I remember the very day that I became colored." She had grown up in Eatonville, a Black community, and was their Zora, "everybody's Zora." At thirteen, after her mother's death, she was sent to school in Jacksonville. She left Eatonville as "a Zora. When I disembarked from the river-boat at Jacksonville, she was no more . . . I was not Zora of Orange County any more, I was now a little colored girl." Like Du Bois, Hurston was lucky and did not suffer as much as many others. Sometimes, she could just be: "I do not always feel colored. Even now I often achieve the unconscious Zora of Eatonville." She does not write of the same double consciousness as Du Bois, but rather says:

> I have no separate feeling about being an American citizen and colored. I am merely a fragment of the Great Soul that surges within the boundaries. My country, right or wrong. Sometimes, I feel discriminated against, but it does not make me angry. It merely astonishes me. How can any deny themselves the pleasure of my company? It's beyond me.

Part of the reason that she was comfortable at the time of her essay is that she was (to borrow a phrase from Du Bois) a "co-worker in the kingdom of culture" during the Harlem

Renaissance. For example, when visiting the library in New York City she can say, "I have no race, I am me . . . The cosmic Zora emerges. I belong to no race nor time."

A more recent version of the doubling can be seen in the work of Gloria Anzaldúa (1942–2004). In her book *Border-lands/La Frontera*, she discusses the literal and metaphorical borderlands and code-switching in contemporary Chicana life. She defines the borderlands as being "physically present wherever two or more cultures edge each other, where people "of different races occupy the same territory, where under, lower, middle and upper classes touch, where the space between two individuals shrinks with intimacy." Anzaldúa's analysis straddles many borders: the linguistic, ethnic, and physical ones that shifted in the history of Texas and Mexico, straight vs. queer feminine sexual identity, as well as switching between prose and poetry in terms of presentation. In a section considering what we call ourselves, she discusses the differing answers we can give: American, Spanish, Hispanic, or Mexican. She says that she answers "Mexican," but that she means it as a race, not as a nationality:

> Deep in our hearts we believe being Mexican has nothing to do with which country one lives in. Being Mexican is a state of the soul—not one of mind, not one of citizenship.

Her identity, she tells us, is grounded in "the Indian woman's history of resistance." She feels able to rebel against the list of binary oppositions because "unlike Chicanas and other women of color who grew up white or who have only recently returned to their native cultural roots, I was totally immersed in mine." Like Zora Neale Hurston, she did not "see" whites until she was a teenager.

Since Clayton Bigsby did not have the same experiences as Du Bois, Hurston, or Anzaldúa, he did not have this double consciousness, this two-ness, and he did not see through a veil (literally or metaphorically). In fact, given his popularity in the white supremacist movement, he too, was a co-worker in the kingdom of culture. What would happen to a white supremacist were he to find out he was Black, not just that he had non-white forbears despite his skin tone, but Black? Well, in the sketch, he divorces his wife, because she is a "n****r-lover." He doesn't really accept the double-consciousness. In a sense, his view is deflationary—deflating the double into a single.

Passing as Black

The opposite situation occurred in June 2015 when a number of controversies swirled around Rachel Dolezal. At the time she was the president of the Spokane Washington chapter of the NAACP, was Chair of the Spokane Office of the Police Ombudsman Commission, and was an adjunct instructor at Eastern Washington University. Dolezal identified as Black, but eventually it was revealed that both of her biological parents (they also raised her) were white, with no known non-white forbears. I consider this an inflationary view. She has added that second soul, thought, and striving. Her part-time contract at the university was not renewed, she resigned her position at the NAACP and was removed from the Ombudsman Commission.

Another revelation of an inflation to double consciousness occurred more recently. Jessica Krug, a History professor at George Washington University, announced via the website *Medium* on September 3rd, 2020 that she was not who she presented as:

> To an escalating degree over my adult life, I have eschewed my lived experience as a white Jewish child in suburban Kansas City under various assumed identities within a Blackness that I had no right to claim: first North African Blackness, then US rooted Blackness, then Caribbean rooted Bronx Blackness.

She says that the assumed identity is the result of trauma earlier in her life, which allowed her to "run away to a new place and become a new person." She then admits "this is harm that I have enacted onto so many others" and her obligation to end "the life I had no right to live in the first place." She relates that she'd never developed an identity separate from that which she purposefully constructed and was unsure how to "heal any of the harm that she had caused." So, she denies that it is a duality or duplicity, because she has only one identity:

> I have not lived a double life . . . I have lived this lie, fully, completely, with no exit plan or strategy. I have built only this life, a life within which I have operated with a radical sense of ethics, of right and wrong, and with rage, rooted in Black power, an ideology which every person should support, but to which I have no possible claim as my own.

As with comments on Dolezal, it's hard not to view this as a matter of convenience—that Krug outed herself before someone else did, in order to possibly save her career by getting out in front of it. It didn't work. The next day, Krug was removed from her classes and replaced with other instructors. On September 9th, less than a week after this started, she resigned from her post at the University.

September 4th, the day after Krug's blog post, Esther Wang wrote "All the Rachel Dolezals" for *Jezebel* "A Supposedly Feminist Website" (as they call themselves). In it, Wang added Jessica Krug to the long list of "racial fraudsters" (mostly white and mostly academics) who have appropriated marginalized identities in recent years. Wang notes something that is worth considering about cases like Dolezal and Krug:

> Underlying many (though not all) of these strange tales, too, is a betrayal of imagination—that one cannot be a white person who cares about the lives of non-white people, that for your moral or even literary concerns to have merit, your experiences need to have the stamp of authenticity too. To go back to Krug, she didn't have to be Black or Puerto Rican or from "the hood" to be a person who is deeply interested in questions of colonialism, to be someone who cares about gentrification and the politics of race. The fact that she thought she did is maybe the whitest thing about her.

This is echoed in a September 7th opinion piece for CNN by Ed Morales, who cites one of Krug's resources, an article "The Jíbaro Masquerade and the Subaltern Politics of Creole Identity Formation in Puerto Rico 1745–1823," by Francisco Scarano. Morales notes that "in the article, Scarano describes how elite Puerto Rican intellectuals used to disguise themselves by writing in the coarse language of rural peasants to make more effective political arguments against Spanish colonialism without endangering their own privileges."

Cognitive Dissonance

Krug seems to deny that she was "playing at" being Black, just as Dolezal did. She will likely still have the benefit of white privilege even after leaving this job. This is an outcome that would most likely be denied to others. In some ways, her case is worse than Dolezal's. In Morales' CNN story and also in a September 5th piece by author Casey Gane-McCalla for *Countere* (that relates his personal dealings with Krug online), instances are cited from multiple sites that Krug would call people out for essentially not being Black enough.

Just as we can ask, "does Clayton Bigsby get to detach himself from his Blackness?" we can ask, "does Rachel Dolezal (or Jessica Krug) get to attach Blackness to herself?" There are a few issues here. For one, Bigsby did not experience his Blackness until late adulthood. In something that can only be described as 'cognitive dissonance', Bigsby cannot incorporate that information into the identity he has constructed and moves to minimize its impact.

Cognitive dissonance was first described by psychologist Leon Festinger (1919–1989) in 1957. In a 1962 article for *Scientific American*, he summarized it this way: "if a person knows various things that are not psychologically consistent with one another, he will, in a variety of ways, try to make them more consistent." It is a motivation, like hunger. Unlike hunger, though, it is often a harder motivation to satisfy. Typically, we try to do so in such a way that we think will put us in the best light. In the Bigsby sketch, when his Blackness is revealed to an audience he is giving a speech to, the head of one attendee literally explodes. Clearly, they cannot incorporate the idea that one of their favorite white supremacist authors is Black.

The situation is not the same with Dolezal or Krug. They were not raised Black and they did not have any of the challenges of the African American experience. Dolezal, for example, attended Howard University, one of the most famous HBCUs (Historically Black Colleges and Universities) from 2000 to 2002 for her Master of Fine Arts degree, it is true, but that is not an equivalence. In fact, she unsuccessfully sued Howard University in 2002, claiming that she was denied scholarships, teaching opportunities, and display of her art, because she was a white woman. So, at least in 2002 she was identifying as white. Most of her detractors in 2015 accused her of cultural appropriation (including plagiarizing artworks) and wearing blackface (she was a pale blonde woman in her youth). As one voice said in the documentary, *The Rachel Divide*, "she can't just appropriate persecution because it's cool."

There is appropriation in *"Frontline:* Clayton Bigsby," too. Jasper, Bigsby's friend and go-between in the sketch, benefits from not telling Bigsby or the white supremacists about the color of his skin. When asked about it by *Frontline*, Jasper tells the interviewer that "he's too important to the movement." Jasper also says it's to protect Bigsby, as he's so committed to the movement that if he found out "he'd probably kill hisself." A few minutes later, Jasper and Bigsby are next to a convertible at a traffic light and the young white men in the car are listening to rap music. Bigsby berates them using a number of slurs.

After Jasper's pickup drives off, the confused men look at each other: "Did he just call us n****rs? Awesome!" This is another example of the kinds of inversions in the sketch.

A different response to our experiences can be seen by the racial unrest in the United States in 2020. Protests arose in all fifty states and many countries after the death of George Floyd while in the custody of Minneapolis Police which followed the deaths of Breonna Taylor by Louisville Police executing a "no-knock warrant" at the wrong address and of Ahmaud Arbery by white motorists in Georgia.

One Drop of Black Blood

What's the proper response to these events from people who have not had the experiences of being African American? A controversy has arisen over celebrities' and companies' various responses and their support of Black Lives Matter. One instance that is particularly instructive is the case of the singer Halsey. Halsey had attended a rally and posted on social media in support of the protests. A Twitter user on June 3, 2020 reproached Halsey because she "never claims her Black side." Halsey is biracial but admits that she is "white passing." In her response to the (now-deleted) Tweet, Halsey stated:

> I'm white passing. it's not my place to say "we." it's my place to help. I am in pain for my family, but nobody is gonna kill me based on my skin color. I've always been proud of who I am but it'd be an absolute disservice to say "we" when I'm not susceptible to the same violence.

The concept of "passing" has a long history. It is usually reserved for those who are not white putting themselves forward as, and being accepted as, white. The philosopher Naomi Zack, in her autobiographical essay (and later in her book *Race and Mixed Race*) discusses the nature of passing within the American racial schema.

In the American racial schema (sometimes called the "one-drop rule"), if a person has any non-white forebears, they are not white. Zack was raised by her white, Jewish mother and did not know her father was Black until she was sixteen. Under the "one-drop rule," Zack would be Black. She was raised as white, her mother was white, she is white on official documents, and she had none of the experiences of oppression that would be consonant with the African American experience. Thankfully, unlike Clayton Bigsby, she did not become a white supremacist. Since there is no specific category called mixed race, what is Zack to say? As she puts it:

> I do not like to explicitly say that I am white because that is a lie—In American society, if one has a black parent, then one is black. I am black . . . I am a Jew and therefore I am white. I am black and therefore I am not white.

To Black people, though if she is culturally white, but racially Black, she is "an inauthentic black person, someone who is disloyal to other black people or who evades or denies racial discrimination by attempting to pass (for white)." Further, she notes that a person operating under "the honorarium of mixed race designation" has an obligation to have her "skills be recognized as the skills of a black person" or else be thought to be agreeing with the devaluing of black people.

Anzaldúa discusses a similar notion. Of those "more tinged with Anglo blood," she understands why the "colored and colorless sisters glorify their colored culture's values—to offset the extreme devaluation of it by the white culture." Anzaldúa, though, will not "glorify those aspects" of her culture which have hurt her or "injured me in the name of protecting me." When returning to academia after a twenty-year absence, Zack was hired as a "Target of Opportunity" in an affirmative action recruitment, in part because of the autobiographical essay discussed above. This appointment and her acceptance of the designation of a woman "of African descent" allowed her "an existential occasion . . . to address racial issues philosophically."

That analysis resulted in the book *Race and Mixed Race* and numerous other works in the following twenty-five years. It also means that Zack no longer passes, either intentionally or unintentionally. In the case of Rachel Dolezal, her detractors maintain that in passing as Black, she appropriated that painful past without having to experience any of its challenges. Dolezal's mother noted, when interviewed, that when Rachel applied to Howard University, she did not claim to be Black, but her art portfolio was indicative of the Black experience, including portraiture. When she applied to be chair of the Ombudsman Commission in 2014, though, she claimed to be multi-racial. When her past caught up with her, the misrepresentation associated with the Ombudsman position led to her being sued by the city of Spokane (eventually settled out of court). So, in some sense, Dolezal's passing is more ethically fraught than Halsey's or Zack's.

Incongruity or Superiority?

But why is *"Frontline:* Clayton Bigsby" funny? One instructive theory that has emerged is called the Incongruity Theory. Contemporary philosopher Noël Carroll describes the theory, which gathers insights from many diverse thinkers as the view that the key to comic amusement is

> a deviation from supposed norm . . . an anomaly or an incongruity relative to some framework governing the ways in which we think the world is or should be . . . [also that] the audience has a working knowledge of all the congruities—concepts, rules, expectations—that the humor in question disturbs or violates.

As a working hypothesis on the nature of humor, the Incongruity Theory provides an explanation of what makes the sketch funny. One of the audience's basic expectations is that a White Supremacist is white. Inside the sketch itself, this expectation is part of the world, too. Like many examples of the best sketch comedy much of the humor comes from drawing out the implications of this basic unmet expectation. In *"Frontline:* Clayton Bigsby," the audience is aware of the incongruity long before the characters in the sketch, including Bigsby himself.

The Superiority Theory provides another explanation. This view finds the origin of comic amusement in a feeling of superiority. This theory is better able to explain humor that belittles than it does the more cognitive or intellectual comedy. One variation on this theory is to be found in the work of the Russian literary critic Mikhail Bakhtin (1895–1975). In his book on French Renaissance author François Rabelais, Bakhtin emphasizes the humor of *carnival.* This kind of humor involves a lot of inversion. An example would be pulling a peasant out of the crowd at a festival and making him "King for a Day." In their essay in the volume *The Comedy of Dave Chappelle,* Gray and Putnam apply this Rabelais/Bakhtin theory to *"Frontline:* Clayton Bigsby" and two other sketches. In *"Frontline:* Clayton Bigsby," there is certainly an inversion, as the figure held in esteem by the white supremacists, is in fact someone who, in other circumstances, would be held as an object of contempt. There is also an inversion in the traffic light scene mentioned above.

The humor in *"Frontline:* Clayton Bigsby" is easier to explain in terms of incongruity. We aren't necessarily laughing because we feel superior to Bigsby, Jasper, or the audience at his unveiling lecture. The element of the unexpected is what produces the first jolt of humor. The rest of the sketch is the unfolding of the consequences of that initial jolt. It has created a stable world out of the incongruous premise—that "What if?" that structures the whole thing. So, although there is an inversion of the type Gray and Putnam attribute to Bakhtin's analysis of *carnival* and some humor at the expense of the residents of the unnamed town (in an unnamed state) in the deep South, I think the humor is more cognitive apprehension of structure than a feeling of superiority. Another question, "Should we be laughing?" Chappelle himself has expressed reservations, after the fact, about this sketch. In an NPR piece from 2006, he said:

> It sparked this whole controversy about the appropriateness of the n-word, the dreaded n-word. You know, and then when I would travel, the people would come up to me and, like white people would come up to me, like man, that sketch you did about them (bleeped out), that was, take it easy. You know, I was joking around. Started to realize these sketches in the wrong hands are dangerous.

The Ethics of Jokes

What happens when a subversive idea is appropriated? Chappelle did bring Bigsby back when he hosted *Saturday Night Live*. In a short movie introduced during his monologue, he gives us a *Walking Dead* parody in which Chappelle-as-Negan tries to decide which one of the *Chappelle's Show* recurring characters to kill off with his barbed-wire baseball bat. Bigsby is the last one introduced and is not the one who got the bat. So, he seems to have come to terms with Clayton Bigsby.

In *Jokes*, philosopher Ted Cohen (1939–2014) discusses a number of issues regarding humor. An insightful passage is a consideration of the ethics of jokes. Cohen argues that the questions of whether a joke is funny or not is a separate question from whether it should be told. All jokes are conditional, in his view. In this context, being conditional means that certain conditions need to be met in order to understand a joke. Minimally, there needs to be a shared language. Beyond that, there are cultural factors (stereotypes, for example) and background knowledge. In order to understand a joke based on stereotypes, you need to be aware of the stereotype. Stereotypes can be harmful. Some jokes should be avoided in some situations as in bad taste (at a funeral or in a religious service). But there might be some jokes that should never be told. To Cohen, that does not mean that they are not funny.

Carroll disagrees with Cohen on this issue. For Carroll, it is possible that understanding the conditions (and intent) of a joke may preclude the "comic amusement" mentioned above. Part of Carroll's argument is detailed in Chapter 3 of *Humour: A Very Short Introduction*. It depends on accepting the conceptual difference between a type (a category) and a token (an instance). He concludes that is not the type of humor that has moral value attached to it, but rather the token. This would explain why a joke might be unacceptable on a certain occasion, as the instance would be inappropriate, but might be acceptable on a different occasion. Is it possible, though, that there might be a type that should never be tokened? There is no clear answer to this question. As with any art form, pushing the boundaries is part of furthering its development. Lenny Bruce's comedy routine in 1964 landed him in jail. It is considered tame by today's standards.

If we return to the idea that jokes (or humor) are conditional, there is another insight to glean from the story of Clayton Bigsby. Much as our racial identity is shaped by our experiences, so is our sense of humor. As we all know, *Seinfeld* was a hugely successful television show, but there were elements that were more resonant with New Yorkers, especially New York Jews. Chappelle seemed less comfortable with the Bigsby sketch, as noted above, once elements of it were appropriated into a different social context. Similarly, this explains why a sketch in which the same *Frontline* reporter spoke with a white white supremacist would not be funny.

Or would it? It might to a white supremacist whose socially constructed sense of humor found it so. For this reason, I agree with Cohen's assessment of the distinction between the aesthetic and moral assessment of humor. I am not sure what the future assessment of *"Frontline:* Clayton Bigsby" will be, but I think it is an example of what social and philosophical comedy can be.

14

The Many Contradictions of Dave Chappelle

Duncan Gale

All fans of Dave Chappelle have their favorite bit, something that sticks with you that you can't help quoting. Mine comes from his first HBO stand-up comedy special in 2000, *Killin' Them Softly*. The bit perhaps has not aged that well, but I think it shows how Chappelle is able to rise above the ranks of good comedians into the pantheon of the truly great. Towards the end, Chappelle tackles that most well-worn subject of stand-up comedians, the battle of the sexes.

He begins with a classic bait-and-switch, talking about how chivalry is dead and getting an applause break from a female contingent of his audience before going on to say, "that's right, chivalry is dead . . . and women killed it." This thesis statement may not be especially original, but it is expertly set up and delivered.

Chappelle then goes into how men and women have different priorities, continuing his delicate game of push-and-pull by talking about the inherently ridiculous notion of women getting advice about how to please men from magazine articles written by other women. Chappelle provides his own pithy advice: "Suck his dick, play with his balls, and then fix him a sandwich and don't talk so much!"

This prompts another applause break and a standing ovation from some men in the audience, and Chappelle even fist pounds a guy in the front row. Such a crude summation verges upon outright misogyny, but Chappelle then deftly pivots to his real problem with the magazines that women read, which is that they make women feel insecure and have low self-esteem about their looks. As Chappelle delivers this, he exudes sincere empathy which elicits some applause yet again. What cements the true brilliance of the bit is what fol-

145

lows when Chappelle offers a "practical application" of the points he has made.

He describes a scenario where he and his friends are at the club and, at the sight of an especially provocatively dressed woman, he might say, "Damn! Look at them titties!" The woman would respond in outrage, saying, "Just because I am dressed this way does not make me a whore!" Chappelle then addresses each half of his audience in quick succession: "Gentlemen, that is true, just because they dress a certain way doesn't mean they are a certain way, don't ever forget it, but ladies, you must understand that that is fucking confusing!" He then makes an analogy to a situation where he is walking down the street dressed in a police uniform and someone comes up to him asking for help. He responds that just because he is dressed that way does not mean that he is a police officer. The audience, getting his point, erupts into thunderous applause, and Chappelle then drops the conclusion of his argument, "All right lady, fine, you are not a whore . . . but you are wearing a whore's uniform!"

This bit is an attempt to break down a certain social phenomenon and is of a piece with much other stand-up comedy, but what puts it in a class by itself is its sheer level of detail and complexity as well as the way that it is structured like a rigorous philosophical argument. It's a complex and multifaceted deconstruction of the contradictory nature of male-female relations, and it makes clear that Chappelle wants to genuinely understand what he is talking about beyond the surface level. It shows the connections of Chappelle's comedy not just to philosophy itself but specifically to the German philosopher Georg Wilhelm Friedrich Hegel (1770–1831) who is known for constructing an elaborate philosophical system to understand the totality of reality by analyzing how the inherent contradictions within all things leads to development and progress. By looking more closely at the connections between Chappelle's comedy and Hegel's philosophy, we may be able to gain a greater appreciation for the unique take that Chappelle has on a number of different topics.

The Dialectic in a Nutshell

The key to understanding Hegel's perspective is the concept of the dialectic. The dialectic is a description of the inherent tension within various aspects of reality and is generally presented as an initial first idea (thesis), a negation of that initial idea (antithesis), and an improved idea that comes about through a resolution of the conflict between those two ideas (synthesis).

One of the most famous illustrations of Hegel's dialectic, and one which is also relevant for dealing with Chappelle's race-based comedy, is the relationship between a master and a slave. If we consider a master-slave relationship as it existed in the American South, the master has all of the power in this relationship. He owns the slave as his property, and the slave is dependent upon the master for whatever food, clothing, and shelter the master deigns to give him. The slave must also be completely obedient to the master and has no opportunity to express his own free will in any way.

However, this relationship is not actually as one-sided as it may initially appear. According to Hegel, because the slave must perform all of the work for the master, he actually has the opportunity to express himself through the performance of his assigned tasks, many of which are quite tangible and physically apparent, such as the picking of cotton. So the slave actually works upon the earth and transforms it in some way, whereas the master does nothing. Furthermore, by forcing the slave to do all of the work, the master actually places himself in a situation of complete dependence on the slave. The master needs the slave just as much as the slave needs the master, which contradicts the nature of the relationship as initially understood. This leads to the final step in the dialectic in which the master and the slave become cognizant of this contradiction and are motivated to bring about a better social situation in which this logically absurd situation no longer exists.

Now let's try applying the dialectical method to Chappelle's bit. Chappelle alludes to the concept of chivalry, which hearkens back to a social arrangement in which men are expected to do everything for women during courtship—pay for food and drinks, open doors for them, place their coats on puddles for women to step over, and so on. This seems to place men as slaves to the mastery of women, but we know that all of this takes place against the backdrop of a patriarchal society where men have all the real power; chivalry reveals itself as an artificial concession to women to make up for their lack of any real social capital. This leads women to try to gain more power within society, but this may come along with a decrease in the chivalric obligations of men towards them.

This is the modern situation, a relationship between men and women in which men desire women sexually and women want to be sexually desired by men, but they also want men to respect them as equals. Sexual desire and respect are not mutually exclusive, but if men perform actions that unduly emphasize one of these, then women might feel that the other is completely lacking. Chappelle's bit is an attempt to explicate and negotiate this delicate dialectical scenario by laying bare the inherent contradictions within it.

As may be evident from the resolution of the master-slave relationship, Hegel's dialectic represents an optimistic reading of history, one that views the story of human civilization as one of slow but sure forward-moving progress. Hegel sees history as a process of gradually realizing what freedom truly is.

Hegel's story begins with the ancient civilizations of the East, vast empires where only one person, the ruler, was free, and everyone else was a slave of the social system. The next stage is the societies of ancient Greece and Rome, where the idea of freedom is understood abstractly and certain social groups enjoy some freedom, but this is undermined by the fact that slavery exists in these societies as well. Only with the advent of Christianity is the full concept of freedom introduced to humanity, the notion that we are spiritual beings not limited by our physical bodies. But this advance is held back for centuries by the Catholic Church which becomes yet another empire inhibiting the freedom of its subjects. Martin Luther liberates Christianity from this by initiating the Protestant Reformation in which every believer is free to interpret the Bible for himself. This leads to the society in which Hegel lived, the Prussian state of the early nineteenth century, which he sees as the culmination of the idea of freedom and therefore as the end of the historical process.

The Prophetic Nature of *Chappelle's Show*

The first episode of *Chappelle's Show* sets the tone for the series with a provocative sketch about Clayton Bigsby, a Black man who, unaware of his own blackness because he is blind and has been misled by well-meaning white people all of his life, becomes a leading figure in the white supremacist movement. The sketch utilizes the deadpan format of a PBS *Frontline* documentary, complete with another well-meaning white man in the form of a reporter who tries to tactfully break the news to Bigsby that he is in fact the very thing that he has dedicated his life to hating. Bigsby does not believe him, and the truth only comes out at a speaking engagement in which Bigsby's adoring white supremacist fans implore him to take off his Klan hood. Once he reveals himself, the revelation causes one man's head to literally explode.

It's difficult to pinpoint exactly what makes this sketch so funny. The premise is inherently outrageous and absurd enough to elicit a chuckle, but probably part of what allowed even someone with Chappelle's reputation of pushing the envelope to get away with it is the fact that in the early 2000s, the white supremacist movement and the Ku Klux Klan were perceived as being on the relative fringe of American society. There was something almost buffoonish about them, so a sketch where a Black man unknowingly infiltrates their ranks simply reinforced the mainstream perception of them as a hopelessly inept relic of the past that was slowly fading away.

Needless to say, much has changed in America since that sketch first aired. The advent of social media has allowed the white supremacist movement to become much more of a presence in our society, regardless of whether or not they represent the views of a significant percentage of the population. The Unite the Right rally that took place in Charlottesville, Virginia, in August of 2017 made explicit what many people had long suspected about Donald Trump vis à vis white supremacy—that he, the sitting President of the United States, has no real problem with these people or what they represent, and may even tacitly approve of their efforts.

These developments are surreal enough to someone attempting to adopt Hegel's approach of finding the guiding thread and purpose of history, but in addition, what about the way in which the Trump era has brought about situations with the strangest of political bedfellows? How is it that Kanye West, an icon of the hip-hop community and by extension the Black community as well, was at one time motivated to lend his enthusiastic support to a President more closely aligned with the white supremacist movement than any other in at least a generation? Is Kanye West the real-life Clayton Bigsby? This may be going too far, but it is worth contemplating how a seemingly absurd sketch from *Chappelle's Show* ended up being much more prescient than anyone would have imagined, with perhaps the exception of Chappelle himself.

Let's counteract this grim example with a more hopeful one, one more in line with the forward-moving progress espoused by the Hegelian interpretation of history. Another classic sketch from *Chappelle's Show* is when Chappelle brings up the topic of whether or not the American government should pay reparations to the descendants of slaves. He imagines a scenario where it actually does happen, which leads into a sketch showing Black people spending their new wealth in all kinds of

frivolous and extravagant ways, such as buying trucks full of cig-
arettes and immediately starting thousands of new record labels.
The resulting economic shift causes FUBU and KFC to merge
and become the largest corporation in the world. The sketch is an
interesting commentary on the way that those who have spent
their lives as part of an economically disenfranchised minority
will act in all kinds of ridiculous ways once they receive an unexpected financial windfall, and is probably based somewhat on the
countless stories we hear about the unwise decisions of lottery
winners. Yet, as with the Clayton Bigsby sketch, the premise also
trades upon an inherently fanciful notion—in this case, that reparations for slavery would ever actually come to pass.

Once again, much has changed since this sketch first aired.
Reparations for slavery is no longer some pie-in-the-sky notion
associated only with militant Black nationalists. The idea
began to gain a certain amount of mainstream awareness when
Ta-Nehisi Coates, a prominent author and journalist who
would go on to receive the prestigious MacArthur Genius
grant, published a long article in the June 2014 issue of *The
Atlantic* entitled, "The Case for Reparations," where he laid out
a complex and detailed argument for why this seeming pipe
dream among the Black community is in fact a long-overdue
and necessary step in America's moral reckoning with itself.

In the summer of 2019, during the debates among the
Democratic candidates seeking the nomination for the 2020
Presidential race, there seemed to be only one real issue on
which the large group of potential nominees were in complete agreement, aside from their hatred of Trump, and that
was on the need for some kind of reparations for slavery. On
June 19th (Juneteenth) of 2019, the House of Representatives held a congressional hearing on reparations with the
intention of voting on a specific bill, HR 40, that would create
a formal commission to investigate the implementation of
reparations for slavery by the US government.

While it remains to be seen whether or not reparations will
ever become a reality, Chappelle was ahead of his time in even
considering the ramifications of such a possibility all the way
back in 2003. As we have seen, the kind of comedic social commentary that Chappelle engages in can be an expression of
both his darkest fears and his greatest hopes, and it is only
with the passage of time that we can sometimes get the full picture on how accurate these may be. This is also fully in line
with the Hegelian interpretation of history, in which progress
and change are inevitable, but the specific manner in which
they happen is impossible to predict.

The Later Chappelle and Post-Woke Culture

I still haven't been cancelled yet, but I'm working on it.

—DAVE CHAPPELLE

The above quote, from the first episode of *Chappelle's Show*, has yet another weird kind of resonance considering all that has happened in our culture between when it was uttered and now. Chappelle was talking about his show being cancelled by a television network, but we are now familiar with another, far more damning form of cancellation—the way in which the culture at large "cancels" actual human beings. The current phenomena of "cancel-culture" and "wokeness" can be seen as the logical extreme of political correctness, and as such they have a naturally adversarial relationship to the kind of raw social commentary that Chappelle engages in with his comedy.

It is here that we can identify a shift in the dialectical relationship that Chappelle as a comedian has with his cultural milieu. He is no longer a young comedic underdog trying to provoke society to deal with uncomfortable issues of race. Our current society has to a large extent taken up those challenges, albeit in often imperfect ways. But Chappelle is now an older, successful and revered comedian who must figure out how to remain relevant in a society that has progressed far beyond what he could have imagined. History did not end in Hegel's nineteenth-century Prussia, nor did it end when the issues that Chappelle brought to light began to gain mainstream acceptance. Issues of race remain a topic of primary concern in American society, but these are accompanied by issues of sexuality and gender as well.

To a large extent, we can regard every one of Chappelle's comedy specials after his long, self-imposed exile from show business as a reaction to this cultural situation. But his Netflix special *Sticks and Stones* released in August of 2019 stands out as an especially explicit response to the problems inherent in a society that may be too sensitive for its own good. The title itself is a kind of provocation, reminding us that as harmful as words may *seem* to be, they cannot actually inflict physical damage. Chappelle comes out swinging, beginning his set with an "impression." Affecting a moronic voice, he says, "Uh, duh. Hey! Durr! If you do anything wrong in your life, duh, and I find out about it, I'm gonna try to take everything away from you, and I don't care when I find out. Could be today, tomorrow, fifteen, twenty years from now. If I find out, you're fucking-duh-finished."

Chappelle then points his finger straight at the audience, saying that he has been doing an impression of them! He goes on to insult the audience and talk about how this is the worst time to be a celebrity and to be doing comedy. This is a perfect illustration of the dialectical relationship that Chappelle has with his own audience—he is negating them! But the audience eats up the abuse, laughing and applauding along with him. Far more challenging is when he begins to talk about the alleged victims of Michael Jackson's sexual abuse and how it may not have been such a bad thing to suffer abuse from one of the most famous and successful people in the world. Chappelle seems to be daring people to walk out, saying things in open defiance not just of wokeness or political correctness but any kind of decency whatsoever. I have to admit that even I, a life-long fan of Chappelle's comedy, turned off the special at this point when I tried to watch it for the first time.

But I gave it another chance, and after that initial gauntlet of unpleasantness I found the same basic Chappelle that has been there all along, just in a different stage of his life now. Instead of seeming to be firmly on one side of the social justice movement, he is now offering bemused reactions to a situation in which social justice may be going too far too fast, but never in a way that questions the overall aims of the movement itself. One of the more inspired bits of *Sticks and Stones* is a bit about all of the different groups involved in the LGBTQ+ movement being stuck in a car together and the absurdity of how they have had to band together out of necessity even though they clearly do not have the same goals or worldview. The bit is sensitive, thoughtful, most importantly funny, and it once again shows how Chappelle's comedic approach is always centered on trying to really figure something out, regardless of whether he may offend some people or say something slightly "wrong" in the process.

Chappelle really is in his own way a kind of dialectical philosopher intent to show contradictions wherever they exist, and we may be able to learn as much from Chappelle's socially conscious comedy routines as from Hegel's philosophical analyses of the historical dialectic.

15

Well, Look No Further, Fella, You Found Me!

JOHN V. KARAVITIS

WARNING: For readers who have mistakenly picked up a copy of this entry in the pop culture and philosophy genre, thinking that they would learn more about their comedic idol Dave Chappelle, please be advised that this chapter contains gratuitous use of philosophical concepts. You'll be subjected to unexpected revelations, which may be followed by moments of disbelief, and then severe, uncontrollable physical outbursts. You have been warned!

Okay. There. I said it. It had to be said, you know. I mean, we live in such a litigious society nowadays; and there are a lot of lawyers who have been out of work since The Great Recession of 2008, that you really have to be careful about dotting your i's, crossing your t's, and reminding yourself that the Fifth Amendment is alive and well–at least for now. Although perhaps, for some of you, a lawyer is a terrible thing to have lying around, collecting dust. But what do I know?

Not that you're going to get into any trouble by reading this chapter. Far from it. I wouldn't call it "trouble," per se, but you are going to find yourself doing some heavy thinking about that thing we casually call "comedy." Call it a mental hike through the backwoods of philosophy. You'll be exhausted by the end, but you'll have experienced something new! Perhaps you'll even adopt a new motto: "Leave only prior misconceptions. Take only new perspectives on Life!"

To help you out on our little romp through the backwoods of philosophy, allow me to scope out the road map for our little adventure. (WARNING: This road map is not drawn to scale, and it cannot be relied on to get you to anywhere in particular. After our hike, you're on your own!) We'll look at one rather famous example of Chappelle's comedic genius, and we'll dissect it and see that it is brimming with messages about morality. And even though we laughed at it, we shouldn't be laughing at anything that Chappelle says or does! (Sorry, Dave! Just kidding!)

The World's Only Black White Supremacist

Let's look at an episode from *Chappelle's Show*: "*Frontline:* Clayton Bigsby." The premise of this comedy sketch (and that officially makes Chappelle a full-fledged comedian, and not just a stand-up comic) is that Clayton Bigsby, a blind Black Southerner, has, for the last fifteen years, "been the leading voice of the white supremacist movement in America." Kent Wallace, a Frontline investigator, begins with Clayton's life in The Wexler Home for the Blind. Bridgett Wexler, the current headmistress, admits that "He was the only n****r we'd ever had around here, so we figured we'd make it easier on Clayton by just telling him, and all the other blind kids, that he was white." Apparently, Clayton never questioned this. "Why would he?" asks Ms. Wexler.

During his interview of Clayton, Kent Wallace asks him "What exactly is your problem with African-Americans?" Clayton launches into a tirade, listing every possible stereotype about Blacks. On the way to a book signing later that day, they stopped at a gas station. There, Kent Wallace asks Clayton's friend Jasper why he doesn't just tell him that he is in fact Black. He answers that Clayton is too important to the white power movement. Jasper also believes that Clayton would kill himself if he ever learned that he was Black, "just so there'll be one less n****r around. His commitment is that deep." Kent Wallace responds, "I'm overwhelmed by the irony."

Later, at the book signing, everyone in the audience is excited and on board, ready to hear Clayton speak. Clayton is admonished by Jasper that he should wear a Klan hood because "it'd be safer, you know, in case some radical unsympathetic to the cause wants to shoot you." Toward the end of his speech, when encouraged by the audience to reveal his identity, Clayton removes his Klan hood. The audience is stunned in disbelief, with one audience member's head exploding!

At the close of the *Frontline* investigation, Kent Wallace informs us that Clayton has divorced his (also blind) wife after nineteen years of marriage because "She's a n****r lover."

Walking Through Life with Eyes Wide Shut

This comedy sketch is hilarious. But by holding Life up to scrutiny, it shows us how morally bankrupt people can be. We learn that Clayton's racial identity was withheld from him and the other blind children at The Wexler Home for the Blind because it was "easier." But easier for whom? For Clayton, who would eventually be out in the real world, dealing with people who would not be blind to his skin color? Or easier for the home's administration, which would not have to deal with Clayton being bullied and harassed by the other children, who would have learned early on that it's "better" to be white than Black? At the gas station stop on the way to the book signing, Jasper admits that he hasn't been told the truth because, "He's too important to the movement." It's easier to let Clayton continue to live a lie as long as his efforts have some utility for others. Clayton himself continues the lie when, upon learning that he is in fact Black, he divorces his wife because "She's a n****r lover."

You'd think that it would be impossible to blame Clayton for his opinions of and behavior toward non-whites. But Clayton is no imbecile. He can think and argue like an adult. And when he does learn that he is in fact Black, we would have hoped that the story would have ended differently. That he would have taken pause to reflect upon his situation, and how skin color is not what determines morality. Unfortunately, his reality has been embedded so deeply in the racist mindset that he was raised in that Jasper firmly believed that "If you tell him he's Black, he'd probably kill himself, just so there'll be one less n****r around." Quite frankly, having Clayton divorce his wife instead of killing himself, as his friend would have predicted, shows just how deep his racist mindset is. Why should he kill himself? He doesn't think of himself as Black—he never has, and he never will! Thus, even with the truth at hand, he remains imprisoned in the lie that his life has always been.

Philosopher John Rawls wrote about a way to cure this moral blindness in *A Theory of Justice* (1971). Rawls understood that the issue here and behind all racism, behind all "us versus them" thinking, would be best addressed by working from a "veil of ignorance." If each of us were unable from the start to determine what social group we would "belong" in, then we would probably be more eager to set up the framework and laws of our society so that, if we happened to have been born into a disadvantaged social group, we would not be punished for this. By working under a "veil of ignorance" of our true social identity, we would be encouraged to create a more equitable world, a world where laws are made part of the social contract objectively. We would understand that the color of our skin is not something that determines a person's self-worth or morality. Skin color would fall into a philosophical category known as "moral luck." If I can't control something, like my skin color, how could I be blamed for it? Would you, gentle reader, agree that discrimination or slavery was *not immoral* if it turned out that, by the luck of the genetic lottery, you found yourself to be a member of the very same group that was to be enslaved? Standing alone, the Clayton Bigsby sketch is one long argument in favor of applying the "veil of ignorance" to our laws and society.

In the Bigsby sketch, we see lie layered upon lie over decades. Instead of doing the right thing, everyone continued the lie. It was expedient to use Clayton instead of telling him the truth. Even Kent Wallace, who should have come right out and told Clayton that he is Black, kept silent during his investigation and interview. You may ascribe his silence to "journalistic professionalism," but journalists are tasked with discovering and eventually revealing the truth. This lie was maintained for years because it was expedient for everyone to do so. It was expedient to keep Clayton "in the dark," for as long as possible, for everyone who came into close contact with him. It would have stirred up too much hatred to simply tell Clayton the truth. And it would have deprived white supremacists of yet one more voice supporting their movement.

But if you take a step back and think deeply about what the Bigsby sketch presents, you'd realize that it is based on something deeper that the audience never realizes. I mean going beyond the surface level messages about racism, moral luck, and Rawls's "veil of ignorance." The deeper meaning of this sketch is that comedy is inherently based on tragedy!

There's Nothing Funny about Comedy!

Have you ever laughed at something that wasn't in some way tragic? Have you ever laughed at a situation where things went the right way in a story, and where no one was hurt? I'm guessing that's never happened. And from early on, there have been ideas about why that is.

First off, there's the superiority theory. We find something funny because we look at a situation and find ourselves superior to it. In the Clayton Bigsby sketch, there's no way you can't see yourself as superior to all of the characters. You can see, of course, how idiotic everyone's position is. But that's not enough to make something funny, is it?

Perhaps comedy makes us laugh because we get a sense of catharsis. Although the word appears in Aristotle's treatise

Poetics, it doesn't really mean what people take it to mean. Things get lost in translation from ancient Greek to modern-day English. Aristotle understood that people had a rational side and an emotional side. But these two sides could be out of balance. Catharsis brought the rational and emotional faculties back into balance. And this was supposed to be why people found tragedies so entertaining. And if tragedy is entertaining, then comedy, which appears to be based on tragedy, should also be entertaining.

The absurd could also qualify as comedy. Bigsby divorces his likewise blind wife after nineteen years of marriage because she's married to a Black man—himself! An absurdity would mean that something is out of whack, and inherently tragic, too.

Irony can also be an element of comedy. Kent Wallace spoke tongue-in-cheek when he said "I'm overwhelmed by the irony" in the gas station. A quick and dirty definition of irony would be something that is the opposite or reverse of what is expected. But it also has to be amusing. So, Kent Wallace may have been referring to one of the three types of irony, situational irony; but he technically misused the word. He found nothing amusing about the situation. The audience, however, does. It's ironic, so, for the audience, it's funny.

At the very least, comedy requires tragedy. But how can all this tragedy be so funny?

Chappelle! What You Really Up To?

You know the drill. The stand-up comic gets up on stage and starts giving us vignettes about life. Sometimes longer stories, but today's audience has a limited attention span, thank you Hollywood and Madison Avenue! At the end of the vignette is the twist that makes the audience laugh. But again, the laughter is what's on the surface. What's really going on is that the stand-up comic is doing something to you, successfully, that other people may have a hard time doing. Stand-up comics are persuading you that their spin on a story is the correct way of looking at the world. And there are a couple of names for people who persuade while speaking in public. Again, it goes back to Aristotle. One such person is a rhetorician.

Rhetoric is defined as the art of persuasion in the sphere of practical affairs. A rhetorician is defined as "a speaker whose words are primarily intended to impress or persuade" (Google Dictionary). Did you realize that? You weren't being catered to, just to cover the charge of admission to the comedy club. It wasn't all about you in the comedy club. You thought that the stand-up comic was playing his act for your amusement. Instead, the stand-up comic tried to persuade you not just what to think, but also what's the right way to act. An attempt was made to persuade you about right and wrong, and that the comic's way was right. Such public speakers rely on the use of emotions to help them sway their audience. You don't agree? Then tell me the last time you found something funny that didn't appeal to your emotions on some level.

In Plato's dialog *Gorgias*, Socrates praises the power of the orator. That's the other type of person who tries to persuade while speaking in public. But for Socrates, the orator would need philosophy, or else his speech would be mere flattery! In Plato's dialogue *Phaedrus*, Socrates defines oratory as "the art of enchanting the soul." (Although oratory typically refers to a long, eloquent speech, I can see how some stand-up routines could be viewed as such.) And you "enchant the soul" by invoking an emotional response, not by offering up a rational argument. It's comedy, not mathematics! Chappelle falls into this mode often during his stand-up routines, as he did when he was awarded the prestigious Mark Twain Prize for American Humor in 2019.

Finally, we get the idea (again from Aristotle) that the purpose of the arts, like poetry, is to not only delight an audience but also to instruct them about Life. Philosopher Francis Bacon (1561–1626) would agree. For him, "the duty and office of rhetoric is to apply reason to imagination for the better moving of the will." So, rhetoric and oratory are not just tools for politicians, as most people might think. Although perhaps there is really just a very fine line between politicians and stand-up comics—or perhaps there's no line at all!

So, let me admit that I for one could not do what stand-up comics and comedians do. It's tough work. You have to be able to spin a story so that people will laugh. You're trying to persuade people who may not be easy to persuade, especially if you are challenging cherished beliefs, or deep-seated ideals. And you have to be sure that, if you do denigrate some social group, it's done in such a way that they want to laugh, too. The audience must believe "It's funny, because it's true!"

But the bottom line is that, when you laugh at a comic or comedian, when you feel that mental high, that "cathartic release," at the pleasure of a good joke or comedy sketch, what you aren't realizing is that you've just been psychologically played.

Will the Real Dave Chappelle Please "Stand Up"?

Comedy has been with us forever. On our hike through the backwoods of philosophy, we've seen that it's based on tragedy. Stand-up comics and comedians present us with tragic aspects of our boring, mundane world, and hold these up for inspection and criticism, and yes, with the "intention to elicit amusement." We are asked to reflect on the meaning of it all. Yet all we do is laugh.

And perhaps we should be doing more than just laughing. Because, as I promised at the start of this chapter, I am going to reveal to you who or what Dave Chappelle is, along with everyone else who ever told you a joke or gave you a comedic performance, at which you laughed.

Dave Chappelle is our world's version of Socrates.

Yes, that's right. (Wait, did I just make you laugh?) In our world today, we don't have philosophers asking the tough questions about life and wondering about the nature of reality, at least not outside of academia. Philosophers in academia are pretty good about writing papers and books, debating with each other, holding seminars and conferences, and being interviewed for the occasional documentary about philosophy. No "philosopher as rock star," as far as I can tell. And their audience tends to be almost exclusively like-minded academics and students of philosophy. But is that what philosophy is supposed to be? Scientists, who should always have the branch of philosophy known as metaphysics in mind as they try to uncover the secrets of nature, rarely bother with philosophy. Today, most scientists see philosophy as what people who can't do real science do. But, for example, the major players who participated in the birth of quantum mechanics were themselves all schooled in philosophy; and their debates were always guided by ideas in metaphysics.

You may balk at this: comedian as philosopher. But I think that's because you've labored all your life under a false assumption. You've probably thought of philosophers as some really smart people who talk about things that most of us can't grasp. And you may have labored under the assumption that philosophers use formal logic as their tool for analyzing ideas. But as philosopher of law Chaim Perelman claimed in 1981, "the methodology proper to the elaboration of philosophical thinking is rhetoric, not formal logic."

In our world today, we don't have Socrates being sentenced to death for asebeia (impiety) against the gods, and for corrupting the youth of Athens. We don't have Diogenes of Sinope (around 404–323 B.C.E.), the Cynic, walking the streets of Athens with a lantern in broad daylight, looking for an honest man. For the *hoi polloi* (that's you and me and everyone else who has no philosophical pretensions), we get our lives dissected and analyzed by comedians.

And all we do is laugh. Sure, you may be at a comedy club, and find yourself turning to one of your friends and saying, "You know, it's funny because it's true." But after that, nothing.

Maybe that's something that you can take away from this chapter. I mean, at the beginning, I gave you two warnings. The first was that you'd find yourself undergoing a lot of emotional upheaval during this chapter. If I've done my job right, you have. You've had a cherished activity, laughing at something funny, dissected and analyzed, and found that you yourself have been "doing it all wrong" from the start. That it wasn't all about you, but about you and your emotions being played to get you to change your ways. The second warning was that, after our romp through the backwoods of philosophy, you'd be on your own. But maybe—just maybe—this shouldn't have been labeled a warning.

Now you can draw your road map through life on your own, at least with the unwitting help of today's versions of the philosophers of old: stand-up comics and comedians. And hopefully you won't find yourself (as often) in the tragic situation of the characters of the comedy sketches that give us so much guilty pleasure. As we saw with Clayton Bigsby and everyone in his world.

[Insert name here], you hardly knew yourself. Well, actually, you didn't. Not really. But if you work at it a bit, you might be able to one day say to yourself "Well, look no further, fella, I found me!"

And that's no laughing matter.

16
Dave Chappelle Meets Sigmund Freud

DRU GRAHAM, BENNET SOENEN, AND
ADAM BARKMAN

Dave Chappelle's *"Frontline:* Clayton Bigsby" skit is one of his best-loved and oft-mentioned skits. It's offensive, funny, and poignant; in it lies the genius of Chappelle. He is, at once, able to shock, entertain, and make important points regarding our preconceived conceptions and philosophical beliefs.

Clayton is found and interviewed by the PBS news show called *Frontline* and they follow his doings as he goes, with his face concealed in a hood, to a book signing and talk, where he accidentally reveals the fact that he is Black to a group of his readers and supporters, causing babies to cry and heads to literally explode. The skit ends with Clayton realizing his Blackness and divorcing his white wife on the grounds of her loving a Black person. This skit is partially about the ridiculousness of racially based hatred, and partly about moral character in this situation.

Freud and Fear of Castration

The question of how these racial views arise is one that philosopher-psychologists like Sigmund Freud, the founder of psychoanalysis, have tried to answer. As a Jew living among those who generally had a low view of Jews, Freud certainly experienced racism. According to Sander Gilman, Viennese society saw Freud and other Jews as "the Negroes of Vienna," and psychoanalysis as a "black thing" (pp. 19–22). This deeply disturbed Freud and, as a result, a lot of his writing can be interpreted as him wrestling with this theory of race in both conscious and unconscious ways.

According to Freud, a race is a group of people with a similar mind or a group mentality. This common mental space is one that is developed throughout history, leaving imprints on groups of people which are passed down through something resembling Lamarckian evolution (the theory that organisms gained or lost traits due to use or disuse during their life). Freud placed great importance on the history of the Jewish people in discovering facts of the mind. He believed that every thought and emotion was influenced by the previous history of humankind to some extent. An example of this can be seen in the correspondence Freud had with other Viennese Jews. These "imprints" are what really make up race, according to Freud—not physical qualities like skin color but a common way of thinking and reasoning. If a community is harassed by a common enemy or has a common hatred for a group of people, these will be passed down the generations, even if the views are not explicitly taught.

According to this psychological definition of race, Clayton's hatred of Black people is based almost entirely upon what he considers to be the character and culture of non-white people. Clayton has many complaints about non-white cultures, ranging from a hatred of hip-hop to a distaste for the cuisine of the East. If race is viewed as a group of people with common intellectual and moral backgrounds, then Clayton, somehow being brought into a white supremacist moral tradition, is predisposed to hating other cultures and hates them as his natural enemies.

We think that some of Freud's other ideas have a lot to say about the problems we face when talking about race. Freud's theory of mind centers around his concept of the Oedipus and castration complexes, and his distinction between the Id, Ego, and Superego. The Oedipus complex is composed of a child's sexual desire for their parent of the opposite sex. This is accompanied by their unconscious desire to see the death of the same-sex parent. Each sex has a different relationship with both the Oedipus complex, as well as to castration.

The castration complex, says Freud, originates from each child's belief that everyone originally has a penis. Freud proposed that all children believe that everyone has a penis. In Freud's own words, "It is self-evident to a male child that a genital like his own is to be attributed to everyone he knows, and he cannot make its absence tally with his picture of these other people." We are able to see how much the boy values his penis in his inability to imagine a person like himself who does not possess one. It is once the boy realizes that not all individuals possess penises that the castration complex emerges. The boy believes that females have had their penises "cut off" and it is this possibility of castration that causes the boy to fear the loss of his own penis. The girl, however, does not fear castration because in Freud's theory she believes that she has already been castrated and is relegated to a life of envy and jealousy towards the male. The fear of castration is primarily caused by the relationship between the father and the son.

For Freud, the circumcision of the Jewish boy becomes the most significant manifestation of the castration process as it results in part of the penis being literally cut off. Freud views this castration as a symbol of the authority that the father has to force his son into submission under him. Thus, Freud views castration as both a literal castration and a symbolic one where the boy submits to the authority and power of the father over himself and loses his penis. Freud then explains how this castration results in the deep hatred the world has for the Jewish people.

The Jewish person becomes a reminder to the world that we can be castrated. The circumcised Jew represents a mutilated person who, because of his own castration, desires revenge by castrating the rest of the world. Those who have been castrated live a life of envy and desire to see those who possess a penis to be castrated. Freud discusses the inevitableness of this belief when he writes, "The castration complex is the deepest unconscious root of anti-Semitism; for even in the nursery little boys hear that a Jew has something cut off his penis—a piece of his penis, they think—and this gives them a right to despise Jews" (*Complete Works*, p. 2026).

Because of the deep nature of the Oedipus complex, not only is this antisemitism inevitable for all males, but it is also quite justifiable in the eyes of Freud. Freud simply relates the problem of race to that of gender. Perhaps this is because the hate that the Aryans had for the Jews came from the same source as males have for females. Freud would see both "isms" as obviously unethical, but perhaps an inevitable consequence of the relationship that men have with women and cultures have with other cultures.

The Leader Can Do No Wrong

The second major part of Freud's theory is his distinction between the Id, Ego, and Superego. First, the Id is the primitive and instinctive component of personality. The Id is the only completely unconscious part of the psyche and is driven by the libido, which is the term Freud used to describe sexual desires or urges. It is impulsive and is concerned with satisfying basic bodily urges and needs. The Ego mediates between the Id and the Superego. It uses rationalization to work out reasonable ways of satisfying the Id's demands. The Superego uses the values of society to impose a set of restrictions on the Ego. The Superego is concerned with repressing the urges of the Id that are considered to be socially unacceptable. The Superego uses either the conscience or the ideal self to accomplish this. The conscience can punish the Ego by causing guilt. The ideal self is a fictitious figure of what a good person is. This can take the form of career aspirations, how to treat people and what behavior is acceptable. If the Ego is not able to live up to the ideal self in a particular situation, the Ego is punished with guilt. However, if the ideal self is realized in a particular situation, the Ego is rewarded with positive feelings such as pride.

For Freud, groups exist because of the libidinal ties that hold them together. This sexual energy is not necessarily directed towards sexual union. Rather, it is directed towards actions that benefit the group, such as empathy and the willingness to help. This libidinal tie, however, doesn't come into existence by itself. For Freud, this libidinal tie is dependent on there being a leader or external object for each of the members to identify with. Freud describes identification as a mental process through which the individual models themselves after the leader by copying traits or qualities.

This identification with the leader gives the group an emotional connection to both each other and the leader. Freud believed that this identification caused the Superego to be replaced with the leader of the group. This replacing of the Superego causes the conscience and moral compass of the individual to be completely replaced by the leader. Freud himself writes:

> A primary group of this kind is a number of individuals who have put one and the same object in the place of their super ego and have consequently identified themselves with one another in their ego. (*The Interpretation of Dreams*, p. 61)

Because this leader is now the Superego, they can do no wrong and nothing done for the sake of the leader produces any guilt from the conscience. Remember that the Superego's main responsibility is to repress the urges of the Id. Thus, the unconscious urges of the Id are free because of the loss of the superego and those individuals who are a part of a group will do things as a part of a group that they would not do as individuals.

We begin to see how the psychoanalytic tradition gives us another lens for viewing Chappelle's depiction of the white supremacist movement. What makes this concept of the "leader" in Freud's psychoanalysis so relevant for our discussion is that it is not necessarily bound to a human leader. It can sometimes be an abstract idea that becomes the Superego of a group. This abstract idea can also join together groups of people through strong emotions. Freud writes:

> The leader or the leading idea might also, so to speak, be negative; hatred against a particular person or institution might operate in just the same unifying way, and might call up the same kind of emotional ties as positive attachment. (*Complete Works*, p. 3793)

To better explain how the Superego can be replaced, think of a young boy in love with a young girl. To the boy, this girl will inevitably have a certain amount of freedom from any kind of criticism or faults as a result of being so highly valued by the boy. The more internalized the crush becomes for the boy the more amazing the girl becomes to him. The girl becomes an increasingly idealized version of herself.

The boy values the girl in much the same way he values himself. Just as he would not think to criticize himself, he would not think to criticize her. Just as he would do anything to protect himself, he would do anything to protect her. In many ways, the girl serves as a substitute for the love the boy has for himself. This crush may increase to the point that the boy is willing to harm himself to protect or satisfy the girl. One might further observe, then, that the boy may be projecting his own ideal self onto his crush. The boy may be said to love the girl for the traits that the boy wishes he had. We see, then, that the boy has replaced his crush with all of the things he holds most important. In the words of Freud, "The whole situation can be completely summarized in a formula: The object has been put in the place of the superego" (*Interpretation of Dreams*, p. 57).

White supremacy can be seen as operating under these pretenses. There is a leading idea (that whites are superior to non-whites) which replaces the Superegos of some white people and binds together a group of people who share this belief. Because this belief has replaced the Superego, this inevitably leads to extreme and harmful actions as there is no longer an internal Superego to regulate the primal urges of the Id as a new external one takes its place. Additionally, when white supremacy replaces a group's Superegos, they can no longer criticize actions done in service to this leading ideal. The new ideal becomes the standard for moral action. Anything done in the name of the new ideal is no longer subject to a guilty conscience. Even more disconcerting, the unconscious desires of the Id exist in all people. Thus, all people are subject to this kind of behavior.

Freud would see white supremacy as an almost inescapable evil that is not concerned per se with race, but with allowing our unconscious evils to manifest. When we understand that hostility is fundamental to human relationships, we begin to understand that the greater the differences between two groups, the greater the hostility. While the hostility between the English and the Scottish is great, it is not quite as intense as that of white people towards Black people. The more obvious the difference, the more hostile the conflict. In the case of Clayton Bigsby, we see that he becomes part of a particular group which has a certain unfortunate abstract idea that replaces the Superego of its followers. To the psychoanalyst, his unconscious drives are able to be released through his writing of books and his hatred for non-whites.

We can see this concept in Bigsby especially towards the end of the skit when he realizes his Blackness. Despite the realization, his hatred for Black people is so ingrained into him that he maintains his ideology although subject to his own hatred. This shows how an ideology becomes the driving force in Bigsby's life, even trumping personal pride, self-preservation, and happiness.

Freud's views on race and white supremacy are definitely a step in the right direction in acknowledging the social factors that create the racism of Clayton Bigsby. Freud's insistence on these patterns of racial and gender inequality being inevitable also seem to align with modern psychology.

Racial Discrimination in Young Children

While many modern psychologists will claim that racial discrimination is a result of both biological and sociological determinants, they will disagree with Freud over what the biological determinants are. For modern psychologists, these biological determinants are not the result of unconscious inescapable drives or some innate inferiority in a group of people, but rather, the result of the patterns that human brains use to engage efficiently with the world.

Because children's brains are underdeveloped, they depend on gathering massive amounts of information and then generalizing from that. Because young children have been shown to be unable to categorize people according to more than one category at once, they stereotype behavior based on the most easily observable differences. Thus, when a child observes that two people are similar in one dimension, they assume that they must be similar in other dimensions as well.

Children as early as six months of age have been found to nonverbally categorize people based on race and gender. These children were observed to look longer at an unfamiliar face of a different race than an unfamiliar face of the same race to a statistically significant degree (*Race, Gender, and Young Children*, p. 55). Children then attach meaning to these social categories. This is an example of a sort of "cognitive puzzle" that children try to solve and then infer that their solution is the norm and is caused by meaningful differences.

What might make the example of Clayton Bigsby so interesting to the modern psychologist is that many of these examples rely on the individual being able to "see" the differences of skin tone and then make generalizations based on that. Bigsby provides us with an opportunity to discuss how powerful the cultural impact is on forming beliefs as he is unable to make these generalizations by himself because he is blind. Many modern philosophers and psychologists agree with Freud in positing societal or cultural factors in determining perceptions of race. Recent studies have demonstrated that the very language that is used to describe irrelevant topics can reinforce generalizations that children then project onto individuals. Associating positive things with the word "white" such as purity or "the good witch," and associating the word "black" with sin or "the wicked witch" can cause children to generalize these linguistic connotations to people.

Dave Chappelle's personal philosophy isn't straight-forwardly stated, of course, but with Freud he certainly seems to lean toward the idea that race is a cultural construct rather than something inherent in our genes. This perhaps isn't too surprising coming from a man who acknowledges his own mixed-race heritage (some white from his mother's side) as well as that of his own children (Chappelle's wife is Filipino).

This is played out brilliantly in his "Racial Draft" sketch from the first episode of the second season of *Chappelle's Show.* In this skit, various races draft celebrities of mixed race into their race, making them officially one or another race. The races of celebrities such as Tiger Woods, Colin Powell, Eminem, and the Wu-Tang Clan are discussed and eventually decided via a sports draft of a sort. All of these figures are either of mixed race or have accepted large aspects of one culture or another. The Black delegation at one point attempts to offload various Black conservatives onto the white delegation while simultaneously trying to take rapper Eminem.

We can see this further in Chappelle's defense of certain Black stereotypes. In his comedy special *For What It's Worth*, Chappelle says, "Just 'cause I eat chicken and watermelon,

> they think there's something wrong with me. If you don't like chicken or watermelon, something is wrong with you, motherfucker. Where are all these people that don't like chicken and watermelon? I'm sick of hearing about how bad it is! It's great!" Dave also has no problem with good natured pokes at cultures. After saying this bit about chicken and watermelon he says, "White people make fun of Latin people for eating. . . . What you all eating? Beans? Rice? Corn? Listen, that's not a reason to hate a motherfucker, all right? It's funny, but it's not a reason to hate.

This is what's important to Chappelle: it is not generalization or jokes; it's the hatred upon which those generalizations and jokes are often based that is the problem. In the same way, Chappelle isn't opposed to stereotyping or generalizations, but rather is opposed to the injustice that can come along with these if we aren't careful. So, let the jokes roll—people with all their differences can be great sources of humor—but, with Freud, we should be mindful of the socially constructed nature of race and certainly avoid injustices that come with imagining that a socially constructed thing is more important than it really is.

V

**Speaking
Recklessly**

17
Revolution or Illusion?

BRANDYN HEPPARD

Dave Chappelle is one of the best comedians of his generation and certainly one of the greatest of all time. Some would go so far as to say that he is a comic genius. Still others regard Chappelle as a revolutionary comic. During a conversation on *Inside the Actor's Studio*, James Lipton tells Chappelle that "Richard Pryor's wife had conveyed Pryor's feeling that he had passed the torch to Chappelle" ("When 'Keeping It Real' Goes Right," p. 145).

In fact, Chappelle's reputation as a revolutionary reaches all the way up to the ivory towers of academia, as well as out into the culture. Esteemed hip-hop artist Talib Kweli, for example, is quoted as saying, "Dave thinks like a revolutionary: He's a comedian, but he thinks in terms of this real hyper-independent, hyper-community way of thought that's really admirable" (quoted by Brian Josephs). And yet, the growing consensus around Chappelle's revolutionary status raises a question that seems to have gone unanswered: what does it mean to describe a comic like Chappelle as revolutionary?

Is a revolutionary comic someone whose work is so influential that it has radically changed the nature of comedy? Or, is the term revolutionary more of a political label for someone who appears to be an agent, catalyst, or prophet of revolution? Despite his extraordinary success, talent, and ability to provide insights into anti-Black male racism, Chappelle's work is not revolutionary in either regard. Moreover, since Chappelle's comedy ostensibly appears to be revolutionary, but actually leads away from revolution, it suggests that we have reached a state of peak capitalism which some scholars have dubbed late capitalism.

Because He Said So

Perhaps the most obvious reason to eschew labeling Chappelle as a revolutionary is because Chappelle himself does. In a conversation with author Maya Angelou, Chappelle downplays his political relevance. As Chappelle tells Angelou, "You're an iconic figure. I'm a pop-culture figure. That's much different" (*Iconoclasts*, 2006). This isn't just humility on Chappelle's part. Chappelle demonstrates an awareness that his role as an artist should not be confused with that of an activist, icon, or revolutionary. Although art is able to influence events in the political spectrum, it doesn't necessarily do so, nor does it intend to do so. Instead, the commitments of the artist remain within the realm of the aesthetic. Chappelle's comedy isn't the expression of a political agenda or the enactment of a revolutionary praxis. Instead, he is committed to his artistic form, the comic.

This again becomes clear in Chappelle's "comedy" special *8:46*. As Chappelle states, "Why would anyone care what their favorite comedian thinks after they saw a police officer kneel on a man's neck for eight minutes and forty-six seconds?" (*8:46*). Chappelle recognizes that he is not the appropriate person to lead the response to an event like this, not because of anything personal to him but because such work is best left to the activists and organizers. Turning to a comedian for leadership in a moment like this is like bringing a joke to a gunfight. In this vein, Chappelle castigates CNN's Don Lemon for explicitly noting the absence of celebrity voices on the front lines of the protests. Chappelle states, "So, the other night I'm in my little clubhouse and I'm watching, ah, Don Lemon, that hot bit of reality. He says, 'Where are all these celebrities? Why aren't you talking?'" (*8:46*). After hearing Lemon specifically name him, Chappelle retorts:

> Has anyone ever listened to me do comedy? Have I not ever said anything about these things before? So, now all of a sudden, this n***a expects me to step in front of the streets and talk over the work these people are doing as a celebrity. Ask me, "Do you want to see a celebrity right now? Do we give a fuck what Ja-Rule thinks? Does it matter about celebrity?" No! This is the streets talking for themselves. They don't need me right now. I kept my mouth shut. And, I'll still keep my mouth shut. But don't think that my silence is complicit to all this shit . . . (*8:46*)

On the one hand, Chappelle rightly balks at the notion that he has been silent on these issues, citing his long record of directly addressing issues of racism and police brutality in his work. He has also been outspoken in his support of those in the streets, particularly young activists, telling the audience that they are "excellent drivers" and that he is "comfortable in the back-seat" (*8:46*). On the other hand, Chappelle draws a clear line between himself, as a comedian, and those actively involved in the work of liberation. And so, the first and most important reason Chappelle should not be regarded as a revolutionary is because he does not regard himself as one.

Revolution, the Renaissance Comedians, and Richard Pryor

Still, in order to make a fair assessment of Chappelle's revolutionary status, it will be necessary to clarify what we mean by revolution. One common misconception is that revolution, in essence, amounts to a major change. Revolutions, however, cannot simply be reduced to change or difference. They are instead predicated upon true novelty. As Hannah Arendt reminds us, "Antiquity was well acquainted with political change and the violence that went with change, but neither of them appeared to it to bring about something altogether new. Changes did not interrupt the course of what the modern age has called history" (*On Revolution*, p. 11). Arendt helps us to understand that the changes that occur in revolution are so radical that they are instead experienced as a disruption in the course of history. As she goes on to say, "Revolutions are the only political events which confront us directly and inevitably with the problem of beginning." And Arendt is not alone in this observation. Enrique Dussel, author of *Philosophy of Liberation*, says of revolution, "It is where ages and epochs begin" (p. 19). Revolution goes beyond change. It marks a new beginning never before experienced, resulting in a time before and then everything after.

Based on this conception of revolution, Chappelle's body of comedic work does not merit the label of revolutionary. Surely, there have been revolutionary comics who have forever changed the game. Arguably, the first revolution in stand-up comedy occurred with the renaissance comedians of the late 1950s and early 1960s. Before the likes of Mort Sahl, Lenny Bruce, and others, stand-up was not so much an art form but rather a mercenary form of entertainment-for-a-living. As Gerald Nachman writes in his book, *Seriously Funny*, "In the fifties, stand-up comedy was merely a show business subdivision" (p. 42). Nachman explains, the "mandate" for comedians prior to the 1950s "was to amuse; survival was their foremost worry" (p. 22).

Nachman continues, "Comedy then was a trade, not a calling. Comics were skillful and resourceful joke tellers, spielers, showbiz brawlers. The aim was to create hilarity, not humor, much less wit. Jokes were only one piece of the craft. They were not always innately funny, but they acted funny. They were one-liner salesmen, guffaw-dealers, joke-brokers" (p. 22). By the late 1950s, however, the renaissance comedians introduced the world of stand-up to more substantive themes, often very personal, often very political, sometimes both. These comedians also brought the story-telling approach to stand-up as opposed to the customary gags and one-liners. Nat Hentoff, former *Village Voice* columnist, described these comedians as "the end of 'the machine-gun one-liner stand-up comic'" (p. 217). In particular, Nachman credits Mort Sahl as the first to bring the story-telling aspect to stand-up. This period was stand-up's coming of age. This is when stand-up truly became comedy. It was a revolution because it completely disrupted the history and trajectory of the field. And now, we can specifically point to a time before and after.

A generation later, Richard Pryor again revolutionizes the world of stand-up comedy, becoming a template for generations of comedians to follow. In Chappelle's own words, he describes Pryor as "the highest evolution of comedy," saying that "the mark of greatness is when everything before you is obsolete, and everything after you bears your mark" (Kimberley Yates, p. 146). Students of comedy can't help but notice the mark of Pryor on Chappelle's career. That said, Chappelle's assessment of greatness also helps us to define revolutionary. In terms of comedy, there is a world before Pryor and the world of comedy beginning with Pryor and after.

But Pryor's status as a revolutionary comic doesn't end with his impact on comedy. If we instead think of a revolutionary comic in its other, more political sense, as an agent, catalyst, or prophet of revolution, we can see that the label of revolutionary comic is still fitting. Long before Chappelle, Pryor was directly confronting issues of race, racism, and police brutality, as he does in the opening of his 1979 feature, *Richard Pryor: Live in Concert*. In one bit, Pryor references the deadly nature of a particular police choke-hold, which can't help but bring to mind the death of Eric Garner at the hands of NYPD some thirty-five years later.

Pryor's performance not only rebukes racism and police brutality, fitting a traditional model of Black masculinity, he also performs a new model of Black masculinity (at least new to non-Black audiences) throughout the show by openly and honestly discussing his fears and insecurities on topics including, but not limited to, parenting, sexuality, health, and diet. In fact, throughout the show, Pryor takes direct aim at "macho" masculinity, a thread he frequently revisits throughout the show. In another bit, Pryor explicitly decries the evils of rape, explicitly stating, "That's some foul shit to take away somebody's humanity like that." Certainly, like every comedian, there are moments when Pryor resorts to low humor that seems to reinscribe the status quo instead of subverting it. However, in the context of the time, 1979, much of it was a radical departure from the status quo. Almost as a nod to the work of revolutionary praxis, there is a moment in the middle of the special when Pryor stops the show and raises the houselights to acknowledge the presence of Huey Newton, co-founder of the Black Panther party, who was in the house that night.

Describing Pryor as a revolutionary comedian seems extremely fitting because he constitutes a radical break in the history of comedy. Chappelle, on the other hand, is an immensely talented comic who has had a long and lucrative career in comedy. He is not only one of the best comedians of his generation, he is one of the best of all time. However, it's hard to say that Chappelle has had the type of impact that the renaissance comedians of the late Fifties and early Sixties did, nor that of Pryor a generation later. Nevertheless, although it would be inappropriate to characterize Chappelle's impact on standup comedy as revolutionary, it is worth looking at his political legacy to determine whether we should understand him as a revolutionary in a political sense.

Chappelle's Ill-liberalism

Throughout his career, Chappelle has been reluctant to take political stances. As he states, "I don't want to be co-opted or subverted. I don't want to be my own worst enemy or be used against myself. But that's what happens to public people" (*Iconoclasts*). Chappelle's comedy, however, is not devoid of politics. Chappelle makes clear, "Yes, I voted for Hillary Clinton. Of course I did. I voted for her because I liked what she said vastly better than I liked what he said" (*Equanimity*). However, Chappelle goes on to qualify his vote, stating, "But to be honest with you, at that point, that shit was like watching Darth Vader do the "I Have a Dream" speech. That bitch is mean as hell. She had already Karate-Kid-swept Bernie Sanders's legs from underneath him. Boy, it was hard voting for that shit" (*Equanimity*). Despite Chappelle's critical tone, his political take on the election falls squarely within the mainstream, representing the views of a large swath of the American electorate, particularly African American voters. In fact, his critique of Clinton resonates with many on both the sides of the aisle.

That said, lest anyone misinterpret Chappelle's critique of Clinton, he also makes it clear that he has never been a Trump supporter. In one bit, Chappelle recalls a call he got from his wife in a panic while in New York City to host *SNL* just after the 2016 election. Chappelle recounts his wife saying, "The paper is saying that you're a Donald Trump supporter," to which he responds, "Don't worry about that shit, baby! Nobody in their right mind would believe that'" (*Equanimity*). However, many people were able to believe it, a notion that was only strengthened after Chappelle ended his *SNL* monologue by saying, "I'm wishing Donald Trump luck and I'm gonna' give him a chance" (*SNL*, 2016). Recalling that moment in a later bit, Chappelle quips, "I don't know what I said but whatever I said I really wish I didn't say that shit" (*Equanimity*).

Perhaps some were ready to believe Chappelle was a Trump supporter because anything seems possible in these days and times. On the other hand, perhaps others were ready to believe Chappelle was a Trump supporter because his comedy at times gives in to overtly reactionary stances which run counter to the spirit of revolution. Nevertheless, I would argue that most of Chappelle's reactionary takes can't be read on the surface. Quite often, when someone interprets one of Chappelle's jokes as landing conservatively, it indicates that they missed the joke and just may be the butt of it. Instead, as we will see, many of these jokes are done with the specific intent of standing up for classic liberal values, such as freedom of speech and expression. So it's not conservatism, which most of Chappelle's traditional fan base would find neither funny nor liberatory, but liberalism which gives his work the air of liberation while at the same time keeping it from being revolutionary.

When Chappelle hosted *SNL* just after the 2020 election, he did a joke affirming that women deserve to be paid less for equal work. Citing the infamous Trump press conference when the President of the United States "tried to guess the cure of the coronavirus in front of the whole world," Chappelle states, "Scariest part about that, one of the leading virologists in the world was sitting as close as you are to me and she just watched him say it. It's crazy. Her face was looking like he might be right . . . I saw that, I said 'Ooh . . . that's why women make half'" (*SNL*, 2020). Doubling down on the joke, Chappelle continues, "I don't know what it is—half, maybe seventy percent, whatever it is—it's too much" (*SNL*, 2020).

For Chappelle, the purpose of this joke, and others like it, is not to express his own reactionary views, but instead, to expose faux-liberal outrage. This is exemplified by Chappelle's mid-joke check-in, when he asks with glee, "Did I trigger you?" (*SNL*, 2020). To this end, Chappelle punctuates the joke saying, "I'm sorry, Lorne. I thought we were having a comedy show. It's like a woke meeting in here" (*SNL*, 2020). Chappelle delivers this joke, and others like it, with intentional irony in order to elicit the ire of virtue-signaling liberals. The subtext then being that Chappelle finds the ire of woke liberals just as ridiculous, if not more, than wage inequality.

On the one hand, these kinds of meta-jokes, which operate on a level beyond what's spoken, help to elevate Chappelle's status as a comedian. On the other hand, these kinds of moral equivalencies are a far cry from a revolutionary stance. That said, although Chappelle pokes fun at woke liberals, his comedy is not operating under a conservative worldview. Instead, this joke should be understood within the broader context of Chappelle's apologetics of classical liberal values, particularly freedom of speech, free expression, and tolerance.

Racialized Capitalism

Despite the growing consensus around Chappelle's revolutionary status, he does not consider himself a revolutionary, but instead casts himself as a sort of liberal humanist. In his own words, Chappelle states, "Contrary to popular belief, in the core of who I am, I don't think in terms of race" (*Iconoclasts*). Perhaps more surprising for fans of Chappelle, he states, "And I must tell you that I've never had a problem with white people ever in my life" (*Equanimity*). When asked if he is surprised that so many white people are fans of his comedy, Chappelle emphatically responds, "No, 'cause it's a human experience" (*Iconoclasts*).

Even though Chappelle never uses this language, there is an underlying recognition of the social construction of race in his comedy. And, as Chappelle is all too aware, race in the United States is largely shaped by capitalism. This becomes evident as Chappelle continues to discuss his relationship to whiteness. "When I make jokes about white people, don't think for a second that I am talking about you" (*Iconoclasts*). As Chappelle goes on to say, "Don't forget, I almost had fifty million dollars once. When you make enough money in America, they'll pull back the curtain and introduce you to the real white people. You guys just *think* you're white" (*Iconoclasts*).

Another example which demonstrates Chappelle's understanding of racialized capitalism is in a bit he does about his
experience as an early voter in his home state of Ohio during
the 2016 election. Chappelle tells the audience that, since Ohio
is a swing state, he knew a week before the rest of the country
that Trump would win the election because of all the trucks
and tractors in the parking lot. In an anecdote describing the
people Chappelle observed while in line to vote, Chappelle
says, "I listen to them say naive poor white people things. 'Man,
Donald Trump is gonna' go to Washington. And he's gonna'
fight for us.' And I'm standing there thinking in my mind,
'You dumb mutherfucker. You. Are. Poor. He's fighting for me"
(*Equanimity*).

However, as Chappelle continues to describe the (poor)
white people at the polls that day, he recounts, "And to my surprise, you know what I didn't see? I didn't see one deplorable
face in that group. I saw some angry faces and some determined faces, but they felt like decent folk" (*Equanimity*).
Chappelle then goes on to explain, "I'm not even saying this to
sound fucked up, but I felt sorry for them. I know the game
now. I know that rich white people call poor white people trash.
And the only reason I know that is because I made so much
money last year, the rich whites told me they say it at a cocktail
party. And I'm not with that shit" (*Equanimity*).

While Chappelle shows a nuanced understanding of how
race is constructed and shaped by capitalism, he nonetheless
reveals his investment in a class system which holds capital as
the key to social mobility. As Chappelle states in his 2016 *SNL*
monologue, "If I could quit being Black today I'd be out the
game. I did the next best thing. I became a rich Black person"
(*SNL*, 2016). Chappelle again touches on this theme in his
2020 *SNL* monologue when he recounts a story about hosting
outdoor comedy shows in his neighbor's cornfield. Despite helping to "save the town" from economic devastation, Chappelle
recounts how his neighbors convened a town meeting because
they felt Chappelle's shows were too loud, despite being held
out in the middle of a cornfield.

As Chappelle recounts, "It was so embarrassing. And I resented it. I resented that these country farmers could decide a
guy like me's fate. These people don't deserve to do that. They
haven't seen enough. They don't know anything. They're probably watching me right now. They're probably at home like,
'Honey, come quick, come quick! The guy from the grocery store
is on television.' No, you big dummy. The guy from television
was at the grocery store" (*SNL*, 2020). Chappelle's resentment

is a result of his frustrated expectation that his wealth and social class, being a rich guy from television, would and should insulate him from the everyday hindrances faced by others stuck on the lower rungs of society. Like many liberals, while Chappelle affirms the dignity and humanity of poor people, including poor white people, his aim is not to eradicate the systems of domination which cause their situations because he is far too invested in them. Instead, Chappelle's politics seek equal access to these systems through the means of capital.

Hetero-Patriarchy

Besides capitalism, Chappelle's work frequently perpetuates the tenets of other oppressive systems, such as hetero-patriarchy. And since these oppressive systems prop one another up, even though Chappelle frequently uses his comedy to contest anti-Black male racism, his work remains trapped within the web of white-supremacist-hetero-patriarchal-capitalism. Chappelle's comedy falls into this trap because it is frequently devoid of an intersectional lens. This creates several lacunae. In a nod to Akasha Hull, Patricia Bell-Scott, and Barbara Smith, Chappelle's work routinely falls into a false binary in which all the women are white and all the Blacks are men, resulting in the silencing and erasure of Black women and queer Black voices.

If we take a closer look at some of Chappelle's most famous sketches dealing directly or indirectly with race, there are hardly any Black women to be found (let alone Latina, Indigenous, trans, or other femme performances). Moreover, the few times Black women are seen, they are certainly not heard. Examples include, but are not limited to, "Frontline: Clayton Bigsby," "Black Bush," "I Know Black People," "Reparations," "Tron Carter's Law and Order," "Pretty White Girl Sings Dave's Thoughts," "What Makes White People Dance," and several others. Another example that helps to illustrate the problematic framework is Chappelle's classic sketch, "The Racial Draft." In this sketch, the only Black woman mentioned is Condoleezza Rice and she is voluntarily given away to "the whites" along with Colin Powell. In Chappelle's "Celebrity Jury Selection" sketch, the only Black women portrayed are R. Kelly's underage rape victim, who is only briefly depicted being urinated on, as well as R. Kelly's grandmother, who Chappelle insists must be a witness for him to believe any crimes against Kelly.

Chappelle's 2016 *SNL* "Election Night" sketch also uses this overly reductive binary frame. All of the women in the sketch are white, or of fair complexion, all the men are Black, and there are no Black women to be found. This example is helpful because it features more contemporary work from Chappelle after his return to the spotlight. In this sketch, Dave joins a party of three women, none of whom are Black, and another man to watch the election night results. As the election results begin to sour, Chris Rock arrives late to the party, introducing another Black male perspective. Over the course of the night, the party inches towards a state of shock from the dual realizations that Trump may win the presidency and that the United States has a problem with racism. Chappelle and Rock are in no way surprised by the election results, but are amused and somewhat bemused by the reactions of their white friends. One particular moment of inflection occurs when one of the women asserts, "This is crazy. I mean, do you even know what it's like to be a woman in this country where you can't get ahead no matter what you do?" (*SNL*, 2016). In response, Chappelle grimaces and remarks, "Oh geez, I don't know. Let me put my thinking cap on—on that one and get back to you" (*SNL*, 2016).

The problem with this sketch is that it remains stuck within a worldview that reduces femininity to whiteness and Blackness to maleness, in effect silencing and erasing Black women. Although this is a consistent thread throughout Chappelle's work, the perspectives of Black women would have been particularly helpful in this sketch since Black women voted overwhelmingly against Trump in 2016 and again in 2020. Disrupting the oversimplified binary that pits white women against Black men with the views of Black women could have potentially offered a third view, giving voice to the disappointment of many voters that night but without the added incredulity. However, since there are no Black women to be found, it allows the joke to proceed unchecked. We should also note that the practicality of adding the perspective of Black women would have been easier than ever since *SNL* featured two Black female cast members at the time, Leslie Jones and Sasheer Zamata. It wouldn't have even required *SNL* to go out of house, as they did with the inclusion of *SNL* alumnus, Chris Rock.

Chappelle's previously mentioned 2020 *SNL* joke about wage inequality also operates under this same framework. However, just as in the previous example, the inclusion of Black women would disrupt this overly simplified framework and derail the joke. It's hard to imagine that Chappelle would do a bit joking that Black women deserved to be paid less for equal work. Not only would it make the joke less funny, it would also undercut Chappelle's authority in addressing matters of white supremacy. But the joke is able to proceed and remain comic because Black women remain absent from the frame.

Additionally, Chappelle has long come under fire for his phobic portrayals of queer and trans people. This only further demonstrates how his comedy operates within a hetero-patriarchal worldview which, knowingly or not, contributes to the erasure of Black women. This, however, necessarily curtails the revolutionary potential of Chappelle's work because, as the Combahee River Collective taught us, "No one is free unless everyone is free." In other words, as Taylor explains, "if you could free the most oppressed people in society, then you would have to free everyone" (Taylor 5). This means that liberation and revolution require the continued analysis of the "the roots of Black women's oppression under capitalism and arguing for the reorganization of society based on the collective needs of the most oppressed" (*How We Get Free*, p. 5).

Although Chappelle's comic worldview does not factually represent the world we live in, we should also recognize that factual representation was never his aim. The projection of the world as flat and binary instead serves an aesthetic purpose for Chappelle. It allows him to punch up at (white) women in ways that are still read by many as comedic. However, from a revolutionary perspective, one of the biggest problems with this framework is that it pits potential allies in the struggle against hetero-patriarchy, Black men and white women, against each other without mediation. This is not to gloss over the historical and contemporary tensions between the interests of Black men and white women, or to reduce either group to a static monolith. However, it is to say that the binary framework that reduces femininity to whiteness and Blackness to maleness necessarily renders an incomplete and inaccurate analysis which obscures any meaningful possible solutions or ways out.

The Illusion of Revolution

Despite my argument that Chappelle is not a revolutionary comic, I still believe him to be a comic genius. Moreover, his comedy undoubtedly has a lot to teach us about ourselves. As Laurie Stone, author of *Laughing in the Dark*, argues, "What we laugh at during any period is a soulprint of the age" (p. xvii). Examining what makes us laugh, then, is like holding up a mirror that allows us to see ourselves from a distance, both as individuals and as a society.

By looking in the mirror of Chappelle's comedy, we can see that the tastes and sensibilities of his audiences are dramatically changing, as evidenced by the amount of ire he directs at cancel culture and woke liberals. It also denotes that, rightly or wrongly, the dominant forces with the power of cancellation have shifted. At the same time, Chappelle's continued popularity makes it clear that his audiences still find the fruits of hetero-patriarchy, including homophobia, transphobia, and misogyny, very funny. Chappelle's clowning shows us that we are still an extremely hetero-sexist society and that jokes at the expense of women, queer, and trans folk are still not deal-breakers for us. It used to be that racism also wasn't a deal-breaker, but anti-racism is having a moment right now.

Finally, the idea that comedy has a lot to teach us brings to mind the ancient Greek notion of aletheia, truth as revelation or disclosure. As Heller states in her book *Immortal Comedy*, "The truth of works of art in general can be associated with revelatory truth, and comic works are no exceptions. Their truth, if they are true at all, is revelatory" (p. 212). This understanding of revelatory truth is particularly helpful for understanding Chappelle's tremendous insights and limitations. The notion of truth as aletheia means that every disclosure comes with a closure. While Chappelle's comedy creates an opening, or access point, which allows us to see anti-Black male racism by centering it, this process also erases other marginalized identities. Like shining a spotlight on the stage in the theatre, Chappelle's comedy simultaneously leaves all the other players on the stage in the dark.

Therefore, audiences beware! Like a moth to a flame, some in the pitch black of late capitalism may see a glimmer of hope in Chappelle's comedy but such hopes turn out to be more illusion than revolution. Although there is no real consensus around the exact meaning of the term late capitalism, one of its trademark features is absurdity. It denotes that we have reached a stage at which the prevailing systems have become so riddled with contradictions that the tragedy has now become a farce, which is reflected in the absurdities that accompany our everyday indignities. For example, like investing our hope of revolution in a comedian.

18
Dave Chappelle Does Not Trust Us

STEVEN A. BENKO AND SCOUT BURCH

I can't even say something true without a punchline behind it.

—DAVE CHAPPELLE, *Saturday Night Live*, 11/7/20

Dave Chappelle's 2019 Netflix comedy special *Sticks and Stones* begins with the comedian quoting the opening lines of Prince's *1999*. Chappelle highlights the last line of the second verse: "Tryin' to run from my destruction, you know I didn't even care." Chappelle's use of the Prince song sets the tone for *Sticks and Stones*. He gets the audience to sing along with him, "positioning his audience to see through his eyes" ("When 'Keeping It Real' Goes Right," p. 152), disarming his audience with what Bambi Haggins calls his lackadaisical candor, sly righteousness, wary hopefulness, and easy-going amiability so that he comes across as "the funny guy on the corner, telling you 'some shit' about life" (*Laughing Mad*, p. 191).

His slow intonation of the song reveals his mindset as he takes the stage: because of previous reactions to jokes about members of the LGBTQ+ community, Chappelle has come to see performing standup as an invitation to his own personal destruction. This could be why he alters the meaning of the line by changing the lyric from "tryin' to run from *the* destruction" to "tryin' to run from *my* destruction, you know I didn't even care" (*Sticks and Stones*, our emphasis). Where Prince locates the chaos outside of himself and not necessarily as a threat to him, Chappelle internalizes the chaos, knows that it's a threat, but states that he's going to take the risk anyways. Prince is going to party while the world falls apart around him; Chappelle is the cause of the self-destruction he is going to celebrate.

The Prince song is Chappelle's way of establishing a different relationship with his audience, one that is more adversarial and confrontational than it is communal. Like other comedians who use humor to address social issues, Chappelle uses "comic misdirection and coded language to ridicule cultural norms that could not be confronted publicly" ("Emancipatory Racial Humor," p. 619). The audience accepts the comedian's violation of social norms, and to a certain extent, the implication that they themselves are being critiqued; however, the audience's laughter is other-directed in that they pretend they are not the butt of the joke. With this understanding the comedian is allowed to violate social taboos and speak difficult truths in an indirect way; the audience understands that the comedian does not mean everything he says and will not turn on them if they or someone else becomes offended. But unlike other comedians who are willing to sugarcoat the truth in exchange for laughter, Chappelle has taken to challenging his audience with truths they should not laugh at.

Chappelle brings to *Sticks and Stones* a frustration with his audience that they are not playing the comedy game fairly. His audience will laugh at the jokes in the club and then disavow their laughter when Chappelle is criticized for his attitudes towards members of the LGBTQ+ community and survivors of sexual assault. His frustration is that the audience will renounce their laughter but hold Chappelle accountable for his satire; put another way, the audience does not hold themselves responsible for what they laugh at while they hold Chappelle responsible for what he says. Chappelle's response to his audience's hypocritical repudiation of their laughter and subsequent indictment of him for using laughter as a mirror to charge them with the racism, homophobia, and transphobia he is joking about, makes him change the game he is playing with the audience. Instead of inviting his audience to laugh at his jokes, Chappelle dares his audience to laugh at truths they do not want to admit about themselves knowing full well that their laughter says more about them than it does about him. Instead of playing the comedy game as it is normally played, Chappelle antagonizes his audience by daring them to laugh at what they think is his truth. Or, as he says in *Sticks and Stones*, "Doesn't matter what I say. And if you at home watching this shit on Netflix, remember, bitch, you clicked on my face."

Confidence Games

Comedians who use comedy of incongruity to generate laughter are playing a confidence game that has two distinct parts.

The first confidence game is in the structure of the joke; the second confidence game is in the nature of the relationship between the comedian and their audience. Comedy of incongruity is a game of misdirection, and the rules are as follows: the audience suspends disbelief and accepts the premise of the joke. The setup of the joke relies on the comedian and audience sharing a worldview or point of view about the topic of the joke. Then, the comedian pivots towards a new way of thinking that has to be within the realm of possibility; this pivot is the punchline. The punchline in comedy of incongruity is another way of seeing things.

The game is to string them along until they are at the precipice of the punchline, and then surprise the audience by taking the joke in a different direction. Laughter and applause are signs that the punchline has deviated from the narrative thread in a way that is both pleasant and remains within the realm of the possible: the state of affairs or perspective described in the punchline is a pleasant, albeit surprising, way of seeing things. Moaning, booing, hissing, or silence are signs that the comedian has failed to offer a different, pleasant, or possible perspective; the joke has failed. It is a confidence game because the comedian knows where the joke is going; the audience is surprised, but the comedian is not.

For comedy of social critique to produce laughter, the comedian and the audience have to play by certain rules. The comedian says less than they mean, but they have confidence that the audience will intuit their meaning. The comedian who uses observational humor to critique existing social mores and attitudes has a difficult job: they can criticize, but they have to say it with a smile. In "When 'Keeping It Real' Goes Right," Kimberly Yates explains the confidence game this way:

> The comedian is granted social license to deviate from the norm, both in behavior and expression. The comic, therefore, can function as an invaluable social commentator who both reflects and shapes community through jokes . . . Having the social license to articulate that which is universally understood but taboo to speak, the comic democratizes discursive spaces, and the revolutionary humorist exercises freedom of speech. (p. 145)

Comedians like Chappelle who use incongruity to address social issues can speak difficult truths, but they can only do so indirectly and in a way that is entertaining and funny. Speaking of how to promote social change, Chappelle talks about the current political and cultural crisis facing America.

As if he is only speaking to his African American audience, Chappelle ponders whether the problem of systemic racism and violence is something that they should try to solve. Ultimately, he concludes that there is a role for African Americans to play: "We gotta be serious. Every able-bodied African American must . . . register for a legal firearm. That's the only way they'll change the law" (*Sticks and Stones*). The laughter results in the resolution of the tension created by a serious sounding Chappelle leading the audience to think that he is going to encourage them to vote. He pivots at the end and encourages Black Americans to buy guns. In doing so, he implies, but does not outright say, that the only way that American liberties or civil rights are restricted is if they are enjoyed by, or benefit, Black Americans. Chappelle does not have to say it forthrightly: he only has to imply it and then let his audience fill in the rest. As a result, the comedian may not get to say everything they want to say, or, the comedian may not get to say what they want to say as openly, honestly, and explicitly, as they want to say it. The trade-off that comedians like Chappelle make is that they accept saying it with a smile in lieu of not having an audience to say it to at all.

This confidence game is not easy. In *The Comedian as Confidence Man*, Will Kaufman describes the pressure the comedian is under to not be a spoil-sport and take away the audience's fun by being too direct or too confrontational. He writes:

> Satire must steer its audience in and out of serious implication; control the degree and balance of optimistic and pessimistic judgments it offers about the actual world beyond the performance; and manipulate the connections audiences experience between its implicating and joking elements. The satirist must instigate and negotiate two conflicting states of mind in his audience: the belief that he is offering more than mere comedy, that is, that 'there is more here than meets the eye,' and, in the interests of self-defense, 'the suspicion that there is less.' (p. 38)

The comedian cannot say all that there is to say because telling it straight is not comedy; telling it straight is a lecture. The game the comedian's playing is that they have to trust that their audience will fill in the blanks and make the connections that cannot be said outright. The game the audience is playing opens them to the possibility of being indicted by the comedian's social critique and becoming the butt of the joke. To keep the confidence game going, the audience will trust that the comedian does not mean them; their laughter allows them to live in the space between the truth of the comedian's critique and the belief (or hope) that the critique does not apply to them.

That's Right! That's Right! That Ain't Right!

Chappelle's relationship with his comedy and audience is one way that comedians can play a confidence game. However, because of Chappelle's history with his material and his audience (including but not limited to the abrupt end to *Chappelle's Show*), subsequent scrutiny over his reasons (and sanity), reactions to his comeback attempts, and criticisms about his language and jokes about members of marginalized communities) he is still playing a confidence game, albeit a different one shaped by a lack of trust between the comedian and their audience. His relationship with his audience is informed by, first, his understanding of race as America's ongoing original sin and, second, what it means to talk about race to a predominantly white audience, and, third, the contemporary moment celebrities and comedians find themselves in, specifically cancel culture.

The opening of *Sticks and Stones* is Chappelle's first comment about cancel culture and signals how he intends to play a different game with his audience. In the opening, after he has transgressed social expectations about believing all victims of sexual assault by saying that he does not believe Michael Jackson's accusers and that being sexually assaulted by the King of Pop is its own form of compliment, Chappelle does two impersonations. The first is of the founding fathers of America waiting impatiently for Jefferson to finish the Declaration of Independence. The second impersonation is the point of the joke:

> You gotta guess who it is, though. Okay, here it goes. Uh, duh. Hey! Durr! If you do anything wrong in your life, duh, and I find out about it, I'm gonna try to take everything away from you, and I don't care when I find out. Could be today, tomorrow, fifteen, twenty years from now. If I find out, you're fucking-duh-finished . . . That's YOU! That's what the audience sounds like to me. That's why I don't be coming out doing comedy all the time, 'cause y'all n***as is the worst motherfuckers I've ever tried to entertain in my FUCKING life. (*Sticks and Stones*)

Chappelle directly challenges his audience and calls them out for their hypocritical behavior: the jokes that they're laughing at in the theater are the same jokes they will repudiate and criticize him for after the show. Knowing that his audience could turn on him at any moment, and likely will after the fact, Chappelle changes the game. According to the rules of this new game, the audience is no longer along for the ride. Instead, the audience and comedian are in a more adversarial relationship. Chappelle is telling jokes that he dares the audience to laugh at. In cancel culture, the comedian is indicted for the jokes they tell: they are the pied piper, using their art to lure people away from decency. Chappelle recognizes that he cannot win at this game. The game he can win is one where he uses the stage as a space to confess his truth and treats the audience's laughter as a confession of their own character. He develops a balance between his adversarial comments and his jokes to ensure that he keeps his audience engaged in the game.

Two jokes highlight the different game that Chappelle is playing. The first joke is typical of the ironic juxtaposition that defines comedy of incongruity and the punchline would not get Chappelle cancelled. After hearing his son describe an active shooter drill at his school, Chappelle walks his audience through his incredulity that anyone would care enough about high school to kill other students. Instead of offering the kind of advice that one might find doled out in an after school special, Chappelle concludes:

> Just do what I did, n***a. Try some things. "Have you skipped school, n***a? Skip school! Take a walk and meet some other kids. Fuck school, n***a. Try drugs. Have you tried drugs out? (*Sticks and Stones*)

The humor comes from the sudden pivot away from what one should say in that situation: positive, life-affirming advice that recognizes the child's pain and tries to ameliorate it with care and concern. Instead, Chappelle surprises the audience by offering worse advice: being a drug addicted delinquent is better than killing someone! The social commentary of the joke is the relativizing of high school social life: being socially ostracized is not the worst thing in the world; go do something else. This is a safe joke to hear, laugh at, and repeat to others.

An example of an unsafe joke, one that no one would describe as woke, is Chappelle's joke about abortion and parental responsibility. This joke is preceded by Chappelle complaining that #MeToo has gone too far by infantilizing women, echoing a comment that he made in *The Bird Revelation* that those who are saying that sexual harassment derailed their careers and dreams have "brittle spirits."

Chappelle's abortion joke is in the same vein: equality is not equal if all parties are not equally burdened. He says:

> What the fuck is your agenda, ladies? Is—Is sexism dead? No, in fact, the opposite happened. I said it was gonna get worse, and they said I was tone deaf. But eight states, including your state, have passed the most stringent anti-abortion laws this nation has seen since Roe v. Wade. I . . . I told you. I told you. I'll be real with you, and I know nobody gives a fuck what I think anyway. —Uh . . . I'm not for abortion. —Oh, shut up, n***a. I'm not for it, but I'm not against it either. It all depends . . . on who I get pregnant. I don't care— I'll tell you right now. I don't care what your religious beliefs are or anything. If you have a dick, you need to shut the fuck up on this one. Seriously. This is theirs. The right to choose is their unequivocal right. Not only do I believe they have the right to choose, I believe that they shouldn't have to consult anybody, —except for a physician . . . about how they exercise that right. Gentleman, that is fair. And ladies, to be fair to us, I also believe if you decide to have the baby, a man should not have to pay. That's fair. If you can kill this motherfucker, I can at least abandon 'em. It's my money, my choice.

Several of the rhetorical tricks that Chappelle uses to reel in his audience and reverse the joke on them are on display here. First, Chappelle repeatedly refers to himself and relativizes the content as being his opinion, based on his experience, and a sincere effort to be honest and authentic with his audience by "being real." Second, Chappelle uses the appearance of reasonableness, fairness, and wokeness to make it seem like he's saying something progressive: abortion is a woman's choice and men have no right to control a woman's reproductive choices. Then, as with all comedy of incongruity, the narrative flips and the punchline becomes clear: if a woman can choose not to become a mother then a man ought to be able to choose to not become a father. Chappelle co-opts the pro-choice slogan: "My body, my choice" and puts it in the service of men who want to apply the logic of choice and sexual freedom to their sexual behavior.

Here, Chappelle is complicating the abortion debate by suggesting that this is what equal representation and participation would look like: both women and men having an equal say in the decision to become a parent. The rules of the stand-up game prevent Chappelle from saying everything he has to say not just about abortion, but about all of the topics he raises in *Sticks and Stones*. Chappelle, like every other comedian, has to trust that his audience will fill in the blanks and continue the conversation that he is having with them. However, it is clear in *Sticks and Stones*, specifically the epilogue, and *8:46*, the short performance Chappelle released where he reveals his thoughts about the murder of George Floyd by Minneapolis police, that Chappelle's dropping of his comic persona to answer questions from his audience (*Sticks and Stones* epilogue) and speak to directly to the crowd (*8:46*) demonstrates that he no longer trusts his audience to follow his lead so he has to say his point straight.

I Don't Mean to Get Heavy, but We Gotta Say Something

The inversion of the confidence game which shifts responsibility from the comedian for the content of the joke to the audience for having laughed at it is a sign of "irony fatigue." Kaufman says that the comedian succumbs to irony fatigue when pessimism makes them give up their confidence game. American humorists often succumb to irony fatigue because they yearn to say things unambiguously, and Chappelle is no different. The rules of the confidence game require that the comedian believes that the audience is with them intellectually and morally; the audience is filling in the gaps the way the comedian intends for them to be filled in. However, there are some topics that are so serious and so grim that they cannot be said with a smile; or the topic is so fraught with moral ambiguity that the truth is required; or the comedian wants to effect change more than they want to make the audience laugh. All of these are reasons Kaufman gives for the onset of irony fatigue (p. 40). Cancel culture, audience hypocrisy, and Chappelle's wrestling with what it means to lead a mixed audience through observations about race in America have contributed to his irony fatigue.

Chappelle is savvier than, for example, comedian Bill Hicks whose irony fatigue grew so intense that he would lecture and attack his audience but keep them in the moment by saying, "by the way there are more dick jokes coming, please relax." Chappelle knows that in order to keep his audience's attention he needs to keep his audience laughing. Chappelle keeps his audience laughing but no longer takes responsibility for them filling, or not filling, in the gaps. The laughter is the point and Chappelle lets their laughter be about them more than it is about him.

Chappelle trusts his audience to do the mental gymnastics that all comedy of incongruity requires in order to make jokes work: they want to laugh (that is why they bought the ticket or clicked on his face) so they are willing to entertain (and be entertained by) the juxtapositions that Chappelle creates to elicit laughter. His antagonistic attitude toward his audience indicates that he does not trust them to understand and share in the ideas, attitudes, and perspective that shaped those juxtapositions, even if their laughter is an admission that they see it Chappelle's way, but maybe only through a glass, darkly.

Dave Gillotta's explanation in "Reckless Talk" of Chappelle's use of the stage as a space to say reckless things and to try to work out in public one's attitudes, ideas and opinions is another indication of how Chappelle's lack of trust in the audience changes the game he is playing. Gillotta concludes that what Chappelle might be doing is modelling a way for his audience to explore their own ideas and opinions. Audience laughter is not the end of the conversation but the beginning of another one. If Chappelle trusts himself to speak his truth on the stage, or, trusts that he can absorb the financial and social ramifications that could come his way if people object to his truth and "cancel" him, then maybe his audience can take his words and speak them as part of their own conversations about race, gender, or politics.

Comedy, in various forms, can become a way to navigate different social situations. Comedy can act as a social lubricant in awkward or gloomy situations. When people laugh at the same jokes, they are showing that more than just having a sense of humor in common, they also have an underlying shared set of perspectives, attitudes, and beliefs. Since not everyone is as gifted a joke teller as Chappelle, people will repeat jokes that they have heard. At least, "that's what she said." Doing so tests whether the joke teller and the audience have a shared set of cultural artifacts and touchstones in common, but also a shared perspective and point of view. Instead of offering his jokes to his audience to be repeated, Chappelle, who has complained about people yelling "I'm Rick James, bitch!" at him while he was at Disneyland with his children, dares his audience to repeat his jokes. Losing confidence in his audience, not trusting that they are filling in the gaps, he tricks his audience into doing his work by either risking being ostracized for telling one of Chappelle's darker jokes or, more interestingly, realizing that they cannot.

Can a white person repeat one of Chappelle's jokes? They would have to be a white person who is comfortable saying "n****r." A lot. How does one sound saying in a group of friends, "If you can kill this motherfucker, I can at least abandon 'em. It's

my money, my choice"? An audience member might be able to
say, outside of the safe confines of the comedy club, "Okay, say
. . . say LeBron James, uh, changed his gender. You know what
I mean? Okay. Can he stay in the NBA, or, because he's a
woman, does he have to go to the WNBA where he will score
840 points a game?" but would raise eyebrows if they repeated
Chappelle's joke likening being born the wrong sex to having
been born the wrong race:

> What if I was Chinese? But . . . But born in this n***a body. That's not
> funny? And for the rest of my life, I had to go around making that face.
> "Hey, everybody, I'm Chinese!" And everyone gets mad. "Stop mak-
> ing that face. That's offensive." —"What?" "This is how I feel inside."
> (*Sticks and Stones*)

For many people in this audience, repeating a Dave Chappelle
joke is no different than wearing blackface. Chappelle's vocab-
ulary, exaggerated facial expressions, and the way he uses his
voice to express frustration and agitation work for Chappelle
because he has made it clear what the African American experience means to him. By telling jokes his audience probably
should not laugh at, and jokes they ought not to repeat,
Chapelle is using laughter as the starting point about race and
identity. To be anybody else and to appropriate and repeat any
part of Chappelle's comedy, reveals the boundaries around different racial groups in America, one's insider/outsider status
relative to those boundaries, and if one is an outsider, ultimately repeats the racist stereotypes Chappelle is exploring.
Inside the comedy club it is (somewhat) safe to play and exag-
gerate; the rules are different outside the comedy club because
it is a different game, one with more intense and real consequences than being cancelled.

Chappelle's clearest expression of his lack of trust in his
audience is on full display in a performance recorded on June
12th 2020. Titled *8:46*, the set contains Chappelle's raw and
unfiltered take on the murder of George Floyd. Chappelle con-
fesses his irony fatigue early in the set by responding to CNN
anchor Don Lemon who asked why celebrities were not speaking out about race in America. Chappelle was indignant:

> I dare you to say me n***a. I dare you. Has anyone ever listened to
> me do comedy? Have I not ever said anything about these things
> before? So now all of a sudden this n***a expects me to step in front
> of the streets and talk over the work these people are doing? As a
> celebrity? Answer me, do you want to see a celebrity right now? Do

we give a fuck what Ja Rule thinks? Does it matter about celebrity? No! This is the streets talking for themselves, they don't need me right now. (*8:46*)

Chappelle's frustration about Lemon's question reveals the limits of the confidence games comedians play when the topics are serious. In *8:46*, Chappelle closes whatever gap there was between what he says and what he means. Gone are the moments when Chappelle cracks himself up and retreats to the back of the stage to laugh at his own jokes. Chappelle pauses to consider and to review his notes before making another attempt to convey how he is feeling. There is little to no logical connection between observations; Chappelle is not making a point as much as he is circling around a set of concerns he does not yet know how to articulate. The jokes are few and far between; the laughter forced and awkward. He refuses to take Lemon's bait and sum up his thoughts and feelings in a tidy story with a punchline.

While he may not trust his audience to get any of his jokes, he trusts that this style of delivery—random, angry, and frustrated—will be the topic of conversation: The fragmented and discontinuous way that Chappelle shares his experience creates a space for people to fill in their own reaction to the murder of George Floyd. By not saying anything, Chappelle's *8:46* creates an opening for others to say their own thing. By frustrating their expectations for a narrative thread wrapped in jokes and tied together with a punchline, he forces his audience to reconsider what they have laughed at and how he has been playing the comedy game.

The current moment that comedians find themselves in is difficult to navigate. Cancel culture and audience sensitivity have changed the rules of the game comedians and their audience have been playing for a long time. Chappelle wants to reach his audience but will not do it at the expense of his truth. As a result, he has chosen to play a different game, one that invites public scorn and condemnation. But Chappelle has also made it clear that he does not give a fuck: tryin' to run from his destruction, you know he didn't even care.

19
Hard Truths and Dangerous Jokes

Lauren Olin

> Our most noted satirists are true columnists and their opinions can be worth more than any well-documented exposé. And whatever they say in jest is taken seriously.
>
> —Umberto Eco

A central and enduring theme in the comedy of Dave Chappelle is his emphasis on the truth. In a memorable essay published in *The Believer*, Rachel Kaadzi Ghansah explores the circumstances surrounding Chappelle's departure from Comedy Central in 2005, and suggests that many of the feelings of loneliness, sadness, and confusion felt by Chappelle's fans at the time centered around these intentions. As she puts it:

> Chappelle did such a good job of truth-telling, on every subject, that nobody knew what to do when he just stopped talking. In no way did his quitting conform to our understanding of the comic's one obligation: to be funny. To talk to us. To entertain us. To make us laugh. ("If He Hollers, Let Him Go")

Questions about the relationship between the funny and the true haven't received a lot of attention from philosophers, for some historic reasons that aren't very surprising. Plato argued a long time ago that comedy should be subject to heavy censorship, if allowed at all, because exposure was likely to corrupt the youth of Athens (*Laws*, 934d–936c). He worried that comedy could distort the truth in dangerous ways, and argued that in his ideal state "slaves and aliens" might be allowed to indulge in humor, but no "composer of comedy, iambic or lyric verse shall be permitted to hold any citizen up to laughter, by

195

word or gesture, with passion or otherwise" (*Laws*, 816e; 935e). Plato did not believe comedy was a friend to truth, and, as the British philosopher Alfred North Whitehead once remarked, the whole of the Western philosophical tradition can be described as a long series of footnotes to Plato.

In this case, Plato was onto something. Satirical treatments of social issues "taken seriously" pervade our contemporary media landscape: the self-conscious mimicry of mainstream journalistic formats is strikingly well-executed by humorists and satirical organizations, right alongside purveyors of "fake news." By the time the first season of *Chappelle's Show* aired, satirical newspapers like *The Onion* were putting stories out weekly in print, and daily online. Satirical headlines were already being regularly posted on Facebook, and re-reported by *The Onion's* mainstream "subsidiaries." By 2004, *The Onion's* editor Carol Kolb was open about the paper's intentions: "That's what we do at *The Onion*. We do print lies to make money. People every single day think *The Onion* stories are real" (Daniel Terdiman in *Wired*). As of this writing, *The Onion's* website nowhere suggests that it's a satirical news outlet; it remains "America's Finest News Source."

Television, like the Internet, seems to have galvanized these scandalmongering trends. In 2014, the Pew Research Center reported that twelve percent of Americans were getting all of their news from satirical programs like *The Daily Show*, roughly the same percentage thought to depend on second-tier mainstream outlets like *USA Today* or *The Huffington Post*. There is also evidence that people had been misunderstanding televised political satire long before that: even very politically conservative individuals liked the *Colbert Report*, but most of those very conservative individuals also believed that Colbert was satirizing liberal pundits like his former boss, Jon Stewart (LaMarre, "The Irony of Satire"). In a *Late Show* interview with President Barack Obama that aired in November 2020, Colbert remarked in reflection: "I didn't know I was a prophet. I thought I was a comedian."

Meanwhile, in 2005, *Chappelle's Show* had become wildly popular. The DVD version of the first season had become the fastest-selling DVD for any TV series ever; more than two million advance orders for the DVD version of the second season had been placed; Chappelle had signed the biggest contract in Comedy Central's history to co-write, co-produce, and singularly star in season three. So why *did* Chappelle stop talking, especially when his brand of truth-telling was in such high demand?

Infamy

You can't get un-famous. You can get infamous, but you can't get un-famous.

—DAVE CHAPPELLE

According to one hypothesis, both popular and enduring, wealthy Black celebrities like Oprah Winfrey and Bill Cosby had been so deeply offended by the *Chappelle's Show* "Niggar Family" sketch that they forcibly orchestrated Chappelle's exit from showbusiness. The sketch itself featured a fictional white family that embodied the upper-middle-class norms celebrated on television shows like *Leave It to Beaver* in the 1950s and early 1960s. The family is introduced with a Black and white montage typical of sitcoms during that era, accompanied by this lighthearted musical theme:

> N-I-G, G-A-R, it's the Niggar Family. We all know, who they are, Frank, Tim, and Emily. Teaching Tim how to ride a bike, these are the Niggars that we like. N-I-G, G-A-R, it's the Niggar Family, it's the Niggar Family. Yeahhhhh.

Jokes in the sketch mostly turn on opportunities to interpret the n-word as implicating racially-based anti-Black stereotypes, on one hand, or the values embodied by the fictional family, on the other. The idea that Bill Cosby could have been offended by Chappelle's character-based approach to comic ambiguity is ridiculous no matter the history: remember, Cliff Huxtable was supposed to be an ideal Black father figure, *and* a respected obstetrician. Even before these revelations, though, the audacity of the rumor dwarfed its plausibility. Chappelle appeared on Oprah's show in 2006 to explain that his decision to leave Comedy Central was squarely his own. Just weeks after he walked away, he insisted in print: "I'm not crazy. I'm not smoking crack. I'm definitely stressed out" ("Dave Speaks").

On the day Chappelle walked away he had in fact been in the middle of filming one in a series of sketches featuring "pixies" that dress, and issue advice, in ways satirically motivated by racially-based stereotypes. That day, the sketch centered on the "Black pixie"—played by a miniaturized Chappelle in blackface and minstrel garb—who appears in a puff of smoke to counsel a Black man sitting on an airplane, also played by Chappelle.

In the sketch, the Black pixie materializes when a flight attendant says "chicken" while soliciting in-flight meal preferences. Chappelle's character first opts for fish in defiance, but the flight attendant promptly returns with apologies: she had been mistaken, they were already out of the fish. At this point the Black pixie rejoices, dancing and shouting "We're back in the game, baby!" The attendant tells Chappelle that the other dish is really quite good, fried chicken, and the Black pixie yells "Hallelujah! Hallelujah!" The sketch concludes when the white passenger sitting in front of Chappelle offers to swap entrées. Chappelle's character accepts and thanks him, but the Black pixie doesn't miss a beat: seemingly in desperate denial, he begins chanting "Catfish! Catfish!"

Chappelle walked off the set of *Chappelle's Show* during the taping of this sketch and then, without notice to anyone, flew to South Africa to visit a family friend in Durban. In conversation with a journalist from *Time* shortly after his arrival there, Chappelle recalls feeling deeply uncomfortable about the laughter of a crew member while filming this pixie sketch because it prompted doubts about whether his work was successfully drawing attention to the pernicious limitations associated with racially-based stereotypes, or just inadvertently reinforcing the ones he had always felt trapped by. He said he felt like his "head almost exploded" ("Dave Speaks"). About a year after that, in that interview with Oprah, he elaborates:

> It was a good spirit or intention behind it. But, what I didn't consider is how many people watch this show and how the way people use television is subjective . . . I know that all these people who're watching TV, that there's a lot of people who will understand exactly what I'm doing and there's another group of people who are just fans like the kind of people who scream "I'm Rick James, bitch!" at my concerts. They're going to get something completely different.

This is not the first time that Chappelle expressed open disappointment with the ways his work was being received. At a show in Sacramento in 2004, Chappelle left the stage when audience members started shouting "I'm Rick James, bitch!" When he returned, he reportedly started yelling "You people are stupid!" and then continued to explain that: "The show is ruining my life . . . You know why my show is good? Because the network officials say you're not smart enough to get what I'm doing, and every day I fight for you. I tell them how smart you are. Turns out, I was wrong. You people are stupid" (Jim Carnes in the *Sacramento Bee*).

It was, however, the first time that Chappelle expressed open awareness of the fact that, *despite* his celebrity, and *despite* his intentions to be truthful, he didn't have control over what people would take away from his comedy. One way of understanding why comedy is misunderstood applies more broadly: the stereotypes implicated in jokes are treated by different individuals in different ways. Reflection on Chappelle's decision to leave, it seems, reflected his awareness of the fact that his intentions to be truthful don't matter so much—not for his fans, not for the industry, and not for his success—so what *does* matter?

Controversy

I never met anyone who said when they were a kid, I wanna grow up and be a critic.

—RICHARD PRYOR

It would be misleading to describe Chappelle's recent return to comedy as anything short of triumphant. At the same time, it would be misleading to describe his return as proceeding without controversy, and I think attention to some of the controversy sheds light on questions about why Chappelle's comedic perspective is so enduring.

Chappelle has not stopped wearing his intentions to be truthful on his sleeve, even in his most recent Netflix specials that include jokes targeting women and members of transgender communities. These jokes have been widely criticized not on the grounds that he is lying, but on the grounds that he's just being insensitive.

For instance, consider the sub-title for *Buzzfeed*'s review of *Sticks and Stones*, the Netflix special for which Chappelle recently won a Grammy: "In his occasionally funny new Netflix special, Chappelle continues to make anti-trans and victim-blaming jokes. Why can't he strive to be more thoughtful?" *Vulture* published the most damning popular assessment I've come across:

Chappelle's retreat to the Ohio plains at the height of the success of his show, and his subsequent return to stand-up a decade later, are a clinic in the ways a lacerating wit can rust and the danger of receding into the comforts of an echo chamber. Jokes about transgender women in recent specials cast the comic, once a hero of the underdog, as an Establishment figure of a sort, punching down in the ways his work used to ridicule and detest. Doubling down when critized put him in the league of millionaire comics who don't get that their anxiousness to fight this generation means the tables have turned.

Some other criticism has been deeply personal. In a moving *Medium* essay, Tyler Foster describes attending one of Chappelle's live performances in Seattle and being upset by Chappelle's apparently callous dismissal of the idea that trans individuals "experienced similar or worse types of discrimination" than members of the Black community. He was upset that Chappelle seemed to deliberately, and derisively, default to using the term "tranny" instead of "trans."

Foster wrote a letter to Chappelle about it, and Chappelle actually replied, but his set didn't then change in ways that ameliorated any of the concerns Foster had shared. A year later, he was making many of the same jokes when he started performing in residence at Radio City Music Hall, then again in his first Netflix special, *Equanimity* (though in that special he does use the term "trans" in lieu of "tranny"). *Buzzfeed* just thought he lacked moral motivation: while Chappelle feigned a willingness to "address criticisms of his earlier sets that were more flagrantly, lazily anti-trans" he stopped short of issuing any apologies, changing his mind, or expressing "any meaningful empathy" (Tomi Obaro in *Buzzfeed*).

The criticism Chappelle has faced for his most recent specials seems to revolve around his insensitivity towards members of a systematically disenfranchised population, towards people that he doesn't appear to engage with empathically. In Chappelle's own words, many of his jokes are dangerous "in the wrong hands" because he understands that few other comedians are able to successfully cultivate the sense in which they are *like* the people their jokes target: Chappelle's empathy, not his honesty, seems to best predict when his jokes will land, and when they will fail.

Protest

Let me tell you the truth. The truth is what is, and what should be is a fantasy. A terrible, terrible lie that someone gave to the people long ago.

—LENNY BRUCE

In *8:46*, a special released in the immediate wake of George Floyd's death, Chappelle's talent for engaging empathically, and its importance, come out in full force. Indeed, in the introductory parts of the performance, there is direct evidence that being honest in the sense of being accurate, or uncensored, is not one of Chappelle's primary goals. Some of the events that he references in the service of building out his narrative are accurately reported, but many are not, and when they're not they're not in ways that seem both comically and rhetorically significant.

He begins by deriding CNN anchor Don Lemon's recent call for Black celebrities to speak out in support of protesters. Chappelle describes himself as screaming at the television when Lemon issued his call, charging that he deserved to be sanctioned for even suggesting that any celebrity "step up in front of the streets and talk over the work" protesters were engaged in. "Answer me:" he shouted, "Do you want to see a celebrity right now? Do we give a fuck what Ja Rule thinks? No!" He elaborates by speculating that people wanted to hear from him because he had no intentions towards dishonesty in a world where "every institution that we trust lies to us."

Still, there is evidence that the special was curated with a careful eye towards cultivating empathy, if not towards telling the truth. Chappelle starts the show with a notebook in hand, but he doesn't refer to the notebook throughout the set. Some editorial decisions also appear to have been made in the service of cultivating empathy rather than getting facts right. The night the special was released, a digital editor for ABC tweeted some of the closed captioning from what appeared to be a homophobic preamble to his bit about Don Lemon that had been excised:

> Don Lemon is a funny newscaster because he's clearly gay, but . . . You know what I mean? He's just gay. He's the anomaly, he's Black and gay but unlike my other gay Black friends, he's got this weird self-righteousness and I'm watching his show and he goes—and he literally says this and I don't mean to make this impression disparaging. He's like, Just kidding.

It's not clear why this part of the performance was removed, or whose decision it was to remove it. It is clear that, throughout the show, Chappelle does a lot of work to identify with almost everyone he discusses. He celebrates the plight of protesters, explaining that he is "comfortable in the backseat" of the car they are driving. He makes a point of identifying with Floyd himself, and intimately. He talks about the tape of Floyd's murder, especially the moment when Floyd started calling out for his mother: "He called for his dead mother. I've only seen that once in my life. My father, on his deathbed, called for his grandmother. When I watched that tape, I understood this man knew he was gonna die."

He doesn't stop with drawing connections between Floyd and his father: he talks about his great-great-grandfather William David Chappelle, who was among the leaders of the first African American delegations to protest the lynching of a Black man at the White House. And he traced the recent history of Black men being murdered, including Trayvon Martin, Eric Garner, Michael Brown, John Crawford. He talked about Philando Castile, who was murdered in front of his daughter in Minnesota; Chappelle has also always been open about the difficulties he's experienced personally as a Black father, and as the father of mixed race children. In a particularly poignant moment in *8:46*, Chappelle shares how disturbing it was to notice that Trayvon Martin looked "just like" his son. He claims: "These things are not old, this is not a long time ago, it's today."

The special doesn't spare everyone, however. And the instances in which his jokes seem to target individuals more mercilessly, it also seems plain that Chappelle is either less able, or less concerned, to self-identify with the those being targeted. For instance: he speaks about police officers negatively in some places, and plenty of misogynistic jokes make the final cut. Chappelle prominently targets three women in *8:46*. The first is Elizabeth Banks, an African American artist who has a reputation for being quite volatile: she uses Twitter in something like the way that President Trump used to, and had just recently used that platform to claim that she had had an affair with Chappelle. He also targets another young Black woman, Candace Owens, who has been making a lot of money over the past several years supporting President Trump, and betraying an insensitivity towards difficulties posed by institutionalized forms of racism. (She says things like "Stop selling us our own oppression. Stop taking away our self-confidence by telling us that we can't because of racism, because of slavery. I've never been a slave in this country" ("Candace Owens at CPAC").

Unlike Banks, Owens has reportedly been influential in shaping the views of some African American celebrities that Chappelle has elsewhere supported very publicly. For instance, she's been credited with engineering Kanye West's confusing relationship with President Trump, and encouraging his controversial claims like "You hear about slavery for four hundred years. For four hundred years? That sounds like a choice." Not so long ago, when Chappelle was asked about a comparison Kanye West had recently drawn between the struggles associated with celebrity, and those associated with civil rights abuses. He said:

]I do see a common denominator in the sense that the issue of privacy in general is everyone's issue . . . I'm a celebrity in some people's eyes, but not to the extent Kanye is. I saw on Yahoo that his wife got tackled in Paris. Like, just crazy shit. I think that he's right in the sense that scrutiny in and of itself is oppressive . . . The metrics are a little wrong to make that comparison. But it is a civil rights issue, in a sense. Because how is he supposed to live his life? ("Dave Chappelle Is Back")

Perhaps because of this influence, Chappelle describes Owens as "the worst . . . she's the most articulate idiot I've ever seen in my fucking life. She's so articulate she can tell you how fucking stupid she is precisely." In particular, he criticized Owens's decision to share Floyd's criminal history in a public forum online, while questioning why the African American community "chose" to make Floyd a hero. Chappelle responded to the charge with vitriol, denying her presupposition:

Why does the Black community make him a hero? Why do you choose him as a hero? We didn't choose him, you did. They killed him, and that wasn't right, so he's the guy. We're not desperate for any heroes in the Black community. Any n***a that survives this nightmare is my goddamned hero.

Finally, Chappelle targets Laura Ingraham, the toxic Fox News host who famously told LeBron James to "shut up and dribble." His attacks on Ingraham involve crude remarks about her body, and other familiar misogynistic tropes. There may of course be a way of charitably understanding what Chappelle is doing in the sense that his jokes are really intended to target individuals on the basis of their characters and patterns of behavior. But with respect to the puzzle I started with—is Chappelle's comedy so successful because of his capacity to engage empathically, or his capacity to tell the truth?—this seems beside the point.

His treatment of Ingraham in *8:46* can be valuably compared to his editorialized treatment of Don Lemon, but also Chris Dorner, an African American officer with the LAPD who lost his position after filing an excessive force complaint against a white female colleague. Chappelle describes Dorner as having exhausted all of his legal options before penning a manifesto in which he called Chappelle a genius, and announced that he intended "to wage asymmetrical war" on LAPD officers and members of their families. Chappelle continues, in apparent disbelief: "And he did it! This MF ambushed two officers sitting in their police car, murdered them. He went to another police officer's house and killed his daughter."

These are, no doubt, absolutely *terrible* things. Yet Chappelle goes on as part of an effort to identify, empathically with Dorner, *and* with the police officers that ultimately killed him. He describes that scene as follows:

> They found him—Big Bear—he was hiding in a cabin. When they figured out where this n****r was, no less than four hundred police officers showed up and answered the call . . . And you know why four hundred cops showed up? Because one of their own was murdered. So how the fuck can't they understand what's going on in these streets? We saw ourselves like you see yourself. He wasn't the only one.

He goes on to run down a series of violent attacks perpetrated against police officers, starting with an account of nine police officers who were killed at a Black Lives Matter rally in Dallas:

> . . . the guy that killed those cops was, like Chris Dorner . . . military. Right after he did it, another four cops were shot dead in Baton Rouge, Louisiana, by a Black man that served in our military. What are they doing? Why would our guys do that? Black people from the military. Because they believe, just like they did when they joined the fucking military that they were fighting acts of terror. These are our people, these are our countrymen.

Chappelle gets some of these facts wrong: five officers were killed in Dallas, not nine, and only three were killed subsequently in Baton Rouge. Inaccuracies aside: Chappelle humanizes terrible acts of violence, in part by emphasizing that they have been perpetrated by *our* people, *our* countrymen.

History

What is it that strikes a spark of humor from a man? It is the effort to throw off, to fight back the burden of grief that is laid on each one of us. In youth we don't feel it, but as we grow to manhood we find the burden on our shoulders. Humor? It is nature's effort to harmonize conditions. The further the pendulum swings out over woe the further it is bound to swing back over mirth.

—MARK TWAIN

When I was listening to the last part of *8:46,* I was reminded of a famous satirical piece from W.E.B. Du Bois. In 1923, following the brutal murder of James T. Scott at the University of Missouri's flagship campus, Du Bois satirically applauded the institution's decision to open "a new course in Applied Lynching" ("Opinion"). While numerous American universities implicitly or silently condoned the practice of lynching at that time, Du Bois argued that most had "not been frank or brave enough actually to arrange a mob murder so that students could see it. . . . We are very much in favor of this method of teaching one hundred percent Americanism; as long as mob murder is an approved institution in the United States, students at the universities should have a first-hand chance to judge exactly what a lynching is." This piece was published the same year that the Dyer anti-lynching bill had started languishing in the US Senate. An anti-lynching bill has never been passed. A hate crimes bill was finally passed in 2009.

One of the things I remembered was Du Bois's choice to use the plural "we" in expressing his satirical endorsement of "one hundred percent Americanism." In *8:46*, when talking about George Floyd and Chris Dorner, Chappelle also uses the language, *we*. And that's not the only place Chappelle uses this plural tactic to identify with members of his audience. When he hosted *SNL* directly following Trump's election in 2016, he surprisingly wished Donald Trump luck, stating: "I'm going to give him a chance, and *we* the historically disenfranchised demand that he give us one too."

Reflection on his long career, and especially on the various ways in which his material has been popularly and critically received, suggest that what's most distinctive about Chappelle's success comedically is not his emphasis on the truth, but his capacity to self-identify with the individuals and groups his humor targets. In as much as an emphasis on the truth is rare in comedy, empathy is rare too: there are plenty of stereotypes according to which stand-up comedians end up being stand-up comedians because they fail to develop the capacities for empathic engagement required to develop and maintain healthy personal relationships in their adult lives. Indeed, there are plenty of jokes about this. One good one is due to Mel Brooks, who gave Chappelle his first significant movie role in *Robin Hood: Men in Tights*. Here is the joke: *Tragedy is when I cut my finger. Comedy is when you fall into a manhole and die.*

Thinking about Chappelle's comedy in this respect helps to understand one puzzling thing philosophers and psychologists have discovered about jokes designed to target members of marginalized groups: members of those marginalized groups often enjoy sharing the same jokes—literally, the same jokes—amongst themselves. The late great Ted Cohen (*Jokes*) wrote a lot about jokes with this point in mind: he often enjoyed sharing jokes that turned on pernicious stereotypes about Jews with his Jewish friends. The same jokes that are used to disparage outgroup members in a comic way can also, paradoxically, be employed to foster intimacy. Especially when he's using his humor to engage complex social issues related to race, Chappelle is more easily trusted as an authority, in part because as a Black man he obviously suffers from negotiating the racial stereotypes that African Americans have had to negotiate for centuries. But Chappelle also seems to really *care* about other people. And isolated failures to communicate don't seem to have undermined his status as one of the most important comedic voices working today.

Indeed: not just after Trump's electoral victory in 2016, but again after his defeat in 2020, Chappelle was asked to host *SNL*. In his most recent appearance on SNL, he took plenty of jabs at Trump, but also encouraged his audience to think explicitly about the many millions of people who did vote for him, and to meditate on parallels between the kinds of disenfranchisement they must be experiencing, and the experiences of African Americans. For instance, he points out that for the first time in recent American history, "the life expectancy of white people is dropping, because of heroin, because of suicide. All these white people out there that feel that anguish, that pain, they're mad because they think nobody cares . . . Let me tell you something: I know how that feels" ("Dave Chappelle's Post-Election Blues").

I mentioned Whitehead's opinion that Western philosophy has been focused on lessons from Plato, perhaps at the expense of sustained attention to questions about the relationship between humor and truth. Whitehead himself thought about humor; he believed humor was called for in any circumstances where the "necessity of irreverence" is manifest.

While Chappelle's intentions to be truthful don't seem to explain his success, it does seem clear that he sees a lot in the world that demands comic irreverence, and that he will continue to share his version of that standing up in "the last stronghold for civil discourse" (*8:46*).

20

Dave Chappelle Says He Doesn't Mean It, So Just Shut Up Already

STEVEN BURGESS

> He was fourteen years old. And Kevin Spacey accosted him at a party . . . Not to victim blame, but it sounds like the kind of situation a gay fourteen-year-old would get himself in.
>
> Or, here's another idea that's going to be very controversial, you could shut the fuck up. I'm sorry, ladies. I just, I got a fucking #MeToo headache.
>
> I feel like they need to take some responsibility for my jokes. 'Cause I didn't come up with this idea on my own, this idea that a person can be born in the wrong body. But they have to admit that's a fucking hilarious predicament. It's really fucking funny.

It's a good thing stand-up comedians don't publish their jokes in written form. If they did, we'd be left with the mean-spirited husks you read above in place of the full Dave Chappelle experience.

His critics tend to point to quotes like these and let Chappelle's own words do the talking. I'm reminded of a time I chided my sisters for supporting Jay-Z, even though his song lyrics include lines like, "I got ninety-nine problems, but a bitch ain't one." I kept repeating this phrase as if it were a sexist smoking gun, until I sheepishly came to understand that Jay-Z may have been using the term "bitch" in its multiple registers of meaning, as poets of course do. Alas, unlocking the layers of meaning in a Chappelle joke is not as simple as telling your brother to listen to a song like less of a dunce.

The philosophical movement called "phenomenology" can help us make sense of such statements. While the natural response to the word "phenomenology" might be to blurt out "Bless you!" the idea is actually quite simple: It is the study of the structure of experience.

Imagine a scenario so utterly commonplace that you would never think to give it a second's worth of reflection. You walk into your place of work at the start of your normal day. You stop into the staff lounge, open the fridge, and leave your lunch there; pick up the coffee pot and pour yourself a cup; hang your jacket on the familiar coat rack; say hi to the office manager who always arrives half an hour before you do. I'm yawning just typing it. What could be less in need of explanation than such ordinary events?

What phenomenology tells us is that there's actually an incredibly rich context of meaning lying in the background that allows us to effortlessly navigate such mundane environments. Notice how each item has its little role to play in the whole space of the workplace: the fridge is for keeping food cold, the coat rack for hanging clothing, the coffee to provide a boost in energy. What's interesting about any of this is that we almost never *think* of these things, yet we have completely mastered all of these tasks as if we were on auto-pilot. We certainly don't need to process the properties of each object like the Terminator (cylindrical object 4.2" tall, 3.4" wide, red glazed ceramic = coffee cup) in order to know what they are and how to use them.

The items in our immediate surroundings are not just isolated objects possessing properties (cylindrical, red, glazed), but gain their significance as things that can be used to complete various practical tasks. Just as the setting and context of our daily routine recede into the background, the world of stand-up comedy, with its shared understanding of American culture and Chappelle's long-term opposition to intolerance serve as the invisible backdrop that gives one of his jokes its bite as hilarious, insensitive, insightful, offensive, or even transformative.

Behind the Scenes of a Chappelle Joke

Let's leave our riveting breakroom example behind and show how phenomenology can illuminate a controversial Dave Chappelle joke. Imagine that you heard someone on the street corner loudly announcing one of the quotations listed at the beginning of the chapter as you walk by. With practically no context, you'd surely be justified in condemning the remarks and the person making them. When Dave Chappelle says these same things during a comedy special, many are just as quick to denounce him in the media or even right there in the venue by shouting from the audience. Chappelle likes to call such people "brittle spirits," implying that the mere words of a stand-up comedian are enough to break them. I think a case can be made that he's right. To build the case we must make visible the layers of hidden context that give Chappelle-isms their full meaning. The story doesn't end there though, as Chappelle reveals his own spiritually brittle tendencies in responding to his detractors.

"Fire, motherfuckers, fire! Get out!" To illustrate the most obvious way that linguistic context matters, I ask the reader to attend to various settings in which I might yell this at the top of my lungs.

> **CASE #1:** I do so while an actual fire has ignited in a movie theater.
> **Result:** I've performed an important public service (though my panicked recourse to a juvenile curse word in an emergency probably says a lot about my character).
>
> **CASE #2:** I scream this suddenly while teaching my Intro to Logic class, with no reason to believe there is a fire in the building.
> **Result:** I've broken about a dozen perfectly reasonable unwritten social rules, making me a completely unprofessional teacher (and a lunatic).
>
> **CASE #3:** For some reason I'm on stage at the Tuesday night stand-up open mic and I'm trying to get a laugh from the crowd by shouting it in my best Dave Chappelle imitation.
> **Result:** I'm more or less falling in line with what's expected of a person in that setting.

Same crude announcement, three very different results. My fellow movie-goers in Case #1 are (mostly) grateful, my students in Case #2 have good reason to be upset with me, and the audience in Case #3 doesn't take my statement in any way seriously, since it's a joke. So, this is the first node in our web of context: Chappelle frequently distinguishes between *joking* and *meaning it*. On stage, the rules are different and we don't hold people to a standard of literal testimony there.

The point is almost too obvious to make and very few critics of Chappelle are guilty of failing to understand it, despite the obligatory kvetching of nearly every stand-up comedian with claims to the contrary. It's not always this simple. Say a distant acquaintance suddenly asserts the following to you before a work meeting:

> Your snub nose makes you the ugliest person I've ever seen, the gap between your teeth makes your voice squeaky and unbearable, and that skin disorder you have makes you smell like old sandwich meat.

After an awkward pause, in which you try to figure out just what you could have done to Jeff in Accounting to make him say such (brutally specific) things, Jeff adds, "Just kidding!" Obviously, this little addendum does not really change anything, even if Jeff really is merely joking. When Chappelle claims he *doesn't mean it,* it is not just an easy out for a thoughtless comment. His mode of telling a joke must be understood in light of deeper commitments to combatting racism, supporting the feminist movement, and even striving for the inclusion of the LGBTQ+ community.

Talking race and racism has always been Chappelle's comedic calling card, but we should appreciate the nuanced angles he takes in doing so. Despite the many lighthearted racialized jokes he tells, Chappelle consistently expresses the deep pain of racism. This comes to light most clearly in his recent *8:46* set in honor of George Floyd, where his raw and visceral outrage at police brutality breaks through the typical screen of laughter. But his most brilliant moments from his earliest comedy specials were also his bits on the police and their interaction with Black communities. While his distrust of the police as a Black man serves as set-up for many a punchline, this distrust is undeniably real and stems from the racism woven into the fabric of American society. Our laughter is conditioned on it.

Although it's fair to say that Chappelle is committed to fighting racism, it's equally clear that he's willing and even eager to exploit racial stereotypes for other reasons. Sometimes (especially on *Chappelle's Show*) he carries these stereotypes through to decidedly absurd proportions. Mostly this works to loosen the grip such racial tropes hold over our social psyche by exposing them as literally laughable. In other cases, the laughter elicited from Chappelle and his audience is at the cost of reinforcing and perhaps strengthening existing racialized associations. The key here is that in spite of expressing the pain of racism personally and holding a fundamental commitment to overcoming racist social structures, Chappelle still believes that Black folks ought to be the butt of his jokes *insofar as they are Black.* This means that he does not even spare himself when it comes to generating a laugh. (I don't mean to associate "being Black" with some kind of inescapable essence that a person is born with, as if it were coded into one's DNA, and Chappelle certainly isn't targeting such a thing in his jokes. These attributes are instead malleable cultural artifacts that have shaped each individual's identity to a greater or lesser degree.)

I suspect the reader has not forgotten my claim above that Dave Chappelle is committed to feminism and the LGBTQ+ movement (in the face of an admittedly large body of evidence to the contrary!). His statements of this sort are normally glossed over in favor of the more bombastic dick jokes, but they are there as additional nodes in Chappelle's web of context. For example: In broaching the issue of abortion, he advises males to "shut the fuck up on this one"; he repeatedly says that women are in the right in their fight for equality, including the aims of the #MeToo movement; he considers himself a feminist. (However, he can't help but temper the bald assertion of his feminism by adding, "as we're known on the streets, 'bitch ass n***as'.")

He claims to only make fun of those in whom he can see himself, such as poor whites, since he was once poor; and if you can get past his slightly cringy terminology, in the comedy special *Equanimity*, he remarks, "If . . . I tell a joke that makes you want to beat up a transgender, then you're probably a piece of shit and don't come see me anymore." Many of his statements that appear sexist, transphobic, or homophobic, come from a place of shared oppression, where he shows genuine concern for the success of a movement that has as its goal the same equality he seeks concerning race. Given that fundamental bond, Chappelle goes on to offer tidbits of advice to women and to the LGBTQ+ community: *slow your roll* or *you're moving too fast*.

At first glance, this sounds like just the sort of advice white politicians gave Martin Luther King, Jr. in the early days of his civil rights activism (roughly, "Well, we believe in your cause, but can't you just work to it more gradually?"). A closer look reveals that Chappelle believes he is speaking to these movements from the perspective of an ally, who can read his own struggles in theirs, and who offers practical advice in hopes of the best way for the movement to ultimately succeed. While it does appear he is advocating regression or at least slower progress, he cites the numerous US states that have recently tried to undermine *Roe v. Wade*, a landmark moment in feminist legislation. His implication is that the rapid rise to ubiquity of the #MeToo movement has caused alarm bells to ring in anti-feminist circles of power, resulting in their quick moves to consolidate the remaining vestiges of patriarchy while this is still politically possible.

There are some points when Chappelle seems envious, as a member of the Black community, of the progress other movements have made in a (supposedly) shorter time. These comments, though frequently harsh-sounding, are made from within a more basic shared commitment to resisting oppression and intolerance. After his 2019 special, *Sticks and Stones*, rolls the credits, a hidden Q & A session is unlocked. During this session, Chappelle recounts the experience of having a trans woman in the audience, which caused him to hesitate before ultimately going through with telling jokes that have been widely condemned as transphobic. He reasons, "If I can't tell them to her face, why tell them at all?" He claims to have sought her out after the show to open up a dialogue, which resulted in a positive exchange. One person does not speak for a whole community, but what's important is that Chappelle reveals genuine concern for her well-being and for the well-being of the entire LGBTQ+ community.

Chappelle distinguishes his own form of comedy from those who tell racist jokes (for example) and "mean that shit." (Despite this fact, he claims to be able to learn something from their "artistry.") Chappelle mentions this in one of the ruminations included in the production for his Mark Twain Prize for American Humor acceptance event. Chappelle's self-professed alliance with marginalized groups hangs on this difference: Those who *mean it* do not work from a perspective of collective opposition to oppression, while those who are *joking* do.

I believe that while in many ways Chappelle is a flawed ally, he refuses to spare others as a mark of respect. For Chappelle, "brittle spirits" are incapable of laughing at themselves, which can be a healthy form of coping with oppression. When he writes jokes at the expense of Black culture (by perpetuating stereotypes, by discussing racism with levity) and his own identity, he is able to expose racist tropes not as fixed and inevitable, but laughably non-binding and impermanent. Often the jokes about other marginalized communities seem to "go too far," but Chappelle regularly repeats the mantra that only in crossing the line will we know where the line is. Think of it this way. Dave Chappelle takes as his starting point his alliance and support for subordinated communities. Then from within that space of shared commitment he maps out the fault lines of social acceptability *by transgressing them.*

Why do any of that? First and foremost, violating social expectations can be *funny.* Most of Dave Chappelle's setups involve building up our customary expectations (You're in a tough neighborhood late at night and you see a baby on the street corner—how heartbreaking!) until the punchline surprises us into laughter by thwarting our expectations (The baby is selling drugs!). But these transgressions can also evoke responses that tell us where our deep sentiments lie (Why did

I laugh at that? Why did that disgust me?). It's important to bring some of the tacit joints of our beliefs into sharp relief, rather than to pretend they don't exist. The latter situation can be especially problematic, as our subconscious beliefs still guide our actions, but without critical awareness of this fact, our ways are unlikely to change.

You Just Can't Take a Joke

Don't confuse what I've just said with apologetics. The main purpose was to illustrate that comedians—and particularly Dave Chappelle—are often lambasted without sufficient attention given to the nuances of their art. Here's the kicker: Stand-up comedians are guilty of much the same thing. When we look more deeply into the same general social backdrop that enabled Chappelle to land his jokes, we see that we live in a world of incredibly difficult intolerance for non-binary genders, queerness, and non-whiteness; a world that enables rapists and shames survivors into silence and guilt. Chappelle is too keen not to realize that his jokes that exploit this cultural vulnerability in many ways reinforce intolerance. The racist feels affirmed in openly laughing at Black and Brown stereotypes; the sexual aggressor is emboldened and assault is made a thing of levity; the trans- and homophobes enjoy the circus of sexual "freaks" from their perch of privileged immunity.

Out of this context, a listener refuses to laugh, disgusted at making light of her trauma. Another cannot help but shout in rage. Still others are reduced to involuntary tears and anxiety. They make use of the same space that enabled Chappelle to latch onto our invisible social lines of normalcy and push past them in laughter. Instead of laughing, they announce their own pain. Chappelle misunderstands this as a call for gag order and censorship, a herald of political correctness, and a sign of thin-skinned brittle spirits, who *can't take a joke*. What if instead this is merely a statement of fact: *Your words caused me pain*. Chappelle has repeatedly shown a lack of interest in engaging with such voices and tends to close off avenues for dialogue. His courage is what opened the door of discourse by vocalizing what is uncomfortable, "off limits." This same courage fails him when the conversation pushes back.

Phenomenology shows us that even the most ordinary experiences are only possible on the basis of a deep well of social assumptions about how things work, how people should behave, which actions are appropriate under which circumstances, and ultimately what counts as 'normal'. For the most part, this background flies under the radar of our conscious experience, but comedy is an important instrument for bringing to light the boundaries of social normalcy by evoking mostly involuntary responses of shock, disgust, delight, disdain, and of course laughter. We have little control over these knee-jerk reactions, and they are often the most revealing way we respond, yet they should not have the last word. Chappelle has rightly bemoaned those who fail to reflect further upon their instinctual response. At the same time, it's fair to ask what kind of ally Dave Chappelle is to those who do let these evocations process and in return communicate disappointment that a supposed ally is capitalizing on an already suffering group.

As Chappelle has made clear, "brittle spirits" are not the ideal recipients of his jokes, as they're unwilling to look past their immediate reactions, recognize Chappelle as an ally, and laugh at themselves. It must also be said, however, that comedians with brittle spirits make for poor allies, as *they* are unwilling to look past their immediate reactions, recognize their critics as comrades in the fight against oppression, and hang in the tough spaces of dialogue. Allies are not defined by their unerring obedience to political correctness or a perfect *offend no one* scorecard. Instead, allies are those who 1. commit their support, even if imperfectly; 2. do not assume that their own experiences entitle them to an automatic understanding of another's oppression; and 3. are willing to listen genuinely and be open to revising their mode of support. Chappelle does indeed succeed on the first measure, and his commitment to alliance is part of the phenomenological backdrop that makes it possible for his jokes to show up in just the way they do.

The other two measures of alliance are more problematic. Chappelle does inhabit a social space that affords him insight into racial oppression, and this, coupled with his discerning eye for illuminating tacit social structures, equips him well as a valuable ally to other communities. Notice that seeing things in this way artificially separates out different oppressed groups (communities of color, trans communities, women, sexual assault survivors, and so on) as though these were not already interconnected, while simultaneously erasing the important differences in the experience of oppression. This indicates that racism is not a monolith; Black women and trans Black persons (for example) do not all experience anti-Black racism in the same way that Black men do; similarly, racialized experience is qualitatively different from gendered or non-straight experiences. These considerations put a damper on how shared Chappelle's "collective" opposition to oppression is. So, the second measure is a complicated and mixed bag, but the third—a willingness to engage in open dialogue—is more decisive. This is not the problem of the *heckler*, who disrupts the flow of joke-laughter-joke-laughter in the space of stand-up comedy. Instead, a willing participant in this space has publicly shared their experience, which is often a triggered trauma, and is met with a spirit too brittle to keep an authentic conversation open. The old saw—*you just can't take a joke*—rings hollow in the face of these legitimate calls for continuing dialogue.

We have arrived at a surprising conclusion. What seemed to be a cut and dried case of comedic freedom against political correctness versus a critique of patriarchy, homophobia, and transphobia, has been complicated by phenomenological analysis. Great, you might be thinking, just what we need—another philosophical theory to muddy the waters! Yet I think this 'complication' of the problem is a richer and truer description of the facts.

Dave Chappelle is not just another comedian who wants to take aegis under the cloak of free speech to entitle him to say hateful things. He believes himself to be in solidarity with marginalized groups and considers laughter at ourselves to be part of the healing process to overcome oppression. This good will alone does not make Chappelle a true ally, but it should allow us to see his more controversial jokes in a fundamentally different light. Much of the remaining work of alliance involves taking to heart one of Dave Chappelle's own wise and enduring counsels: Don't be a *brittle spirit* in the face of hard words.[1]

---

[1] I would like to thank Chez Rumpf for her comments on an early draft of this chapter, my sisters Carolyne and Shainna for making me a Jay-Z fan, and my wife Jess for quality control on the liberal use of Dad jokes herein.

VI

Revealing People
to Themselves

21

Why Do You Feel Guilty for Loving Dave Chappelle?

Eliza Wizner

B efore I even knew what I would write for this chapter, I was talking (boasting) to my friends about the cool project to which I would contribute. When they asked what the project was about, I casually (braggadociously) mentioned the name Dave Chappelle.

This struck everyone in the group differently. One friend raised her eyebrows and said, "Well he's certainly . . . controversial." Another friend shivered with excitement (I'd never actually seen someone *shiver* with excitement before, but it's a real thing) and exclaimed, "Oh my god, Dave Chappelle, I LOVE him!" I agreed on both counts. And suddenly, my topic was right in front of me: people are afraid to love Dave Chappelle because he says controversial things on stage, but we can't help ourselves.

In my experience, people can agree that the guy is smart. He's tuned in and certainly has a knack for what he does. It's also hard to dismiss him as a bad person. I mean, he's done his fair share of humanitarian work (see Dave Chappelle's Block Party, his advocacy for civil rights, and other accomplishments). And yet most would probably also concur that he's said some pretty eyebrow-raising stuff on stage (jokes about the LBTQ+ community—transgender individuals especially—jokes about victims of sexual assault, and so forth).

Dave does disclaim most of these jokes with an "I'm not hateful, I swear" statement He says both, "If you're in a group I make fun of, just know that I will probably only make fun of you because I see myself in you" and, in reference to the LGBTQ+ community, "Everybody loves me and I love everybody" in his special *Sticks and Stones.* Yet despite such disclaimers he can still feel really shocking to watch.

I can always tell when something Dave says during a set will get him in trouble. Because I know what public opinion will deem 'good' or 'bad', I sometimes feel guilty for finding the 'bad' stuff funny. But then, of course, I feel angry that I feel guilty, because I can't be sure that the guilt comes from me. On the one hand, I want to support only good people. On the other hand, I really don't believe he's not a good person. So, then, something is conditioning me to respond to him with fear of public reception more than anything else.

The Sanitization of Language and the Present Age

The thing about Dave Chappelle is that he seems to say whatever he wants to say. People laud him most for his honesty, amd I definitely feel that truth-telling is the biggest factor in his charm. His honesty is one of the things that people laud him most for. While reflecting on what made him so charming, it was the number one thing on my list. But what exactly is it about his honesty that's so valuable? The reason we're drawn to truth-telling is related to a sort of crowded suffocation identifiable in our culture, both in celebrities and in our friends and families. So, we are comforted when we see someone telling the truth, especially a truth different from repeated phrases and statements we are used to hearing.

It's almost freeing to see *him* free. There are two parts to understanding this process, though; first, we need to identify what exactly makes us feel so suffocated. Then, we need to uncover what about Dave Chappelle helps us to escape that. For some help in both of these regards, I'm turning to Søren Kierkegaard's essay, "The Present Age."

"The Present Age" actually isn't about *this* present age at all—it was written in 1846—but I think we can find some similarities between the description in the essay and American society as we know it today. Kierkegaard proposes that the past, the previous age, could be characterized by passion and rebellion. He argues that people used to take concrete action on issues they cared about, but that this age, the "present age" is completely different. The present age, according to Kierkegaard, is superficial and devoid of passion. It is characterized by publicity about everything, though nothing really happens. This causes certain phrases and opinions to make their way through society, reflected from person to person and without any individuality expressed (pp. 252–54). In some ways, this really reminds me of progressive talk in the US today, especially among younger generations.

In their article "The Coddling of the American Mind," the beginnings of a 2018 book of the same name, Greg Lukianoff and Jonathan Haidt examine a phenomenon on college campuses around the US the authors dub "vindictive protectiveness" (*The Atlantic*, 7/31/17). Their definition of the phrase is a sort of impulse to crack down on any language which makes people uncomfortable, as a pre-emptive defense against bigotry and the like. However, they argue, this is creating a culture in which people are afraid to voice nearly any opinion at all, lest they suffer abuse.

Don't get me wrong—we should absolutely be holding people accountable for racism, sexism, and bigoted language. However, as Lukianoff and Haidt argue, vindictive protectiveness is ultimately allowing the emotional response to serve as an end-all be-all authority on what is right and what is wrong. Without fostering helpful dialogue because of, on the one hand, a state of "constant outrage," and, on the other, fear of backlash, speech is more and more confined to a list of acceptable words and phrases.

There's nothing wrong with calling out those with hateful ideals and who use hateful opinions. In fact, the only way to better our country is to call for that betterment. However, the process of "calling out" need not be one of aggression and spite. Rather, we should be focusing on allowing everyone room to grow by making the very call for growth as gentle and understanding as possible. Thus, when we limit speech at all, even with the best intentions, the space for growing is shrunk down to nothing, and both parties lose out on the opportunity to learn.

The negative characteristics of Kierkegaard's "Present Age" as identified in our own society are further exemplified by the use of social media. It is easier than ever to become locked into echo chambers of opinions we agree with, and even easier to demonstrate support for a cause without taking any concrete action. Just as Kierkegaard points to his "Present Age" as devoid of passion and without any real rebellion, it is easy to see how this description could fit our own age as well. Often it can feel as if we're all so tuned in to social media, and media in general, that we all voice the same opinions over and over until they don't mean much anymore. So, when we find someone who can snap us out of this sort of complacency, we are instinctively drawn to them.

This, I believe, is what I was trying to put my finger on during my reflection on the shock-value of Dave Chappelle. The things that he says on stage are not necessarily things that I would ever say, or even consider, but I don't want to feel guilty or ashamed because I like him. I want Dave Chappelle to say things that he finds funny, and I want to be able to take or leave those things without dismissing his entire career or value as a human being.

The Public and How Chappelle Avoids It

A key point of Kierkegaard's essay is what he calls "the public." The public is a sort of undefinable yet all-encompassing entity. All who exist in the present age interact with the public in some way—a person can be a part of the public and not notice it, or a person can try to voice a dissenting opinion and experience defeat at the hands of the public. Any opinion held by the public is fleeting and superficial, so although everyone may feel that they are correct for holding the beliefs of the public, there is rarely any substance involved (p. 262). When we think about some of the problems with safe space culture and the like, it becomes clear that limits to speech, even if that speech is harmful, necessarily reduce access to varying opinions. When we don't have access to varying opinions, then we don't have the ability to see what's right and what's wrong for ourselves.

So, although I most certainly would not go as far as to say that Dave Chappelle is an honorable man for making jokes about transgender individuals or about the victims of sexual assault, I am most certainly comfortable saying that he's brave for doing so. Chappelle is a complex case in this sense, because usually when someone in the public eye says something unsavory, we witness a fall from grace and the aftermath of the fall. However, Chappelle never claimed to be perfect. He never claimed to have it all figured out. Rather, he admits that he is confused by some ideas. In *Sticks and Stones*, Chappelle says, "I feel bad for T's. But they're so confusing. And it's not all my fault—I feel like they need to take some responsibility for my jokes. Because I didn't come up with this idea on my own—this idea that a person can be born in the wrong body—but they have to admit that's a hilarious predicament."

What he doesn't do is approach the situation from a place of hate. He unequivocally will not apologize for what he says, but he also doesn't hold hate for the groups he makes fun of. "The T's hate my fucking guts. And I don't blame 'em, it's not their fault—it's mine. I just can't stop telling jokes about these n * * * as." (*Sticks and Stones*). And this, for me, is why it's okay to love

Dave Chappelle (or at least why it should be): he makes it okay not to know everything about everything, and to mess up.

A lot of people, especially those speaking on civil rights or progressive ideas, talk from a place of teaching. Individuals in the public eye make statements that never contain an admission that they came from a place of ignorance and then grew into the knowledge they now share. Even more than that, there are almost never sincere admissions that one may *still* be ignorant. Rather, the "vindictive protectiveness," as Lukianoff and Haidt call it, scares us into believing we are completely bad people if we do not know and understand every facet of every social issue.

The space for judgement-free growth is now littered with eggshells upon which people must walk. Phrasing a sentence incorrectly or asking a sincere question for the sake of understanding, are so daunting that some are afraid to speak at all. The public, in this case, has required everyone to behave the same and to vocalize the same opinions, even if those opinions are held falsely or in name only. Just as Kierkegaard said, the present age has become "superficial." We're more concerned with the perceptions of ourselves than with the actual content of our minds, which can only serve to limit growth that people *could* be doing. So, the public serves to let the landscape of society remain the same, but "subtly drains the meaning out of it" (p. 225). We're left not with inspired action, but with empty and constant reflection. This is why we experience so much relief when we come across a genuine truth teller.

This is where Dave Chappelle's comedy comes into play. He avoids being a part of the public by offering his *own* thoughts. He doesn't play it safe or work hardest to preserve his image. He doesn't pander to communities on which his comedy is based, nor to his own audience. Rather, he shares himself on stage. He shares even the parts of himself that can make an audience member wince at his insensitivity—the parts that are not easy to love. By admitting that he is not perfect and still growing, he allows us to also admit that we, too, are still growing.

I would obviously prefer that all people, myself included, could truly educate themselves on all important topics and be able to speak definitively on them. However, that is not the nature of the country at the moment and, moreso, I'm not sure it's even the nature of human beings. We are continually growing, learning, and making mistakes. So, for now, I think it's better to have someone who can both acknowledge the important issues of the day and offer up his own genuine reflections to the country than someone who avoids touchy topics or pretends to be completely unflawed. This, in my eyes, makes Dave Chappelle a far braver and, yes, even more honorable celebrity than those who make statements through social media accounts or publicists with the same words and phrases over and over again.

It's an impossible standard, to be all caught up and all on board with every social issue of the day. But part of the work lies in the ability to understand there's work to be done. It is easier for me to accept as "good" a person who loves even that which he does not understand than any person who claims to have learned all there is to learn.

In "The Present Age," Kierkegaard writes that satire, if it is helpful in any way, "must have the resource of a consistent and well-grounded ethical view, a sacrificial unselfishness, and a high-born nobility that renounce the moment" (p. 254). This is a difficult call to action. Renouncing the moment seems easier said than done. I think, though, that if we consider Chappelle's track record, he does just that. Whether he renounces the moment by refusing to be silent about normalized racial discrimination in the country, or by daring to admit that he does not fully understand transgender individuals, he allows the complexity of his personhood to be made clear to his audience.

This is completely "unselfish," as it opens him up to all sorts of attacks from all sorts of people (on both the political right and left). But it also makes his viewers feel more comfortable with our own rates of growth. This, in turn, allows for a trust between Chappelle and his audience that not a lot of celebrities can achieve. Whether or not we agree with what he says, we can count on the fact that he is always unfiltered and speaking from his heart. Chappelle, I believe, understands this more than anyone. In his most recent set, *8:46*, named for the amount of time Derek Chauvin had his knee pressed to the neck of George Floyd, Chappelle says,

> I figured out why people want to hear from me, and it's serious. The only reason people want to hear from people like me is because you trust me. You don't expect me to be perfect but I don't lie to you. I'm just a guy and I don't lie to you. And every institution—every institution that we trust—lies to us.

Here, Chappelle identifies the meaninglessness and superficiality of the present age in our own institutions. We don't trust them a lot of the time because we recognize the work of the public in them. Everything is real and firm but ultimately empty, and we see this all the time. It's scary to witness, but it is made more comforting with presences like Chappelle's given platforms to voice their opinions.

However, Chappelle is clear: this courtesy to allow stand-up comics to speak their minds is not to be extended only to those with whom we agree. At the end of his acceptance speech for the Mark Twain Prize for American Humor, after many of his closest friends and colleagues lauded his incredible honesty on stage, he said,

> There is something so true about this genre, when done correctly, that I will fight anybody that gets in a true practitioner of this art form's way, because I know you're wrong. This is the truth, and you are obstructing it. Not talking about the content, I'm talking about the art form. (*Mark Twain Prize*)

Chappelle understands that real truth-telling, no matter the opinion conveyed in that telling, is of the utmost importance. The quote with which Lukianoff and Haidt end their article is attributed to Thomas Jefferson when founding the University of Virginia: "This institution will be based on the illimitable freedom of the human mind. For here we are not afraid to follow truth wherever it may lead, nor to tolerate any error so long as reason is left free to combat it" (*The Atlantic*, 7/31/17).

Although Lukianoff and Haidt (as well as Jefferson) were discussing the American college through the lens of this quote, Chappelle's statements on comedy echo the sentiment. When people are afraid to speak, we end up limiting the ability of all others to grow from either mistakes that they make or from truths that they identify. Individuality in speech is what can counter the role of the public in the present age. Kierkegaard says that an author or an artist who speaks in the present age will never offer his own opinion. Only a repetition, in some form, of the public's opinions will be reflected in the content of his material (p. 265).

So, when Chappelle produces content in which his own opinion is easily discernible at every turn, he manages to avoid being the type of artist that Kierkegaard would have identified as part of the public. He allows us to hear what he says and to think about it for ourselves. He could give into the fear that those in the public eye are so very familiar with— the fear of criticism, of losing favor with a fan base. Instead, he offers up his opinions, freely and honestly, and invites the criticism.

So, people like me, upon hearing some of his comments, can reject what he says. Or, I can allow his words to resonate with me, and discover a new truth for myself. This process, this truth telling and acceptance of multiple views in the public eye without the pressure to be perfect, is what can bring some action back to our own present age. Once we feel free to make mistakes, to learn from them, and to discover on our own the injustices of the world, maybe then our present age can be one devoid of *reflection*, and full of rebellion.

Maybe then we can stop talking in circles and holding our breath; maybe then the country can admit that human error is inevitable, and that we will all crack the eggshells sometimes. And then, maybe we can move forward, with *real* progression. I guess for now though, we can continue to listen to comedians like Dave Chappelle and try to be proud of it.

22

How Dave Chappelle and Saint Augustine Help Us See Ourselves

CONOR W. HANSON

My daughter is never watching *Chappelle's Show* or his stand-ups. Hopefully, she'll never know they exist. Call me a prude or paint me a conservative, I don't care. I myself often worry how the show (along with other shows or movies I've watched) may have warped my imagination in troubling ways. Garbage in, garbage out, they say.

I also find myself twelve years after high school in the paradoxical position of indebtedness to Dave Chappelle. The show was all the rage when I was in high school (2005–2008), prompting many conversations with friends of all races. What made it so fun was repeating the ridiculous and idiotic phrases to each other. The hilarious one-liners were endless.

Given my absolute unwillingness to allow my daughter to even know about the show, or watch Chappelle's stand-up specials, why am I thankful to him? Why, after years of soaking in the vulgarity and profanity, am I glad I watched Chappelle? The answer is simple: Dave Chappelle helped me see myself. Specifically, by watching his show, I was led to see the tendencies and habits within my own heart that were, quite simply, racist.

And when I did see those things, I was a little shocked. I began to see that the jokes I laughed at perpetuated a view of Black people as lazy or violent, Latinos as dirty or illegal job stealers, or Asians as bad drivers. I began to realize I had Latino friends whose parents didn't speak a lick of English, their kids being the bridge between them and the world of so-called economic promise around them (they worked really hard for their kids to have a decent life in America). I began to realize that I viewed my Black friend's lives as an exotic or foreign commodity to be consumed. I began to become aware of how I responded to the presence of a Black person or Black people. The n-word seemed magical to white kids like me. Like if my Black friends ever called me the n-word I'd be "in." I began to realize that we lived in quite distinct and disproportionate worlds. The one meeting place for us, however, was Chappelle.

So how did such an obscene show pull this off? How did Dave Chappelle get a white kid like me to see himself with a new clarity, and who is now more self-critical, more willing to listen to and engage in conversations with friends of different races? I think there's a simple logic to *Chappelle's Show*, brilliantly used by Chappelle, that encourages such self-knowledge.

The logic goes something like this: create a semi-caricatured scene, bring in characters that are a little too real, say the things out loud we'd rather not say out loud, in a ridiculous way or by way of self-deprecation, make it even more absurd with some crazy additions so we all feel comfortable laughing, all dealing with a topic or theme that is highly controversial. Within the drama world, there's a category of comedic drama that is structured like this, utilizing absurdities and outlandish scenes, called a *farce*. Chappelle blatantly utilizes this dramatic method, although there's a very clever twist to it that I think makes it very powerful. Let's see how this plays out in one of Chappelle's well-known skits: Black Bush.

War on Terror

Immediately following September 11th, then-president George W. Bush was seeking retaliation on those responsible for the September 11th terror attacks. The "War on Terror" sought to target al-Qaeda and their leader, Osama bin Laden. There were also arguments tossed about that Saddam Hussein, then dictator of Iraq, was amassing weapons of mass destruction (WMDs). Because Hussein had been listed as a sponsor of terrorism since the 1990s by the State Department, squashing him was part of the war effort as well. However, no WMDs were ever found and the arguments offered by Bush's administration ended up being baseless covers for some other motives which were never quite clear (many suspected Iraq's oil supply was the primary goal). Altogether there was a perfect recipe for deception and general shadiness from our elected leaders: a war against an invisible enemy ("terror"), semi-legitimate sounding arguments as well as half-baked concerns regarding national security, and a public that was, for the most part, simply seeking revenge for September 11th.

In times of crisis Americans expect their leaders to have a clear plan of action, all while maintaining a decorum that shows they are sincere and looking out for what's best for the American people. However, this was undermined for many by the Bush administration's "War on Terror." When combined with an American ethos that simply distrusts authority generally (we didn't care for the British Empire very much), the result is a public that sees their leaders as having a faux-decorum that's simply a cover for other motives which may or may not be good for the American people.

With that context, how does Chappelle's farce play out within the skit? He takes key moments from the "War on Terror," typically press conferences by then-president Bush or TV news reports, and replaces the president and his advisors or allies with Black people. But it's not just any Black people; it's stereotyped *gangsta* Black people. This is crucial to his farce. Bush is transformed from a monotone, emotionally sterile run-of-the-mill white politician into a stereotyped Black guy who speaks African-American English (as well as his advisors played by Mos Def, Donnell Rawlings, and "some Black dude").

The comedic effect is immediately felt with Black Bush's administrative board speaking about the region of the Middle East being "ripe for a regime change." This sounds like an official-sounding sentence a typical white politician would use. But Black Bush asks if he can be "real," to which his advisor (a bit of a hype-man) says, "Be real real, son." "He tried to kill my father, man." He then pulls down the microphone, presumably that the news crews are using or the show itself, breaks the fourth wall, and shouts, "That n****r tried to kill my father!!" It's hilarious because a serious foreign policy issue has now become a personal dispute. To see a depiction of a president who is so emotionally expressive and blatant in his communication making such decisions is both funny and a sharp contrast with our expectations (which is part of Chappelle's method).

Or take the scene where Black Bush seeks to justify the invasion of Iraq at a press conference because of the WMDs that Saddam Hussein allegedly has. He begins by overtly gesturing with lots of body language, "the n****r bought aluminum tubes! Do I have to tell you what the fuck you can do with an aluminum tube? Aluminum!" It's so funny because I think many of us would expect some complicated description of a complex military device with loads of scientific-sounding technical language. Of course many of us have discovered that, when broken down, a very easy and layman description is actually more helpful and appreciated, even from our so-called professional leaders. I can even hear it being called an "extended propulsion incendiary device" or something. But the thing is really just an aluminum tube. To have a leader, whom we expect to be "professional," speak so straightforwardly is actually quite nice and relatable. Combine that with the profanity and it's pretty funny.

The reporters are unmoved by the aluminum tube accusation against Saddam and Black Bush notices. "That don't scare you? Fine, I didn't wanna say this: the motherfucker bought some yellow cake. Okay? In Africa. He went to Africa and he bought yellow cake." The reporters are skeptical, with one woman pressing further "Are you sure?" Black Bush stares at her incredulously for a moment and then shouts, "Yes I'm sure, bitch!" It's interesting to watch this skit in 2020, because I would immediately describe Black Bush as someone who "tells it like it is" or speaks straightforwardly and without reservation. Which is exactly how President Trump is described by many of his supporters. I wonder how many Americans would be willing to say that about a president with non-eurocentric mannerisms. It's this kind of tension that Chappelle intends to draw out in us and get us to see.

The immediate response I have as a white guy to this skit is laughter because I'm thinking, "That's funny because it's not professional or how leaders should run a country." But wait, where did I get this idea of how a country 'should' be run, or this idea that says, "Here's how *real* leaders act if they truly are leaders"? This is where we must see how the farce is actually functioning as we watch the skit. The farce makes us both vulnerable and yet comfortable enough to see that a door has been opened through Chappelle's brazen humor. So we wander over to the door and find a serious question waiting: why do we privilege white ways, white mannerisms and characteristics of leadership in the way we do? Why think that politicians or elected officials should speak "professionally" and not like regular people? Or if they do talk like regular people, what standard of "regular" are we using?

For me it was a standard of regular that was privileging white culture: you say things in a very objective and straightforward manner with regulated emotions, and every word is sterile in its description and tone. In other words: European mannerisms and habits that come from the inherited thought of the European Enlightenment. These ways of being a leader are seen as sophisticated and "civilized" (echoes of colonization here), or even if they do "say it like it is" it's being said with a gritty white working-class attitude that is respectable because it's relatable to most white Americans. But this is precisely white hegemony! It's the assumption that white ways of speaking, whether "professional" or "saying it like it is," are normative. But is that way of talking relatable to Black Americans? Does a white leader talk in ways that speak to the shared experience of much of the Black community in America?

The farce has brought us to this point by creating a scene in which we see the stereotyped Black person and know it, though it's sort of running in the background while we laugh. It's at this point that the farce can really do its work, because as we begin to ask why this is funny, we realize that what the humor is really about is stereotyped Black behavior coupled with what we think is a contradiction, namely, a Black leader in a position of power whose actions and words do not fit our expectations (what's normal and "right"). It's here that we're each being revealed to ourselves: Surely a leader wouldn't be like that, right? Do I think this is funny because I think it's *true* we shouldn't have leaders who differ from the norm I conceive? But wait, why? Would I be willing to submit to Black leadership that wasn't in the mold of white European habits and practices?

The Truth in the Farce

In these questions it's clear that there is a power imbalance. It's easier for me, a white guy, to just say, "of course that couldn't happen because here's how leaders should be and I know it. End of story." And then I can stop thinking about it. But a Black leader may feel immense pressure to conform to such mannerisms or expectations and can't *not* stop thinking about it, because it's the water in which they're always submerged and navigating. By ignoring this dynamic I perpetuate it. And to ignore it is to utilize white hegemony to dissolve my discomfort, squash the situation, and "get back to normal." So what will we do with what Chappelle's farce has given us? Will we maintain white hegemony, laugh at some hilarious skit, and walk away? Or will we question ourselves more and go further through that door of ourselves which the farce has brought forth?

The form Chappelle uses is deceptively simple. It's the creation of a farce, an absurd and ridiculous fictional comedic scene. But what exactly does Chappelle do with this dramatic method that makes it so effective (at least in my case)? I think the twist Chappelle uses is simple but profound: the farce itself isn't quite a farce; the farce was a sham! It's the ole bait-'n'-switch, with the farce drawing our attention only to find that the scene is actually *full of truth*. The farce draws us in and the absurdity acts as a sort of waterslide that dumps us in the deep pool that is, we now find, more real and serious than we first thought. A farce is attractive because it creates conditions for vulnerability, easing psychological tension and alertness. It is precisely this that Chappelle recognizes and utilizes. It certainly worked on me.

Chappelle has done something quite impressive in his show: he's gotten us to a place to potentially see ourselves, particularly white people, giving us the chance for self-examination. Even those of us who would avoid talking about racism are drawn into the show's absurdity (how many white conservative Americans are listening to Childish Gambino or Trevor Noah or watching *Key and Peele*? Probably none). This is done through the farce-but-not-quite-a-farce that disarms us and opens us up to dialogue, both with ourselves and those around us.

Augustine on Chappelle

A very famous Christian theologian and philosopher would applaud Chappelle's accomplishment: Saint Augustine. No doubt Augustine would have some serious criticisms to level against Chappelle, which I think would be well-founded. Even so, it wouldn't be lost on him that Chappelle had done something deserving of applause: he's created something with the immense potential for us to see ourselves and self-scrutinize, something Augustine understood quite profoundly.

Augustine was a Christian bishop of the North African town of Hippo (in what is now northeastern Algeria). He wrote a very popular book called *Confessions*, in which he recounted his life before and after converting to orthodox Christian faith. However, before he responded to what he understood as God seeking him, he found himself teaching in Carthage (a town in what is now Tunisia). In book III of *Confessions* he recalls how he was in Carthage and his "soul was in rotten health." I suppose that's understandable if, like he was, you're dunked into a "cauldron of illicit loves." He slept around quite a lot yet never was satisfied because his "hunger was internal," not something satisfied through mere sexual intercourse. Yet he found a surprising companion in Carthage: the theater. "I was captivated by theatrical shows," Augustine says, because he found his own miseries in life played out on stage, which allowed him space to experience the pleasure of commiserating with the actors in the stories. Who doesn't enjoy the satisfaction of realizing, "you too?!"?

The theater, Augustine says, presents something that none of us would actually want to go through, yet we love to watch it as a spectator. Augustine says that by watching the scenes played out on stage, the spectator is actually experiencing pleasure from the fiction *while not being called on to actually do anything*. Typically, humans see other humans (or perhaps animals) in distress, and respond with compassionate (the word means "suffer with") action that is a form of mercy. Not so with the theater, since there's no action for us to take in response to the pain or suffering or various other scenes. The fiction portrayed is not meant to spur us on to charitable or merciful action, but rather to give us an internal satisfaction or pleasure at the intensity of the scenes. And why is this a problem? Because, Augustine says, "the more anyone is moved by these scenes, the less free he is from similar passions." The passion grips us in chains through the viewing pleasure, all the while keeping us from acting for the good of our fellow humans and neighbors who may be in real distress.

That's quite a negative view of the theater in his own day and I don't think he's the guy who would be the first to suggest a Netflix night. Yet what would Augustine think of *Chappelle's Show*? Obviously, he was not some clairvoyant writing about the show 1,600 years before it aired, so there's no way to know with certainty. And we can't ask him since he's dead. But based on his comments on the theater, I think we can say a couple things about how Augustine might view *Chappelle's Show*. Given the intense care of his theological and philosophical inquiry of himself throughout the *Confessions*, which reveal how Augustine *sees*, I think Augustine would extend a praise and a criticism.

First, the praise. Augustine's concern with the theater was that it encouraged a person towards things which were not good for them. It did this through arousing passions and leaving the viewer to stew in those passions, never giving a guiding hand towards what is actually good and helpful for living well (not just what the person *thinks* is good; Augustine thinks there is truly an objective Good for human beings). Not only this, but Augustine found the theater concerning because it did not "pierce him deeply." Rather, it only scratched the surface and brought about strong feelings *as if* it were piercing him deeply. But it wasn't. The fact that Chappelle actively seeks to bring us to see racism and white hegemony, then, is a good.

To see a spade as a spade is, to Augustine, to begin to see truthfully, the first step towards reorienting your life towards what is Good (ultimately, God is the true Good for Augustine, but things that are in line with the life God requires of us are also good). To see our racism, to have it brought before us and see it for what it is, is a gift that pierces us deeply. Racism is absurd. To be shown how absurd, through the farce-but-not-quite-a-farce that is the show, is a gift. To be shown that our vision was wrong, that we were seeing the world improperly, is to begin the process of healing our hearts. You see the heart, for Augustine, must love the right things in the right way. But it must *see* the right things properly, which involves dealing with the garbage that obscures our vision. This is the problem Augustine had with the theater in Carthage: it did not assist in clearing the obscurity of our moral vision, but maintained the veil that prevents us from seeing ourselves rightly. Chappelle encourages a real *seeing*, and this is what, I think, Augustine would applaud.

Now to the criticism. I think Augustine, while praising Chappelle for challenging the implicit racism and white hegemony many white Americans participate in, would have a major criticism. The criticism could be put in the form of a question: where do we go from here? Chappelle has done us the service of revealing racism at work in our social and cultural practices, and ultimately at work within our own selves. But what are we supposed to *do* with that? What's the *goal* towards which we should point our lives and hearts? There's a lack of direction at work in *Chappelle's Show*, a lack of positive vision of what life *should* be. It's easy to be negative, to openly deconstruct things. And make no mistake: this needs to be done. But to leave things there is a disservice. A positive vision, filling the void left by the tearing down, must drive us towards something. And for Augustine, that goal must be objectively good for humans, not just what we think is good for us.

The Problem of Evil and the Problem of Good

You might be familiar with the famous "problem of evil" as it's called in modern philosophy of religion. If there's a God who is good, all powerful, and all knowing, then surely there *shouldn't* be any evil in the world since this God would be good and want to stop it, powerful enough to stop it, and smart enough to know about it. It's usually then argued that, since all of those together produce a contradiction, you must give up one of those three items (God is good, God is all powerful, God is all-knowing) or give up God. It can be exciting to feel as if you've finally got God backed into a corner.

While this is interesting and can bear fruitful discussion, there's a more profound problem than this one which is often overlooked: the problem of good. Specifically, what is this concept of goodness? Is there a *true and objective* good? Or are all conceptions of good merely human projections or social constructs? For Augustine, God is the "greatest and chiefest Good." Indeed, God is Goodness itself; there is no higher good, nor is goodness something separate from God. What this means is that God is the final goal, the resting place towards which all good things lead. Various actions or movements of human life can be more or less good depending on their congruence with and participation in the way of the revealed Good of God (Augustine thinks that philosophy can only do so much; revelation is needed, received by faith).

What does all this mean regarding Chappelle? Two things. First, there must be a positive vision towards which we move in our actions and lives. No one can live in a completely deconstructed world because nothingness is lifeless. Second, this positive vision must be in accord with what is truly good for humans. Now perhaps this second point is sort of implied in Chappelle: a good for humans is to recognize the humanity within each fellow human, the equal dignity possessed by each race and ethnicity. But if this is implied it is not put forward as something we can grab on to and work towards; it lacks coherence and solidity. Indeed, this lack of positive vision in *Chappelle's Show* threatens to undermine the work he does in exposing white hegemony and getting us to see our complicity in racist practices.

Chappelle wraps real life in an absurd fiction, a farce. Since we come to the show recognizing the scene as a fiction we aren't ready for the truth and reality found within the farce. I was surprised just how much I saw my own complicity in the practices discovered within the show, specifically the way I responded to Black Bush. I didn't expect to see more of myself than I bargained for, a self that had adopted habits of practice and thought that were racist and assumed a white normativity.

Though Chappelle doesn't offer much in the way of where to go from there, he does us the service of exposing the truth, a crucial first step toward rectifying ways of life that are harmful. The first step to course correction is to recognize you're going the wrong way.

Augustine, while having a major problem with the lack of goal or direction in *Chappelle's Show*, would applaud this. He knows that the human heart is kept in chains by its own sinful and disordered passions and desires, racism being a prime example. To *see* those bonds, and thereby see ourselves, is the first step on the path to true freedom.

23
Original Gangsta

Marisa Diaz-Waian

Laughter without a tinge of philosophy is but a sneeze of humor. Genuine humor is replete with wisdom.

—Mark Twain, Quoted in *Mark Twain and I*

There are two types of OG's (Original Gangstas)—those who're alive and those who're dead. One of the most famous OG's was Socrates, also known as the father of Western philosophy. Socrates rocked a toga, got his talk on in the town square, and inevitably (due to style or content) always stirred up some shit. In the end, he died—sentenced to drink hemlock.

He had other choices. He could have left Athens and never practiced philosophy again. But he chose death instead. (And a horrible one at that. Hemlock is no joke!). For him, the alternatives would have betrayed everything he was about. Socrates was committed to the art of critical thinking—of following reason wherever it led. As an OG, he embodied this commitment—in life and death—and he did so excellently.

Dave Chapelle rocks the same metaphorical toga as Socrates. He's a living OG. And while not a street philosopher in the sense that Socrates was, he's earned his stripes in similar ways—most notably through his dedication to truth (or relationship to reason) and authenticity (how he shows up in the world). It's easy to see why these things matter in philosophy. But what do they have to do with Chapelle's comedy and his OG status as an artist?

Chapelle is what I like to refer to as a "laughter and tears" comedian. Comedy of this sort draws deeply from the wells of life—a reality which is thorny, absurd, hilarious, messy, inspiring, beautiful, and often overwhelmingly heartbreaking and infuriating. Of equal import, his genre of art has an overtly educational goal of transformation and improvement. It's a mirror and moral corrective that invites us to laugh, think deeply, and grow. Because of these ends, a commitment to truth and authenticity is necessary (in ways that they might not be for other genres of comedy).

For artists of this kind, there are some that stand out as exemplars—as paradigmatic figures who navigate the space between laughter and tears brilliantly, who like the best of teachers cultivate our hearts and minds and help "lead us out" from darkness. Chapelle is one of these. To see how, we'll need to start with knowing and being—both of which are critical players in the truth and authenticity game.

Knowing and Being

In 2006, Chapelle was a guest on James Lipton's *Inside the Actor's Studio*. Near the end of the interview a young audience member asked him how he stays so down to earth. He replied:

> I'm famous today, people like me today, they might not like me tomorrow, you never know. You can't count on it, the world can't tell ya who you are. You just gotta figure out who you are, and be that for better or for worse.

This is no easy task—knowing and being; it takes courage and dedication and sacrifice. Here's what I mean by this.

Inscribed in the Temple of Apollo was the maxim "Know Thyself." This imperative demands that we stand and live according to our nature. And in order to figure out what our nature is, we must first look within. That's hard. What's more, knowing thyself is an ongoing process and contextual—we exist as individuals, within systems and relations, as part of a whole. So inevitably, looking within also means looking outside of ourselves—at the ways in which we're connected and distinct and evolving.

Oh yeah, and then there's still the whole living according to our nature thing. It's not enough to just know, we must be. Seriously? That takes stones, especially when you have to "be your be" in a public forum! For Socrates, this resulted in lovers and haters, in discomfort and delight. The same goes for Chapelle. Comedy, like philosophy, can be rousing. Some like what it awakens, others do not. Either way, the comedian has a tough job. As Chapelle says, "The hardest thing to do is to be true to yourself, especially when everybody is watching."

In a podcast called Wisdom at Work, philosopher David Storey and his guest Sal Giambanco talk more about this. For Giambanco, Socrates was missing something crucial to the philosophical life. He had the whole "knowing thyself" thing down but lacked in the "being thyself" department. This is where, according to him, Nietzsche had the upper hand. While I happen to disagree (I think Socrates held his own on both), the discussion between Giambanco and Storey is worth mentioning.

Nietzsche was very focused on emotions and the sticky mess of living. To some, his work was a reaction against Socrates for being too rational or too "cognitively oriented" and "not enough in touch with the body and the emotions and the wild and what cannot be fully grasped and framed" (Storey, Wisdom at Work podcast, May 2020). For Nietzsche, the heart (our passions) and being thyself was where it was at. And this, says Giambanco, is something entirely different from "knowing thyself."

> I think when we are really engaged in reflection we can figure out and know who we are. But we need courage to be who we are. And being who we are often separates us from the herd and the crowd. Which is truly what Nietzsche was talking about . . . he's encouraging us to be thyself . . . and with cost. He recognizes that when you're yourself you may make other people uncomfortable. And that may lead to rejection. Which means that you really have to have that inner work done. (Sal Giambanco in an interview on Wisdom at Work, 2020)

Giambanco's general point is a good one. There's a difference between talking game versus playing it, of knowing a thing versus living it. The irony here has to do with the comparison. In my opinion, Socrates is the one that had it going on, not Nietzsche. Alexander Nehamas speaks to this when he contrasts the ways in which each of them lived: Nietzsche practiced philosophy alone and withdrawn from the world, rarely leaving his desk; was perpetually sick and cold; regularly rejected by women; never fought in a war, and couldn't even stomach a beer. Socrates fought in at least three battles; was the embodiment of health and vigor; had three kids; could drink prodigiously without getting drunk; was devoted to his friends, and lived his philosophy by putting it to task in the streets, with people (*The Art of Living*, p. 153).

Ultimately, while I side with Nehamas's portrait of Socrates over Giambanco's, the podcast does a nice job at drawing out some distinctions between knowing and being. "Knowing thyself" and "being thyself" are indeed different things. For Socrates, they were inseparable. There was no one without the other. And the way in which he lived and ended his life revealed this; homeboy talked the talk (he knew his shit) and walked the walk (he put his money where his mouth was)! I don't know about you, but I can't think of anything more courageous than being willing to die for what you believe in and then actually doing so. This is part of what makes Socrates such an OG.

The same goes for Chapelle. His investment in knowing and being, and commitment to truth and authenticity are remarkable. These have propelled his work as an artist and have, like Socrates, put him in some precarious and revealing situations, from his controversial decision to walk away from a fifty-million-dollar contract, to his television special in response to the killing of George Floyd, to his benefit concert in Ohio for mass shooting victims. When asked by broadcaster Polo Sandoval what he hoped to achieve by throwing the concert, Chapelle said:

> CHAPELLE: I grew up in Washington, so that city always makes the news. Then I moved to New York . . . And Los Angeles, which can't stop talking about itself. And these people are often forgotten. You know what I mean? And then . . . something like this happens in your city and then you think of all the other times it happens . . . and it makes it all very real. You realize these aren't numbers, these are people's lives. And . . . it hurts. Like not even in a political way, but just in a human way . . .

> SANDOVAL: What do you hope, after everything is said and done tonight . . . whether it's politically or socially, what do you hope lasts after this?

> CHAPELLE: Man, politically I could care less at this point. I mean, it's ridiculous. But socially . . . I think that people do need to understand just the ethics of being a neighbor or being a friend. I think we just gotta be kind to each other, like deliberately and willfully kind, even when it's hard to do or if you're afraid to do it. Somebody gotta put their god damn dukes down so we can live better lives. So . . . that's what we hope we can start. (CNN Exclusive Interview, 2019)

Like Socrates, Chapelle talks the talk and walks the walk. His willingness to "put in the work" (intellectually and emotionally), to live his philosophy, and to throw his "god damn dukes down" for what he believes in is part of what makes him such an OG.

Crossing Lines

Being an artist is a tricky thing, especially when your medium is comedy. And even more so when your comedy is not afraid to cross the line. But where is this proverbial line really? Does comedy have one? Should it? In a 2019 interview at London's Royal Albert Hall (alongside John Stewart), host Christiane Amanpour talks with Chapelle and Stewart about this.

> AMANPOUR: It has been said by Steve Martin that "comedy is not always nice. It can be really mean. And it can push boundaries, to a place where some people are really offended." Is that because everyone's a snowflake? Or does comedy . . . should comedy have certain boundaries at all?

> STEWART: Well, I think they are somewhat separate comments. Comedy's boundaries should be excellence.

In other words, whether or not people are offended (and by what) is an entirely separate question from whether or not there are or should be boundaries to comedy. The first query is concerned with people's subjective experiences and comfort zones. And to this, there is no shortage of commentaries in literature and media. I am more intrigued by the question of comedy's boundaries. This is a much deeper question which, at its core, is about purpose and aim.

Answering this is complicated. First, comedy comes in many forms. The only obvious shared purpose or aim of all comedy is laughter. Second, if more than one form of comedy exists, each with its own aims, then more than one boundary exists. Boundaries—as parameters and rules—are relative to their ends. Third, excellence is tied up with purpose and aim in the same way that boundaries are. One could easily be an excellent prop comedian but a horrible satirist in the same way that one could be an excellent trumpet player but a horrible pianist. Excellence depends upon what it is being applied to.

So, what might this mean in terms of Stewart's comment? Like Chapelle, Stewart engages in "laughter and tears" comedy, which has the aim of helping us become better people. As a vehicle for education and moral development, its boundaries and sense of excellence have to do with the single-pointed focus of truth. Such practitioners structure their comedy in a way that leads people to these kinds of examinations and discoveries. That seems "easy" enough. But here's where it gets sticky. If the boundaries of comedy are excellence as "the quest for truth" then all bets are off in terms of content and style so long as whatever is being explored is being done in a way that does not impede our moral growth or manipulate and obstruct the truth. It is here that shit gets kicked around, that lines and boundaries blur and begin to lose significance.

> STEWART: I think people are defining those lines (left, right, red, blue, boundaries) as if they're not supposed to be blurred. But if you don't define those lines, then he's not blurring them.
>
> AMANPOUR: But . . . those lines can be defined by another . . . and, in fact, they are. . . .
>
> CHAPELLE: The lines don't . . . [pregnant pause] . . . in a life well lived, I think these lines will mean less and less.

Here, the point is that while lines and boundaries exist—be those self-defined or impressed upon us in some other way—if truth is what we're really after, then many of those are going to fall away. "Sometimes," says Chapelle, "what's going on in the immediate present, is not as important as the long term. The truth is permanent, and then everything else will fall by the wayside" (interview with James Lipton for *Inside the Actor's Studio,* 2006). In the process, discomfort may (and likely will) occur. But few transformative experiences happen without this.

More intriguingly, that "excellence" and fading lines are referred to in the context of "a life well-lived" is captivating. There is something profoundly philosophical going on in Chapelle's work. Some of this has to do with what this qualifying statement intimates. A "life well-lived" implies that certain things must be present in order for good living to occur. For Chapelle, like Socrates, the pursuit of truth is an important component. But the profundity of this claim also has to do with something much subtler. How is just as important as what and why. Part of what makes Chapelle such an OG is the masterful way in which he threads the needle between his particular craft's aims (education and moral development) and its boundaries (truth). As a result, his art aligns itself with "the beautiful."

Looking at music can be a helpful way to make sense of this. "Even if you look . . . in the early days of jazz," says Chappelle "the bandstand was integrated decades before the country was."

> Art is such a beautiful thing to look at that one can forget such lines that one should not transgress socially. In the pursuit of art, if someone's good at something, you want to be with that person. No matter what color, race, gender. If they got the gift, they got the gift. Art transcends everything. (Interview with Amanpour, 2019)

The power and magnetism of this bandstand scene is more than just the notes being played. It's the irrelevant lines of race and creed being crossed and cast off in pursuit of art. It's the integration of parts into a unified whole, and the expression of human excellence and beauty. Chappelle's comedic pursuits and cratsmanship can be viewed similarly.

Making Love with the Form

During his acceptance speech for the Mark Twain Prize in 2019, Chapelle said:

> There is something so true about this genre when done correctly, that I will fight anybody that gets in a true practitioner of this art form's way. 'Cuz I know you're wrong. This is the truth and you are obstructing it. I'm not talking about the content. I'm talking about the art form. Do you understand? Do we have an agreement? (*Mark Twain Prize*)

Chapelle's request for understanding this deeper sort of relationship is said in earnest. But what does it mean and look like for a true practitioner of art to participate with a form? Plato's *Symposium* might help us understand Chapelle's point. In this dialogue, a group of friends come together to discuss the nature of love. Several conceptions are offered, culminating in a definition of love that links beauty to "the good," which for Plato has to do with living a life of reason. Eventually, an explicit connection between love, beauty, and wisdom emerges—with the desire for (and love of) wisdom equating to beauty (which by virtue of being beautiful is something that we are drawn to) and reasoning being a form of Love. This is a lot to unpack and, perhaps, not immediately clear as to how it relates to Chapelle's love for the art form of comedy and his defense of its "true practitioners." But at least two interesting parallels exist.

The first has to do with the experience of beauty. A beautiful piece of music can transport you. A beautiful painting can make you cry. A beautiful story can help you see the world in new ways. Beauty is beauty. It's transformative and magnetic. We all want to be around it, in whatever form it takes. This experience is illustrated in the *Symposium* through the arguments of Socrates. Some people are "pregnant in body," he says, while others "are pregnant in soul" (*Symposium*, 209a). The offspring of the latter is "wisdom and the rest of virtue" or, for simplicity sake, ideas. He then describes how such a soul pregnancy and birth might track with the more typical trajectory of physical love, noting that people are wired to procreate (be it ideas, persons, or in some other way) and naturally go about seeking beauty. If someone "has the luck to find a soul that is beautiful and noble and well-formed," he says, "he is even more drawn to this combination" because such a soul "makes him instantly teem with ideas and arguments and virtue" and give "birth to what he has been carrying inside him for ages" (*Symposium*, 209b–d).

Chapelle's comment about jazz mirrors this: "In the pursuit of art, if someone's good at something, you want to be with that person . . . If they got the gift, they got the gift." Well, Chapelle has the gift. His craftsmanship is superb. You can't help but be drawn to it, respond to it, and engage with it, in much the same way as lovers are drawn to their desires. The soul children produced by his comedy are laughter and thought.

The second parallel concerns the transcendence of beauty. In her book *Nine Gates: Entering the Mind of Poetry*, Jane Hirshfield writes of art being a path not just to beauty, but to truth (*1997*). Chapelle echoes this sentiment when he says: "There's something divine about artistry" . . . "it's like the god-like part of a person that can write a song or tell a good joke, it's the best part of our nature" where you can "touch a higher part of yourself" and "connect with people on a more profound level" (Interview with Lauren Poteat for New York Amsterdam News, 10/22/19). Here, in this process is where art transcends. Think about the integrated bandstands again. Jazz artists weren't just playing music, they were participating in something greater than themselves, in the same way that lovers do. Chapelle's comedy does the same thing. Be it jazz, philosophy, or comedy, any activity aimed at truth and beauty is always an act of making love. Some make love so well that you can't help but come back for more.

Whole-Assin' It

Excelling in comedy requires certain habits of body and mind. On the short list are courage, resolve, sincerity, epistemic humility, and vulnerability—all of which are wrapped up in Chapelle's unique and robust brand of authenticity. The idea of authenticity first got some wings in the Western world around the seventeenth and eighteenth centuries. It remains a nebulous concept and a ubiquitous ideal that impacts socio-political thinking. In its fledgling years, it was an attribute valued as a means to an end. Later, it took on a different flavor and became a thing worth pursuing for its own sake. A person was considered authentic (real, sincere, true to oneself) if they were unique and distinctive, even if doing so clashed with social norms. This is similar to how we use authenticity in everyday language—as originality.

In his *Mark Twain Prize* show, Chapelle gives a shout-out to his comedian friend Tony Woods, citing Miles Davis in the process: "Miles Davis said so much cool shit. But one of the things he said that I always loved . . . it took me years to learn how to play like myself." Tony was to Chapelle what Dizzy and Bird were to Miles—an inspiration. And for years, Chapelle was trying to play (perform) like him. Eventually, he found the rhythm to play like himself. This sentiment and metamorphosis capture an important feature of originality as authenticity, not to mention the "O" of OG. While we are all inspired in some important sense by the notes and beats of others, becoming an authentic self means finding your own rhythm and flow.

This "becoming" is not something that happens instantaneously, but over time and through great amounts of effort. Søren Kierkegaard offers insight here when he says, "The self is a relation that relates itself to itself . . ." (Kierkegaard, *Sickness unto Death*) and an unfolding project defined by concrete expressions over time. "Becoming what one is" is not a matter of simple introspection but a matter of passionate commitment to a relation to something outside of oneself. It is through this commitment that our existence is given meaning. This resonates with me. It is both forgiving and unforgiving; an invitation and a challenge; an individuation of self and integration of self with the whole; and something which requires that you bring your whole self to the game—warts, smiles, hairs, tears, scars, fears, and all. There is no room for half-assin' it. Authenticity is a "whole-assin' it" gig and not for the faint of heart.

This is how I see Chapelle—as a "whole-asser," in the Kierkegaardian sense, who actively and publicly lets it all hang out on stage as an extension and concrete expression of his life. This can be unnerving. Comedy is the kind of gig "that'll show you where you're at," says Chapelle. And when aimed at the "beautiful" it can show society where it's at by helping to reveal the gap between who we are and where we aspire to be. This is comedy as a mirror and moral corrective in a nutshell. At times, the reflection might be painful and hard to look at. How we respond to the reflection is up to us. Either way, the artist must be willing to bare it all. "All art is a kind of confession, more or less oblique. All artists, if they are to survive, are forced, at last, to tell the whole story; to vomit the anguish up" (James Baldwin's Interview with Studs Terkel, Studs Terkel Radio Archive, 1961).

Monk and Miles

Musicians and comedians have a lot in common. Both require impeccable timing and a good ear. In his 2005 documentary *Block Party*, Chappelle played Thelonius Monk's famous song "'Round Midnight." He is "one of my favorite musicians," he tells the crowd, "because his timing was so ill. Every comedian is a stickler for timing, and Thelonious Monk was off-time yet perfectly on time. You should study it if you're an aspiring comedian." This idea of being "off-time yet perfectly on-time" is mesmerizing, in large part because it involves an ability to hold two opposing things (off-time and on-time) together at once. Anyone who has ever experienced both (simultaneously) the sorrow of losing a loved one who has been ill and the joy of knowing that they are no longer suffering can relate with this. Life is both of these. Whether music or comedy, art that honors these rich and complex dichotomies in harmonious ways is powerful.

Being able to pull something like this off requires having a good ear. Miles Davis is a prime example, and like Monk, another favorite of Chapelle's. His autobiography opens with a single word—"Listen." This was central to his artistry. By deeply attending to his surroundings and being fully present he was able to "see" the notes and the spaces in between. This ability to be both in the moment and above the moment at the same time is rare. But it's also what contributed to Miles's gift of knowing what notes needed to be "left out" (*Miles Beyond*, 2001). The importance of this cannot be understated. So much of life happens in the grey—in those pregnant pauses in between. Miles was a musical genius because he held this space so masterfully.

Chapelle's comedic artistry takes on a similar "Monk-and-Miles" vibe, adding another complexity of hue to his OG ranking and the unique way that he "shows up" in the world. Sure, many of his pieces—like the brilliant and disturbingly hilarious Clayton Bigsby or Cyrus Holloway Bathroom skits—are about as "in your face" as you can get; they're comedic concerts full of notes on blast. But there is a subtler side to Chapelle's work that, like Monk and Miles, is both "off-time yet perfectly on-time," that leaves space for the grey, and allows room for its message to percolate and take hold. "The Racial Draft" skit is a great example.

In this sketch, Chapelle, Bill Burr, and Robert Petkoff play commentators for a draft where sports and entertainment figures are claimed by representatives from various races—Blacks, Jews, Asians, Whites, and Latinos—as "one of their own." The skit is riddled with moments of layered hilarity that purposefully play on and with racial stereotypes, beginning with the commentators opening back and forth about the Black Delegation drawing the first pick.

> **Bill:** Believe it or not, the Blacks have actually won the first pick.
>
> **Chapelle:** Wow! That's the first lottery the Blacks have won in a long time, Billy.
>
> **Bill:** Yes, and they'll probably still complain. [*Commentator laughter*].
>
> **Chappelle:** [*under his breath, laughing, smiling*] Man . . . fuck you!

Then the camera pans to the podium where Rondell, the talking head for the Black Delegation played by Mos Def, selects Tiger Woods. The Black spectators go wild. One person breaks into the Robot, another busts out some kind of move that resembles the Cabbage Patch, and the Asian spectators stand by in quiet disappointment. "Wow! The Asians have got to be upset!" says Robert. "There's no doubt about that, Robert!" says Chapelle. "But you gotta think about it. He's been discriminated against in his time. He's had death threats. And he dates a white woman. Sounds like a Back guy to me!" [*Track laughter*].

The skit continues in this same vein with few races or stereotypes spared. Everyone has their time on the chopping block. Because of this it might seem as if nothing has been left out, that the extremes and opposing views about others take up the whole bandwidth. But not so. Too many, too nonsensical, or too one-sided of notes would have left the skit impotent, imbalanced, and rhythmically out-of-whack. Too loud or poorly timed, would have silenced the subtler undercurrents in play—the selection by the Asian Delegation of the entire Wu-Tang Clan; the hand-wiping by Rondell post-agreement with the White Delegation rep; the finger dap by the two white commentators in celebration of OJ going back to Black; the loss of endorsements once Tiger became one hundred percent Black; the Condoleezza Rice give back to the White Delegation; and, my personal favorite, the Black Delegation's request for Eminem.

But there's more to the "Racial Draft" skit than just its technical beauty. There is a lesson and an invitation for growth. As a mirror, the skit reveals the ridiculous absurdity and pervasiveness of racism and shows us that even if social progress has been made . . . this is where we are, still. As a moral corrective, it pokes holes in the ideas (or categories) of "race" and "class," encourages us to think about our preconceptions and justifications, and invites us to grapple with the various ways in which racism manifests, which need not be loud to exist or be felt.

Chapelle's "Monk-and-Miles"–like dexterity paves the way for its edifying force by helping us tune into the fact that "the background noise" and "subtler forms" of racism are just as relevant and toxic as its "more overt policies and practices" (Camille T. Dungy in an interview with Airica Parker, "Poetic Justice," *The Sun*, 2018). What's more, he manages to do so in a way that helps us see a way out. Embedded in its playful and serious critique of humanity, there is direction on what is needed to grow. First, we must tune in and listen. We must see racism for the absurd, harmful, and egregious cancer that it is—not only (though unequivocally) for those who are its targets, but for all who participate in it. If we care about surviving, flourishing, and living a good life, the skit implores, then we—as a people—must fully own this. Then we must make a change. It's as black-white (and grey) and simple (and complex) as that.

Medicinal Art

"The true and lasting genius of humor," said Mark Twain, "must be antiseptic." There are countless artists who've approached comedy in this way and a handful who have done it exceptionally well. Here comedy is about more than just laughter. It's about comedy as therapeutic, as something that can help us grow and prosper. Comedians of this sort have a tough job. The best of them resemble the best of teachers—educating not by telling us what to think but by showing us different ways to look at things and inviting us to think.

Chapelle stands out as an exemplar. His ability to inhabit the space between laughter and tears, to make that space visible and accessible, and to do so in ways that encourage and invite us to be active members of the symposium is extraordinary.

Each dose of his comedy contains the brushstrokes of philosophy and the signature of an OG. It may not always go down so easily. And it may not always feel like medicine. But, its aim and execution is beautiful. And, if we're up for the challenge, it will transform us.[1]

---

[1] Thank you to Mark Ralkowski for your encouragement, guidance, good spirit, and keen philosophical eye. Thank you also to David Nowakowski and Barry Ferst for your thoughtful perspectives and critiques, to my late father Lee B. Waian (my own and favorite Original Gangsta), and to J. Angelo Corlett who (whether you know it or not) planted the seeds for thinking about Chapelle as an OG back in the day.

24

How Dave Chappelle Uses Absurdity to Make Us Think

ALEX R GILLHAM

I'm embarrassed to say that it took me a PhD in philosophy to get the joke. I was a teenager the first time I watched *Chappelle's Show*. I remember thinking the Clayton Bigsby skit was hilarious. Years later, when I first saw the call for papers inviting the submission of possible chapters for this book. I thought, "I like Chappelle and I'm a professional philosopher. I should do this." So I started watching *Chappelle's Show* again.

I still found the Clayton Bigsby sketch hilarious, but it was funny this time for different reasons. I tried to remember why I found it so funny when I watched it the first time. I can't remember exactly, but I think that I just found the mere thought of a blind and Black man being a white supremacist utterly ridiculous. The sheer unlikelihood of there ever being such a person made me laugh. Fifteen years later, this was not what caused me to laugh. The sketch was funny this time because it captured the very absurdity of racism. Now Clayton Bigsby makes me laugh because his character shows just how utterly nonsensical white supremacy is.

Defeating Clayton Bigsby

Why did I find the sketch funny for one reason fifteen years ago but for very different reasons a few months ago? I chalk the difference up to spending the last ten years or so becoming a professional philosopher. The sketch is funny for different reasons now because I know a lot more philosophy.

Philosophers want to know stuff. To know stuff, we must have true and justified beliefs. If I want to know that it's raining, for example, I must satisfy three conditions. First, I must believe that it's raining. Second, it must be true that it's raining. Third, I must be justified in believing that it's raining. Per this last condition, having a justified belief requires me to have evidence of a certain kind and strength. Philosophers disagree widely about what sort of evidence I require for my belief to be justified and how much of it I need, but there is general agreement that the belief must go undefeated. The belief only goes undefeated if there is not some evidence easily discoverable that would make me believe otherwise. For example, if I were to walk outside right now and see that it's not in fact raining, then my belief that it's raining would be defeated. This business about justified belief and defeaters isn't just philosophical grandstanding; it explains my change of heart about why Clayton Bigsby is so funny as a character: I laugh at him now because he so strongly and absurdly holds a belief that cannot be justified because it could be so easily defeated. Clayton Bigsby adamantly believes that it's raining, although he wouldn't if he just went outside and checked.

If you're reading this book, you're probably familiar with the Clayton Bigsby sketch. In it Chappelle plays a blind white supremacist who is Black but does not know this. Bisgby believes that white people are superior to Black people. How could Bigsby justifiably hold this belief given how easily it could be defeated? After all, if Bigsby were not blind, he would know that he is Black, and if he knew this he probably wouldn't think that Black people are inferior to white people. Chappelle complicates this later in the sketch. Bigsby does find out that he's Black and not white. We would expect Bigsby to abandon his white supremacy at this point, but he doesn't. He keeps believing that Black people are inferior to whites and therefore decides to divorce his wife. His wife married a Black man, which is incompatible with his own white supremacy; generally white supremacists do not support whites marrying nonwhites.

All of this is absurd and funny, but the sketch drives at two underlying philosophical points about belief and justification. First, white supremacists are often resistant to evidence that would defeat their beliefs to the point of irrationality. Bigsby exemplifies this, which makes the sketch funny. In revealing the absurdity of Bigsby's decision not to change his mind, the sketch encourages us not to be like Bigsby. This nudges us to aim for justified beliefs, which requires being responsive to the evidence and correcting our judgments when they are defeated. Second, the sketch points to how absurd white supremacy is in the first place. The beliefs of white supremacists like Bigsby are always on the verge of being defeated because there is such poor evidence supporting them in the first place.

Suppose we were all blind like Bigsby. Would anyone be a white supremacist? Probably not. We couldn't see anything, so we probably wouldn't even know if we were white or not. My point is that it's bad epistemic practice to maintain belief that can be so easily defeated, and believing that whites are superior to nonwhites is such a belief. The belief can be easily defeated because if there were a slight difference in everyone's circumstances, as there would be if everyone were blind, then no one would hold it. The upshot of the last three paragraphs is this: I never would have understood what I take to be these deeper points of the Bigsby sketch without knowing some basic epistemology. In other words, embarrassingly enough, it took me ten years getting a PhD in philosophy to understand one layer of one joke from the first episode of *Chappelle's Show*.

The Absurdity of Denying White Privilege

In other words, knowing philosophy helped me understand some of what Chappelle is up to in his work. Knowing some philosophy could provide a similar benefit to others. This occurred to me when I recently revisited his 2000 special *Killin' Them Softly:* familiarity with the basics of mapping arguments goes a long way towards understanding one of what I take to be Chappelle's theses from the special, namely that white privilege exists. As with the Clayton Bigsby Sketch, I was a teenager when I first watched *Killin' Them Softly*. Again: I thought it was hilarious. But when I recently watched it, it was funny for very different reasons. I paid close attention to the structure of the argument that Chappelle seemed to be making. Chappelle was using a style of argument commonly used by philosophers to reveal the absurdity of denying that white privilege exists.

Philosophy is fundamentally about arguments. Philosophers want to prove a point by arguing for it, which requires them to provide claims supporting their point. Arguments come in many forms. One popular form is the reductio ad absurdum, which is Latin for reduction to absurdity. The point of a reductio is to show that a claim is false by revealing that something absurd follows from it. Put otherwise, a reductio pushes us to reject a claim because it has ridiculous consequences. Suppose I wanted to prove to you that my car is in the driveway. I could accomplish this by getting you to realize that the denial of this claim must be false. This is what I mean: suppose now it is false that my car is in the driveway. Now I ask you to get up and look out the window toward where my car would be if it were in the driveway. You see that it is there. If my car were not in the driveway, then you wouldn't see it when you look out the window. But you do see it when you look out the window, so my car must be in the driveway.

I have just run a reductio. I showed you that it would be absurd to deny that my car is in the driveway, which means you must accept that it is indeed there. I take Chappelle to be developing this style of argument in *Killin' Them Softly*. He pulls off the task of showing that white privilege exists, but he does it backwards. Suppose that white privilege does not exist. If white privilege does not exist, then people of color would be able to get away with everything that white people very often get away with. A major aim of the special is to show that this last clause is indeed false: that people of color would be able to get away with everything that white people often get away with. Logically this means it must be false that white privilege does not exist, and if it is false that white privilege does not exist, it is true that white privilege does exist.

Sometimes philosophers find it helpful to map out an argument by its premises to see how it attempts to prove its point. The argument I attribute to Chappelle above goes like this:

1. Suppose that white privilege does not exist.

2. If white privilege does not exist, then people of color would be able to get away with everything that white people often get away with.

3. But people of color are not able to get away with everything that white people often get away with.

4. So white privilege does exist.

Premise 1 is what the argument aims to reveal as absurd. If the reductio is successful, then we will have reasons to reject Premise 1, and once we do, we must believe its opposite: that white privilege does exist. Premise 2 offers a definition of white privilege. It claims that white privilege exists if white people can do things unscathed that people of color cannot. Academics disagree widely about what white privilege is, but Premise 2 offers a very intuitive definition: group g enjoys a privilege that group f does not if g can do something that f *cannot*. Premise 3 is what Chappelle spends the majority of *Killin' Them Softly* trying to prove. A barrage of jokes gives us evidence to accept Premise 3, reasons to believe that people of color cannot get away with everything that white people often get away with.

If we accept Premises 1–3, we must accept Premise 4, since Premise 4 follows logically from Premise 3 due to the Law of

Contraposition. The Law of Contraposition tells us something important about conditionals. Conditionals are just if-then statements. Philosophers call the if-part of a conditional the antecedent and the then-part of a conditional the consequent.

Here is an example of a conditional: if it is raining, then there is at least one cloud in the sky. In this example, "it is raining" is the antecedent, and "there is at least one cloud in the sky" is the consequent. The Law of Contraposition tells us that if we have sufficient reasons to reject the consequent of a conditional, then we must also reject its antecedent. To return to the previous example, if we know that there is not at least one cloud in the sky, then we know that it is not raining. Premise 2 offers a conditional explaining when white privilege exists. Premise 3 denies the consequent of that conditional, and contraposition tells us that we must also deny its antecedent. This is precisely what Premise 4 does: it rejects the antecedent of Premise 2, which justifies denying the truth of Premise 1. Thus *Killin' Them Softly* reduces the denial of white privilege to absurdity.

Premise 3 is the most controversial move in the argument. I suspect this is why Chappelle spends so much time trying to prove it throughout the special. In order for Premise 3 to be true, there must be things that people of color can't get away with doing that white people can. Many of the jokes from *Killin' Them Softly* show that this is the case. One of the first jokes of the special notes that there are far more white people in Washington DC then there used to be. In the 1980s, Chappelle jokes, white people were looking at DC with binoculars through their windows from Virginia, noting that DC looks dangerous. "Not yet," they said about it being time to make the trip over. White people in Virginia enjoyed the privilege of avoiding the dangerous DC area, a privilege that many people of color in DC certainly did not enjoy.

This joke in turn sets up a larger theme of *Killin' Them Softly:* many people of color have to navigate obstacles that white people generally do not. Chappelle jokes that he can no longer scare white people, even though he has really tried. "Those days are over," the white person responds. Chappelle is driving at something deeper here: white people generally do not have to be afraid of the things that people of color generally fear. Chappelle's white friend Chip does not have to be afraid of the police. Chip can even get high in front of the police, touch them to get their attention, confess to them that he is high, and then ask them for directions. As Chappelle concludes, "A Black man would never dream of talking the police high. That's a waste of weed." Chappelle is afraid of just being sleepy around the police; they might get the wrong idea and think he's on PCP. He would not think of talking to them while high. Chip enjoys this privilege because he's white.

Chappelle goes on to tell a bunch of similar jokes. Chip can race while drunk, get pulled over for driving recklessly, blare "We're Not Gonna Take It" while pulled over, but then get off the hook by lying and claiming that he didn't know he couldn't do that. These anecdotes are probably not even true. Plus, Chappelle is not claiming that any white person is always guaranteed to get away with something that no person of color ever would. Nor is he claiming that people of color don't enjoy privileges that white people lack; he admits that in circles of friends, white guys must do more to earn the respect of Black guys.

Chappelle is making the general point that racial privileges exist. Generally people of color have less leeway with the police. Generally people of color deal with fears that white people don't. White people enjoy these privileges and people of color don't. Thus the consequent in Premise 2 is false, and white privilege exists. In this way, Chappelle reduces the denial of white privilege to absurdity by pointing out what most of us already know: generally people of color face certain disadvantages that white people do not. How could anyone realize this but then deny that white privilege exists? Chappelle's point, I think, is that no one reasonably could. To do so would be absurd.

As a teenager watching *Killin' Them Softly*, I didn't see the full picture of these jokes. What made me laugh was the ridiculousness of someone doing all of the things Chip does. Now I see that it's the very denial of white privilege that's ridiculous. As did the Clayton Bigsby sketch, *Killin' Them Softly* alongside some fundamentals of philosophy taught me a lot about race.

Has Chappelle Gone Too Far?

Given what Clayton Bigsby taught me about white supremacy and what *Killin' Them Softly* taught me about white privilege, I've had some trouble making sense of Chappelle's more recent work. On the one hand, I think we can learn a lot from Chappelle about certain social justice issues. His material went a long way toward enlightening me about racial inequality, leading me to realize the absurdity of white supremacy and reflect on how I benefit from white privilege. On the other hand, perhaps we ought to exercise caution before looking to Chappelle for guidance on other social justice issues.

Many jokes from his 2019 *Sticks and Stones* are about women, sexual assault victims, Asians, transgender individuals, and the LGBTQ+ community more generally. Some critics have claimed that the special was offensive and insensitive to a morally objectionable degree. I'm sensitive to these worries. If Chappelle's jokes are indeed offensive and insensitive to a morally objectionable degree, perhaps we shouldn't find them funny. Even stronger, if this is so, perhaps we ought to reconsider how we esteem Chappelle's corpus.

I think there is a way to interpret many of Chappelle's jokes from Sticks and Stones that makes him much less vulnerable to charges of offensiveness and insensitivity than we might think. Maybe there isn't this kind of interpretation for all the seemingly objectionable jokes; I've come up empty handed searching for redeeming features of his joke that he thinks Michael Jackson is innocent because if Chappelle himself were a pedophile then Macaulay Culkin would be the first kid he would target. My aim here isn't to defend Chappelle or *Sticks and Stones* from all the criticism he's recently received. It's simply to show that we might have missed the point of some of the jokes, and that if we really were to get them then we might realize that our criticisms missed the mark in the first place. In framing them, Chappelle wasn't coming in for cheap laughs. He was pushing us to address some questions that deserve our consideration.

Take for example Chappelle's first few bits of the special. It seems like he's suggesting that it didn't make sense for Anthony Bourdain to commit suicide, whereas it would make sense for his friend who lives with his mother and works at Foot Locker to commit suicide. Taken in isolation from one another, these jokes might appear objectionable. One suggests that someone was wrong to commit suicide; the other alleges that someone else was wrong not to have considered it. However, when we take them together and realize how Chappelle was making use of them alongside one another, they seem less offensive and insensitive, perhaps not at all. He concludes by sharing the insight that whether life is worth living isn't tightly correlated with how it seems to be going from the outside.

Chappelle wasn't endorsing the claim that Bourdain was wrong to commit suicide or that his friend was wrong not to commit suicide. Chappelle was using these claims to run a reductio against the principle that whether one should commit suicide depends on how well one's life seems to be going to others. If this principle were true, then Bourdain should not have committed suicide and Chappelle's friend should have. But it would be insensitive to make either judgment, so we must reject the principle entailing both. Chappelle was making a deeper point about our inner lives and what makes life worth living, not charging Bourdain with being unappreciative of his lifestyle or encouraging his friend to kill himself.

Chappelle does something similar later in the special. He defends Kevin Hart, who had been pressured to apologize for seemingly homophobic comments, by claiming that Hart was clearly joking. Then Chappelle explains that during the filming of *Chappelle's Show*, he was told by an executive that he couldn't say the f-word (f****t) in a sketch. Chappelle asked why he was allowed to say the n-word (n****r) but not the f-word on the network. The executive explained that this is because Chappelle is not gay. Chappelle responded that he's not an n-word either.

On reflection, Chappelle's point in defense of Kevin Hart was to bring some contradictions to our attention about the usage of slurs against different groups. His suggestion was that since he can use the n-word but not the f-word, there seems to be more tolerance for racism than homophobia, and he wanted us to wonder why this is so. Then he ran a reductio against one of the common explanations. Suppose you can only say a slur when it describes you. If this is so, then Chappelle cannot say the f-word. However, if this is the case, then neither can Chappelle say the n-word. But Chappelle can say the n-word, even though he is not what the n-word describes, so it cannot be the case that we can only say a slur when it describes us. Perhaps his aim was not to defend homophobia, but to expose an inconsistency in how we monitor slurs. If so, then the joke makes a worthwhile contribution to discourse about fairness in censorship.

Chappelle has a related aim in his discussion of LBTQ+ issues, especially when he explains his confusion about what it means to be transgender. What confuses him, and what he claims to find so funny, is how someone could have an identity that is different from what their body indicates. It would be hilarious, he says, if there were a Chinese man trapped in his body. But the real problem he points to is that this creates a conflict between our goals. He accomplishes this by running another reductio. Suppose that a man can be trapped in a woman's body or vice versa.

Chappelle wonders why it is so obvious that he should be comfortable with that, but he goes on to point out that if it is true, then our tolerance towards transgender individuals might conflict with our goal to promote fairness. If LeBron James were to change his gender, Chappelle jokes, then LeBron would score 840 points a game in the WNBA. Chappelle is pushing us to realize that there are sometimes conflicts among the beliefs that we are expected to adopt without hesitation, the ones that his detractors like Kang and Martin condemn him for criticizing. Maybe they are right about some of his bits. If my interpretation of the joke is correct, then Chappelle should have said that gender expression has confusing entailments, not that transgender individuals are confusing. And perhaps some of his jokes have no such charitable interpretation, such as the one about bisexuals being gross. In fact, maybe none of Chappelle's recent jokes admits of charitable interpretation and all of them are objectionable. Again: my aim is not to defend Chappelle. I just want to use the tools of phiosophy to understand him before I decide whether he has done something worthy of comdemnation.

Still, I suspect that Chappelle is up to something deeper in many of his jokes. He's pushing us to acknowledge the tensions among our beliefs, often by pointing out that if we accept them then we're committed to various absurdities. That's what's so funny about Chappelle's Jussie Smollett joke. How absurd would it be, after all, for Trump-loving Nigerians wearing MAGA hats and carrying rope around Chicago to commit a hate crime against a gay Black man walking to Subway in subfreezing weather around 2:00 A.M.?

VII

Standing
Back from the
Elephant

25

Dance Like Nobody's Watching

Mark Ralkowski

> I love Dave Chappelle unconditionally . . . I don't know of anybody who cares more deeply and anyone who gives less of a fuck. Dave is a touchstone because he is a seeker of knowledge. He's a man who seeks people and experience and knowledge, and he wants to touch it and feel it and be with it on the ground so that he can channel that through his art and redirect that back to you as something completely different and new.
>
> —Jon Stewart, *Mark Twain Prize*

Everybody loves Dave Chappelle. Even his harshest critics seem to look at him as the ally that they would love to have. He has been criticized by progressives for being out of touch with today's values, but he keeps winning Grammy and Emmy Awards, and in October 2019 he was given the prestigious Mark Twain Prize for American Humor at the John F. Kennedy Center for Performing Arts.

Years ago, Maya Angelou called him her "soulmate" (*Iconoclasts*, 2006). His friend Bradley Cooper said he felt lucky to be alive at a time when he could watch Chappelle "be a human and an artist," and Eddie Murphy called him "the voice of his generation, without question. Nobody even comes close to him" (*Mark Twain Prize*). After quitting *Chappelle's Show* and walking away from fifty million dollars in 2005, Chappelle left the business for twelve years. It was a hard time for him; he wondered whether he had made a mistake and destroyed his own career. "Have you ever worked all your life for something and have it not work out? That happened to me . . . It was hell . . . I watched the world go on without me" (*Mark Twain Prize*).

But since returning in 2016, Chappelle's popularity and cultural significance have grown. His current deal with Netflix pays him twenty million dollars for every special he releases, and on June 12th 2020 the world turned to Chappelle's *8:46* for emotional guidance in the wake of George Floyd's murder. "I was shocked that nobody ever talked about what it *feels like* to watch a man get murdered that way by a man in a police uniform" (*My Next Guest*, Season Three, Episode 3). Chappelle may not want to be a leader in this country, as he told David Letterman. But it is clear from his stature that people *see him as one*, whether he likes it or not. His ability to "remix cultural boundaries" and connect with people across lines of race, class, and politics makes him into a kind of "American folk hero" (*New York Times*, 4/19/17). This same quality seems to be the reason Lorne Michaels keeps asking Chappelle to host *Saturday Night Live* after our presidential elections. His monologue in 2016 was controversial, but others liked it for exactly that reason. And in 2020, as he looked back at his 2016 appearance on *Saturday Night Live*, he reminded his audience of the virtues of being a "humble winner" while he promoted a "kindness conspiracy" for Black Americans and told despairing white people that he understood their suffering. Everyone finds something to relate to in Dave Chappelle. Or, as Dame Dash of Roc-A-Fella Records once said, "I think he's good for the community and culture. He's the truth. He knows how to be political in a funny way" (*MTV News*, 6/1/2004).

The contributors to this book do not treat Dave Chappelle as "the truth," and do not always agree with each other on the pluses and minuses of Dave Chappelle, but many of us do believe that he's good for the community. This book looks at how the comedy of Dave Chappelle intersects with a wide variety of philosophical ideas. It does not present a philosophy of Dave Chappelle, as if there were a philosophical theory underlying all of his jokes. We respect his vision as an artist, and we use philosophy as a tool for helping the rest of us non-artists see things the way he does.

So, each of these chapters has looked closely at a sketch from *Chappelle's Show* or a bit from one of his comedy specials, and talked about the philosophical significance of Chappelle's ideas. Not all of these chapters present a flattering portrait of Chappelle or his comedy. Some authors challenge his jokes about the LGBTQ+ community; others discuss whether his comedy reinforces racial stereotypes, and a few authors comment on his jokes about the victims of sexual assault. There's an open debate about the ethics of Chappelle's comedy. It's one that he himself has entered with his reflections on the importance of absolute artistic freedom for comedians. His position makes him a hero to other comics and fans, and it seems insensitive or worse to others. You'll have noticed that this book has a range of diverse opinions.

Get Your Africa Tickets Ready, Baby!

One of the most remarkable things about Dave Chappelle is that he walked away from fifty million dollars at age thirty-one, and he did it to stay true to himself. At the time, everything was going well for him. He was "the biggest comedian in the world" (*MTV News*, 9/20/2004), and *Chappelle's Show* was wildly popular. As Dick Gregory said at the time, "when you mention his name among young folks, it's like mentioning Jesus in a Christian Church" (*Time*, 5/14/2005). He made appearances on *The Tonight Show with Jay Leno* and *The Daily Show with Jon Stewart*. Sketches from *Chappelle's Show* had become memes in American culture—to such an extent that Chappelle confronted a fan in Disney World for saying, "I'm Rick James, bitch" to him in front of his family—all before the era of Twitter, Facebook, YouTube, and Instagram. His most recent stand-up special at the time, *For What It's Worth*, was popular and well-reviewed for its insightful cultural critique. And just a few months after signing his contract with Comedy Central, he put together his *Block Party*, a "hip-hop and R&B Woodstock," which celebrated the music and culture of New York, featuring many of Chappelle's favorite artists. "All of my friends and heroes are going to be there," Mos Def said after being invited. The world of pop culture was revolving around Dave Chappelle; he was Comedy Central's fifty-million-dollar man; the third season of *Chappelle's Show* was eagerly anticipated—and he *walked away from it all*.

Chappelle says his breaking point on *Chappelle's Show* was a sketch called "The N****r Pixie" (Season Three, Episode 2). In the skit, he's dressed as a minstrel show performer, wearing blackface and white gloves, a red vest and a Pullman Porter hat. After filming it, he could no longer tell whether he was challenging or promoting racial stereotypes. "Hearing the wrong laugh while you're dressed that way—it makes you feel ashamed" (*My Next Guest*, Season Three, Episode 3). And thanks to the long and loud laughter of a white crew member on the set, he realized that he didn't really know *what* his audiences were laughing at in any of his sketches—how they were interpreting his jokes—and he felt overwhelmed by the social responsibility that critics and fans had placed on him to be a moral and intellectual leader. "As a matter of fact, that was the last thing I shot before I told myself I gotta take fucking time out after this. Because my head almost exploded."

Neal Brennan, the co-creator and co-writer of *Chappelle's Show*, says that in the middle of taping Season Three, Chappelle started to second-guess all of their sketches: "he was calling his own writing racist." It was an overwhelming situation for Chappelle to be in: he had lost confidence in his own judgment; he was uncomfortable with how big he had gotten, and he didn't trust anyone. "Everyone around me says, 'You're a genius! You're great! That's your voice!' But I'm not sure they're right" (*Time*, 5/14/2005). And so, he stopped showing up for work at *Chappelle's Show* in April of 2005, and he never returned.

Looking back at this time in Chappelle's life and career, Letterman said he admired what he saw in it. The more he thought about all of the factors, "the better this thing sounded to me, because what bigger, cool, badass thing to do than just say, 'Goodnight, everybody,' and then adios. How cool is that?" Chappelle's response to Letterman is telling. He didn't feel like a hero at the time. "Initially, it was terrible." Yes, things worked out for him in the long run: here he is today making more money than ever before. But at *that* time, he worried that he had become "a parable of what not to do" with your career (*My Next Guest*, Season Three, Episode 3). "It was cold out there," he says in *The Bird Revelation*. People were calling him "crazy"; rumors spread that he had been using drugs and that he was having a nervous breakdown. He told James Lipton in 2006 that he had learned all about "where art and corporate interests meet," and he had had his heart broken. "Get your Africa tickets ready, baby, because it's coming. You have no idea" (*Inside the Actors Studio*, 11/7/2006). When Chappelle quit his show in 2005, he immediately went to stay with a family friend in Durban, South Africa for a couple weeks. Away from home, he could avoid media scrutiny and find space to be anonymous and reflect. It wasn't an easy decision to live with then, but it was something he felt he had to do for himself. Fifteen years later, he sounds more confident than ever about the wisdom of moving on.

CHAPPELLE: I'm very happy that I did what I did, you know, in hindsight.

LETTERMAN: It was the biggest thing that has happened in your life so far, other than the birth of your kids.

CHAPPELLE: It was a very, very, very formative event, or sequence of events. It wasn't any one part of it. But if I had finished the show, feeling the way that I felt, I would never have been the same. (*My Next Guest*, Season 3, Episode 3)

"You don't have to be awake all the time," Chappelle told the students at the Duke Ellington School of the Arts, the high school he credits with making him "wildly prepared" for his professional life in television and comedy. "But three or four times in your life, just pay attention." This was Chappelle's advice to these aspiring artists as he donated one of his Emmys to the school and received a key to the city of Washington DC from Mayor Muriel Bowser in 2017. It also seems to be the wisdom he was acting on when he left *Chappelle's Show* in 2005. He took a look at his life, and at the impact his show was having on popular culture and public discourse, and he didn't like what he saw. Moving on wasn't just an option at that point. It was essential to him being true to himself. As Cornel West says in *Why We Laugh: Black Comedians on Black Comedy*, "I thought [Chappelle's walking away from fifty million dollars] was courageous . . . You got to be true to yourself . . . William Butler Yeats says what? 'It takes more courage to be true to yourself than it does for a soldier to fight on the battlefield.'"

Going Hard in the Paint

Chappelle told Charlie Rose in 2004 that the comedy he and Neal Brennan did on *Chappelle's Show* was more cultural than political. They wrote sketches about politics from time to time—a sketch called "Black Bush" (Season Two, Episode 13) was a fan favorite during the presidency of George W. Bush—but they were more interested in writing comedy about issues in pop culture. So much has changed since then, and some people have wondered whether Chappelle has failed to evolve with the times. Critics have called him transphobic and homophobic; they've said he is undermining the #MeToo movement; they have been critical of his jokes about the victims of sexual assault, and they've said he is insensitive to the suffering of the most marginalized Black people because he never includes Black women or Black trans people in his material, even when he addresses the issue of police brutality.

Some of these criticisms are nothing new to Chappelle. As he told the *New York Times* in 2004, "I'm not trying to push people's buttons. But at the same time when we're making this, I don't want to hold back. Our MO is to dance like nobody's watching." He said something similar to Letterman on *My Next*

Guest: "You know, Dave, I like to go hard in the paint." In the early days of his career, he always felt that his show could be cancelled at any time, so he decided to "err on the side of excess, and there are instances when you go too far. You're playing with powerful shit, doing jokes about racism and this ism and that ism. To me, I looked at it as an occupational hazard."

Chappelle never intends to offend people, and it pains him to learn that his jokes or specials have hurt people emotionally. But this will happen in comedy, because comedy reflects life, and Chappelle thinks it is not his job to protect people from hurtful ideas. "I feel like the attempts at these jokes—they're like Evel Knievel tricks. I *hope* to land them." He is an artist, not a schoolteacher, and "so much of the work of art is on the viewer to interpret. But in this time, we cut people's meat for them so much that we do too much of the audience's work." The job of the artist, Chappelle told students at The Duke Ellington School of the Arts, is to reveal people to themselves, not to tell them what to think or how to live (*Mark Twain Prize*).

Chappelle seems to treat jokes as if they were items in an implicit bias test: how we respond to them sheds light *on us*, not on him. It is on us to do the work of understanding why we laugh at some jokes and not others, why we find some humor offensive but look past other kinds. We need to "cut our own meat." Chappelle's progressive critics may not learn anything about *themselves* from this exercise (apart from how much they disagree with Chappelle on certain issues), but there is a lot to learn about *others* from the popularity of Chappelle's comedy. And if the last two elections tell us anything about Americans, it's that we have a lot to learn about each other.

Chappelle wants us to "go hard in the paint." This is a basketball metaphor. Chappelle is talking about a style of basketball that is physical and requires toughness. He says he wants Americans to be "soldiers" on the battlefield of ideas—people who are willing and able to say what we think and explain why—not "brittle spirits" who want to cancel everything we disagree with or feel offended by (*Mark Twain Prize*). He calls the comedy club sacred ground because it is one of the few spaces left in American life where people can say what they really think and laugh when they want to, without social pressure to conform to one way of thinking and feeling. It is a space of absolute freedom, and it is imperative that we maintain it, even at the cost of offending some people.

As Chappelle says in the *Mark Twain Prize* special, "there's something so true about this genre, when done correctly, that I will fight anybody that gets in the way of a true practitioner of this art form. Because I know you're wrong. This is the truth and you are obstructing it. I'm not talking about the content. I'm talking about the art form. Do you understand? Do we have an agreement?" Sometimes Chappelle gives what looks like a utilitarian defense of this position: our country will be better off if we can "let some air out of the ball" by laughing together over issues that we find troubling and challenging, and this will make us function more effectively as "countrymen." Other times he defends the freedom of comedy independent of these social benefits: we shouldn't *ever* obstruct the truth (*My Next Guest*).

Needless to say, many people disagree with Chappelle on these issues. They have argued that we do real harm to marginalized and powerless people when we laugh at them. Some critics may want to see Chappelle "cancelled" on social media, but others simply expect more from him because they think he knows better, or he should know better thanks to his own experiences with racism as a Black man. Regardless of which position you take in this debate, it's notable that Chappelle's comedy has been at the center of it throughout his career. He left *Chappelle's Show* in 2005 when similar debates started about his racially charged sketches. At the time, he did not know himself well enough to have confidence in his own judgment about what was and wasn't appropriate for his show. But now he is back in the game, and he is at least as bold as he was when he surprised us with *"Frontline: Clayton Bigsby,"* "When Keeping it Real Goes Wrong," "Charlie Murphy's True Hollywood Stories: Prince," and "The Racial Draft."

Some of the material in his new Netflix specials raises hard questions about the ethics of humor: is it ever wrong to laugh? Should some jokes be censored? Should some comedians be cancelled if they go too far? How should we respond to a comedian who tells offensive jokes? Should the comedy club be a safe space for *all* humor? Chappelle says "no" to all cancellation (*Mark Twain Prize*), and he invites us to "go hard in the paint" and avoid being "brittle spirits." This volume has given you several opportunities to "cut your own meat" and explore what *you* think.

A Kindness Conspiracy

On January 6th, American citizens stormed the Capitol . . . Watch the tapes. Watch that crowd that told Colin Kaepernick he can't kneel during a football game try to beat a police officer to death with an

American flag. Look at that shit . . . Who's the terrorist now that they're looking for? It's you, not me.

—DAVE CHAPPELLE, *Redemption Song*, 2/11/21

In one of Plato's dialogues, Socrates says that the "true craft of politics" is not about passing legislation or making arguments in the Assembly. It's about changing the way people think. He thought that if he could change the way his countrymen thought, he could change everything in his city. Something like this idea of politics seems to motivate Chappelle's critics. They appreciate the power of comedy to influence the way people think, and they worry that instead of using comedy to turn people toward justice, Chappelle has been using it to "punch down." They look at shows like *Sticks and Stones* and *The Bird Revelation* and they see missed opportunities. Chappelle could be so much more; they think he *used to be* so much more, but now he is just a relic, washed up and out of touch.

One wonders whether any of these folks have changed their minds since the murder of George Floyd and Chappelle's extraordinary cultural upswing as an important voice in the Black Lives Matter movement. In his *8:46*, Chappelle is careful to insist that it is not his role "to step in front of the streets" and serve as a leader in the movement.

> I want to shout out all of the young people who have had the courage to go out and do all of this amazing work, protesting. I am very proud of you. You kids are excellent drivers. I am comfortable in the backseat of the car. (*8:46*)

"I'm far from a leader," he said to David Letterman. "I'm having way more fun being whatever the fuck I am than being somebody that people would look to for moral or intellectual guidance" (*My Next Guest*, Season Three, Episode 3). But it's hard to deny that people turned to him for leadership when *8:46* was watched more than twenty million times over the weekend that it was first released on YouTube. It's even more difficult to deny it after watching his 2020 post-election *Saturday Night Live* monologue in which he did quite a lot of "punching up" at white Americans—for their refusal to wear masks during a pandemic, for their support of Donald Trump, and *for being more like Donald Trump* than most of them would care to admit, for their role in mass shootings, for their addiction to opioids and heroin, and for their entitlement attitudes (one of his neighbors in Ohio filed a noise complaint against him for putting on community-benefitting comedy shows in a cornfield, "in *a cornfield*!!!")—while also recommending a "kindness conspiracy" as an overdue corrective to the centuries of anti-Black racism in this country. These bits sound like examples of Socrates's "true politics."

When Chappelle visited his alma mater to donate his Emmy Award, he gave the students in the audience advice about being an artist, but he also told them not to be afraid and to be kind to one another. Kindness is important to him, and so is community. He talks about both a lot, especially when he is addressing young people. "I'm trying to tell you, community is everything, and fostering trust amongst each other—that's everything. Whatever you guys argue about the specifics, we gotta trust that there will be a livable level of decency" (*My Next Guest*, Season Three, Episode 3). In his 2020 post-election *Saturday Night Live* monologue, he offers "good whites" an opportunity to help with the cause of anti-racism. It is a way to be an ally that doesn't involve virtue signaling on social media or burdening Black friends or coworkers with conversations they would prefer not to have. All it asks of "good whites" is that they perform random acts of kindness for Black people who don't deserve it. "Do something nice for a Black person, just because they're Black. And you gotta make sure they don't deserve it. That's a very important part of it. They can't deserve it—the same way all them years they did terrible things to Black people just because they're Black and they didn't deserve it." This is a classic Dave Chappelle bit: it's funny, but it also makes us think. And in this case, it makes us think about American history, anti-Black racism, white privilege, white responsibility, anti-racism, and a lot more. This is the kind of humor that Chappelle's detractors have been waiting for!

Chappelle is clearly dunking on his critics here, these people he told "to shut the fuck up forever" after winning two more Emmy Awards in September 2020. "All these n***as trying to get everyone to sing these fucking songs. I know these songs. I was raised on these songs" (*8:46*). His great grandfather was born into slavery and went on to become a bishop and the president of Allen University. His mother helped design and then completed one of the first Black studies PhD programs in the country. She was also the first American to work for the government of the Democratic Republic of Congo, where she was promoted to the highest office open to a foreign citizen.

When Chappelle says we need to "cut our own meat," he's reminding us that he is an artist and that it is on us to think about the meaning of his art. He may sometimes write jokes that fit with our preconceptions of what is true and good, and he may create charged humor that punches up at the powerful and makes progressive audience members feel like he is speaking directly to them and serving their causes. But on other occasions, it's the progressive critics themselves who are his targets. A show like *Sticks and Stones* is not for them; *it is about them.* He wasn't just punching down at the LGBTQ+ community in *Sticks and Stones.* He was baiting cancel-culture liberals, knowing how they would overreact and demonstrate their own *illiberal* intolerance. As President Obama said, "this idea of purity and you're never compromised and you're always politically 'woke' and all that stuff, you should get over that quickly. The world is messy; there are ambiguities." Chappelle's alternative to the excesses of cancel culture is to leave room for honesty and forgiveness. "This tightrope walk just makes everybody not want to get caught" (*My Next Guest*, Season Three, Episode 3).

Chappelle says he's not making any predictions about this country's future. He says he's hopeful that there will be real change, but he also reminds us that any change will be "uncomfortable before it is comfortable again. It will be quite the negotiation." Some people may be irredeemable—"How the fuck do you negotiate with Derek Chauvin?"—but Chappelle encourages the rest of us to keep "storming the streets" for justice, because "if the people that execute your laws are kneeling on people's necks, you have no country. You have to stop that shit." Even if there is no hope for the Derek Chauvins of the world, we can build our own communities and work on ourselves. "All politics are local, community is everything" (*My Next Guest*, Season Three, Episode 3). And we must work on unlearning our hatreds for one another. "That's what I fight through. That's what I suggest you fight through. You gotta find a way to live your life. You gotta find a way to forgive each other. You gotta find a way to find joy in your existence in spite of that feeling" (*Saturday Night Live*, 2020).

In the end, where does Dave Chappelle leave us? It's not easy to answer this question. The authors who have contributed to this book would each have very different things to say. But in a few words, Chappelle leaves us with hope for a kindness conspiracy, sound advice to get our Africa tickets ready, tough love for white America, and courage to dance like nobody's watching.[1]

---

[1] I would like to thank Lizzie Capeda and Michelle Vassilev for help with copy-editing this book.

Bibliography

Anderson, Luvell, and Ernie Lepore. 2013 [2011]. Slurring Words. *Noûs* 47:1.

Anzaldúa, Gloria. 1987. *Borderlands / La Frontera: The New Mestiza*. San Francisco: Aunt Lute.

Arendt, Hannah. 1963. *On Revolution*. New York: Viking.

Aristotle. 2014. *Nicomachean Ethics*. Indianapolis: Hackett.

Assunção, Muri. 2019. Transgender Actress, Activist and Comedienne Daphne Dorman, Referenced in Dave Chappelle's 'Transphobic' Netflix Special, Commits Suicide. *New York Daily News* (October 12th).

Augustine. 2009. *Confessions*. New York: Oxford University Press.

Bakhtin, Mikhail. 1984. *Rabelais and His World*. Bloomington: Indiana University Press.

Baldwin, James. 1965. The White Man's Guilt. *Ebony* (August).

———. 1992. *The Fire Next Time*. New York: Vintage.

Bergin, Lisa. 2009. Latina Feminist Metaphysics and Genetically Engineered Foods. *Journal of Agricultural and Environmental Ethics* 22:3.

Berman, Judy. 2018. 'Nanette' Is the Most Discussed Comedy Special in Ages: Here's What to Read about It. *New York Times* (July 13th).

Bigler, Rebecca, et al. 2007. Developmental Intergroup Theory. *Current Directions in Psychological Science* (June).

Bilsker, Richard. 2002. *On Jung*. Belmont: Wadsworth.

———. 2002. *On Bergson*. Belmont: Wadsworth.

Block, Walter E., and Roy Whitehead. 2019. Resolving the Abortion Controversy. In Block, Walter E., and Roy Whitehead, eds., *Philosophy of Law: The Supreme Court's Need for Libertarian Law*. Palgrave Macmillan.

Boxsel, Matthijs van. 2003. *The Encyclopedia of Stupidity*. London: Reaktion.

Campbell, James. 1982. Du Bois and James. *Transactions of the Charles Sanders Peirce Society* 28:3.

Carnes, Jim. 2004. Dave Chappelle Lets Rude Crowd Have It, Sticks Up for Cosby's Comment. *Sacramento Bee* (June 18th).

Carroll, Noël. 2001. *Horror and Humor.* New York: Cambridge University Press.

———. 2014. *Humour: A Very Short Introduction.* Oxford: Oxford University Press.

Chappelle, Dave. 2000. *Killin' Them Softly.* HBO.

———. 2004. *For What It's Worth.* Showtime.

———. 2017. *The Age of Spin. Dave Chappelle Live at the Hollywood Palladium.* Netflix.

———. 2017. *Deep in the Heart of Texas.* Netflix.

———. 2017. *The Bird Revelation.* Netflix.

———. 2017. *Equanimity.* Netflix.

———. 2019. *Sticks and Stones.* Netflix.

———. 2020. *The Kennedy Center Mark Twain Prize for American Humor.* Netflix.

———. 2020. *8:46.* YouTube.

———. 2021. *Redemption Song.* Instagran.

Cohen, Ted. 1999. *Jokes: Philosophical Thoughts on Joking Matters.* Chicago: University of Chicago Press.

———. 2018. *Serious Larks: The Philosophy of Ted Cohen.* Chicago: University of Chicago Press.

Conley, Dalton. 2005. A Man's Right to Choose. *New York Times* (December 1st).

Coser, Lewis A. 1977. *Masters of Sociological Thought: Ideas in Historical and Social Context.* Second edition. Long Grove: Waveland.

Critchley, Simon. 2002. *On Humour.* New York: Routledge.

Deggans, Eric. 2019. Barbershop: Dave Chappelle's Controversial New Special. NPR (August 31st).

Descartes, René. 1989. *The Passions of the Soul.* Hackett.

Du Bois, W.E.B. 1923. Opinion. *The Crisis* (June).

———. 1926. *Criteria of Negro Art. The Crisis* (October).

———. 1998 [1935]. The Propaganda of History. In *Black Reconstruction in America 1860–1880.* Free Press.

———. 1990. *The Souls of Black Folks.* New York: Vintage.

———. 2013 [1935]. *Black Reconstruction in America: Toward a History of the Part which Black Folk Played in the Attempt to Reconstruct Democracy in America, 1860–1880.* New Brunswick: Transaction.

Dussel, Enrique. 1985. *Philosophy of Liberation.* Eugene: Wipf and Stock.

Ellison, Ralph. 1952. *Invisible Man.* Random House.

Farley, Christopher John. 2005. Dave Speaks. *Time* (May 14th).

Feldman, Susan. 1992. Multiple Biological Mothers: The Case for Gestation. *Journal of Social Philosophy* 23:1.

Feinberg, Joel. 1989. *Harm to Self: The Moral Limits of the Criminal Law*. New York: Oxford University Press.

Festinger, Leon. 1956. *When Prophecy Fails: A Social and Psychological Study of a Modern Group that Predicted the Destruction of the World*. New York: Harper.

———. 1957. *A Theory of Cognitive Dissonance*. Stanford: Stanford University Press.

———. 1962. Cognitive Dissonance. *Scientific American*. 207:4.

Foster, Tyler. 2018. I Wrote Dave Chappelle a Letter About His Terrible Transgender Jokes. Sadly, He Didn't Really Listen. *Medium* (January 2nd).

Freud, Sigmund. 1960 [1900]. *The Interpretation of Dreams*. New York: Basic Books.

———. 1961 Humour [1927]. In *The Future of an Illusion, Civilization and Its Discontents and Other Works*. London: Hogarth.

———. 1990. *Complete Works: Standard Edition*. New York: Norton.

Gadsby, Hannah. 2018. *Nanette*. Netflix.

Gane-McCalla, Casey. 2020. Jessica Krug, the Fake Black Professor, Once Questioned My Blackness. *Countere* (September 5th).

Garcia, Mayte. 2017. *The Most Beautiful: My Life with Prince*. New York: Hachette.

Ghansah, Rachel Kaadzi. 2013. If He Hollers, Let Him Go. *The Believer* (October).

Gilman, Sander. 1993. *Freud, Race, and Gender*. Princeton: Princeton University Press.

Gillotta, David. 2019. Reckless Talk: Exploration and Contradiction in Dave Chappelle's Recent Stand-Up Comedy. *Studies in Popular Culture* 42:1 (Fall).

Giorgis, Hannah. 2019. The Fear in Dave Chappelle's New Special. *Atlantic* (August 28th).

Glaude, Eddie, Jr. 2020. The History that James Baldwin Wanted America to See. *New Yorker* (June 19th).

Goffman, Erving. 1959. *The Presentation of Self in Everyday Life*. Garden City: Anchor.

Greene, Mark Anthony. 2014. Dave Chappelle Is Back (This Time We're 100% Sure It's Maybe Totally for Real. *GQ* (November 13th).

Haggins, Bambi. 2007. *Laughing Mad*. New Brunswick: Rutgers University Press.

Haidt, Jonathan. 2013 (2012). *The Righteous Mind: Why Good People Are Divided by Politics and Religion*. New York: Vintage.

Harwood, Erika. 2017. Dave Chappelle Apologizes for Saying 'Give Trump a Chance'. *Vanity Fair* (May 16th).

Heller, Agnes. 2005. *Immortal Comedy: The Comic Phenomenon in Art, Literature, and Life*. Lanham: Lexington.

Herbert, Cassie. 2015. Precarious Projects: The Performative Structure of Reclamation. *Language Science* 52 (November).

Herman, Alison. 2019. Dave Chappelle's Provocations Have Turned Predictable. *The Ringer* (August 29th).

Herrick, Paul. 2015. *Think with Socrates: An Introduction to Critical Thinking*. Oxford: Oxford University Press.

Hirshfield, Jane. 1997. *Nine Gates: Entering the Mind of Poetry*. Harper.

Hobbes, Thomas. 1994. *Leviathan*. Hackett.

Hosking, Taylor. 2019. You Can Definitely Skip Dave Chappelle's New Netflix Special 'Sticks & Stones'. *Vice* (August 26th).

Hurston, Zora Neale. 1928. How It Feels to Be Colored Me. *The World Tomorrow* 11 (May).

Iconoclasts. 2006. *Dave Chappelle and Maya Angelou*. Season Two, Episode 6.

James, William. 1950. *The Principles of Psychology*. Two volumes. New York: Dover.

Jenkins, Craig. 2020. Dave Chappelle's *8:46* Is Powerful but Not Quite Perfect. *Vulture* (June 12th).

Josephs, Brian. 2017. 'He Thinks Like a Revolutionary': Talib Kweli, Hannibal Buress, W. Kamau Bell, and More Share Their Favorite Memories of Dave Chappelle. *Billboard* (March 21st).

Kang, Inkoo. 2019. Dave Chappelle's Sticks & Stones Fights for the Rights of the Already-Powerful. *Slate* (August 27th).

Katz, Phyllis A., and Jennifer A. Kofkin. 1997. Race, Gender, and Young Children. In Luthar et al. 1997.

Kaufman, Will. 1997. *The Comedian as Confidence Man*. Detroit: Wayne State University Press.

Kaur, Harmeet. 2018. Kanye West Just Said 400 Years of Slavery Was a Choice. *CNN* (May).

Kierkegaard, Søren. 1978. *The Essential Kierkegaard*. Princeton: Princeton University Press.

Kimberley, Margaret. 2020. *Prejudential: Black America and the Presidents*. Lebanon: Steerforth Press.

King, Martin Luther, Jr. 1954. Propagandizing Christianity. Stanford: The Martin Luther King, Jr. Research and Education Institute.

Kolers, Avery, and Tim Bayne. 2001. 'Are You My Mommy?' On the Genetic Basis of Parenthood. *Journal of Applied Philosophy* 18:3.

Krug, Jessica A. 2020. The Truth, and the Anti-Black Violence of My Lies. *Medium* (September 3rd).

Kukla, Rebecca. 2018. Slurs, Interpellation, and Ideology. *Southern Journal of Philosophy* 56.

LaMarre, H.L., K.D. Landreville, and M.A. Beam. 2009. The Irony of Satire: Political Ideology and the Motivation to See What You Want to See in The Colbert Report. *International Journal of Press/Politics* 14:2.

Lamsweerde, Inez van, and Vinoodh Matadin. 2017. On Set: Dave Chappelle. *New York Times Style Magazine* (August 19th).

Letterman, David. 2020. *My Next Guest Needs No Introduction: Dave Chappelle.* Season Three, Episode 3. Netflix (October 21st).

Lipton, James. 2006. *Inside the Actor's Studio: Dave Chappelle* (November 7th).

Littleton, Darryl J. 2008. *Black Comedians on Black Comedy: How African Americans Taught Us to Laugh.* Applause.

Lombardini, John. 2013. Civic Laughter: Aristotle and the Political Virtue of Humor. *Political Theory* 41:2 (April).

Lukianoff, Greg, and Jonathan Haidt. 2018. *The Coddling of the American Mind: How Good Intentions and Bad Ideas Are Setting Up a Generation for Failure.* New York: Penguin.

Lumpkin, Lauren. 2020. GWU plans to replace Jessica Krug, the Professor Who Admitted to Falsely Claiming Black Identity. *Washington Post* (September 4th).

Luthar, S.S., et al., eds. 1997. *Developmental Psychopathology: Perspectives on Adjustment, Risk and Disorder.* New York: Cambridge University Press.

Lynskey, Dorian. 2017. Father John Misty. *The Guardian* (March 30th).

McFarland, Melanie. 2019. What Happened to Dave Chappelle: The Cruelty of 'Sticks & Stones' Is a Sign of the Times. *Salon* (September 5th).

Mead, George Herbert. 1934. *Mind, Self, and Society from the Standpoint of a Social Behaviorist.* Chicago: University of Chicago Press.

———. *On Social Psychology*, ed. 1956. Chicago: University of Chicago Press.

———. *Selected Writings*, ed. Andrew J. Reck (Indianapolis: Bobbs-Merrill, 1964).

Mills, Charles. 1997. *The Racial Contract.* Ithaca: Cornell University Press, 1997.

Morales, Ed. 2020. The Most Hurtful Part of Jessica Krug pretending to be Black. *CNN* (September 7th).

MTV News Staff. 2004. Dave Chappelle: The Reason Grandmas Know Who Lil Jon Is. *MTV News* (June 1st).

Nachman, Gerald. 2003. *Seriously Funny: The Rebel Comedians of the 1950s and 1960s.* New York: Pantheon.

Nehamas, Alexander. 1998. *The Art of Living: Socratic Reflections from Plato to Foucault.* Berkeley: University of California Press.

Nietzsche, Friedrich. 1961. *Thus Spoke Zarathustra: A Book for Everyone and No One.* Penguin.

———. 2003. *Beyond Good and Evil: Prelude to a Philosophy of the Future.* Penguin.

Noroozi, Mona, I. Singh, and M. Fazel. 2018. Evaluation of the Minimum Age for Consent to Mental Health Treatment with the Minimum Age of Criminal Responsibility in Children and Adolescents: A Global Comparison. *Evidence-Based Mental Health* 21:3 (August).

Nussbaum, Emily. 2017. How Jokes Won the Election. *The New Yorker* (January 15th).

Obaro, Tomi. 2019. Dave Chappelle Doesn't Need to Punch Down. *Buzzfeed* (August 27th).

Patel, Joseph. 2004. Fugees—Yes, Even Lauryn—Reunite for Dave Chappelle's Block Party. *MTV News* (September 20th).

Powell, Kevin. 2017. Dave Chappelle Is an American Folk Hero. *New York Times* (April 19th).

Plato. 1997. *Plato: Complete Works*. Indianapolis: Hackett.

Pew Research Center. 2014. Political Polarization and Media Habits. (October 21st).

Ralkowski, Mark. 2016. *Louis C.K. and Philosophy: You Don't Get to Be Bored*. Chicago: Open Court.

Rand, Ayn. 1957. *Atlas Shrugged*. New American Library.

———. 1966. *Capitalism, the Unknown Ideal*. New American Library.

———. 1984. *Philosophy: Who Needs It*. New American Library.

Read, Opie. 1940. *Mark Twain and I*. Chicago: Reilly and Lee.

Rogers, Melvin. 2012. The People, Rhetoric, and Affect: On the Political Force of Du Bois's *The Souls of Black Folk*. *American Political Science Review* 106:1 (February).

Roiphe, Katie. 2012. Unexpected Pregnancy, Morality, and the Law. *Slate* (June 8th).

Rossing, Jonathan P. 2015. Emancipatory Racial Humor as Critical Public Pedagogy: Subverting Hegemonic Racism. *Communication, Culture, and Critique* 9:4.

Sanger, Margaret, ed. 1919. *Birth Control Review* (January).

———. 1918. *Birth Control Review* (December).

Sartre, Jean-Paul. 1956. *Being and Nothingness*. New York: Philosophical Library.

Scarry, Eddie. 2019. Dave Chappelle's Netflix Special Is a Giant Middle Finger to Social Justice. *The Federalist* (September 6th).

Schlosser, Markus. 2019. Agency. *Stanford Encyclopedia of Philosophy*.

Seitz, Matt Zoller. 2018. Bill Maher Is Stand-Up Comedy's Past. Hannah Gadsby Represents Its Future. *Vulture* (July 12th).

Siegel, Robert. 2006. Dave Chapelle Back in the Spotlight. *NPR* (March 24th).

Sims, David. 2020. Dave Chappelle's Post-Election Blues. *The Atlantic* (November 8th).

Stanley, Jason. 2015. *How Propaganda Works*. New Jersey: Princeton University Press.

————. 2018. *How Fascism Works: The Politics of Us and Them*. New York: Random House.

Stone, Laurie. 1997. *Laughing in the Dark*. New York: Ecco Press.

Taylor, Keeanga-Yamahtta. 2005. *How We Get Free: Black Feminism and the Combahee River Collective*. Chicago: Haymarket.

Terdiman, Daniel. 2004. Onion Taken Seriously, Film at 11. *Wired* (April 14th).

Thomson, Judith Jarvis. 1971. A Defense of Abortion. *Philosophy and Public Affairs* 1:1.

————. 2008. Normativity. Chicago: Open Court.

Turner, Jonathan H. 2003. *The Structure of Sociological Theory*. Seventh edition. Belmont: Wadsworth.

Wang, Esther. 2020. All the Rachel Dolezals. *Jezebel* (September 4th).

West, Cornel. 1989. *The American Evasion of Philosophy: A Genealogy of Pragmatism*. Madison: University of Wisconsin Press.

Wiesniewski, K.A., ed. 2009. *The Comedy of Dave Chappelle: Critical Essays*. Jefferson: McFarland.

Wilstein, M. 2019. Candace Owens at CPAC: Racism Is Over Because 'I've Never Been a Slave'. *The Daily Beast* (March 1st).

Yates, Kimberly. 2009. When 'Keeping It Real' Goes Right. In Wisniewski 2009.

Yglesias, Matthew. 2017. 'Tax Reform' Is the New Euphemism for Inequality. *Vox* (October 24th).

————. 2019. The Great Awokening. *Vox* (April 1st).

Zack, Naomi. 1992. An Autobiographical View of Mixed Race and Deracination. *American Philosophical Association Newsletters* 91:1.

————. 1993. *Race and Mixed Race*. Philadelphia: Temple University Press.

————. 2016. Why I Write So Many Books about Race. *Journal of World Philosophies* 1.

"The Worst Motherfuckers"

That's why I don't be coming out doing comedy all the time, 'cause
y'all n***as is the worst motherfuckers I've ever tried to entertain in
my *fucking life.*

　　—DAVE CHAPPELLE, *Sticks and Stones*

ADAM BARKMAN is Professor of Philosophy and Chair of the
Philosophy Department at Redeemer University, Ontario. He is the
author and editor of more than a dozen books, most recently *A
Critical Companion to Robert Zemeckis* (2020). Like Chappelle,
Barkman has an Asian wife, but unlike Chapelle, Barkman doesn't
find it safe (literally) to joke about it.

LUIS FELIPE BARTOLO ALEGRE is a Peruvian philosopher interested
in almost every topic, although he has mostly written and presented
talks on topics such as philosophy of language, theory of science,
philosophical logic, and argumentation theory. His current research is
focused on the problem of inconsistencies in empirical science, especially in relation to internally inconsistent theories. He is also a
founding member and current president of the *Peruvian Society for
Epistemology and Logic* and has organized events to promote
research on logic and philosophy of science. In this volume, he presents his first foray into ethics.

STEVEN A. BENKO is a Professor of Religious and Ethical Studies at
Meredith College. His research focuses on ethics, subjectivity, and culture. He is co-editor of *The Good Place and Philosophy: Get an
Afterlife* and editor of *Ethics and Comedy: Essays on Crossing the
Line.* He has published articles on authenticity and *The Good Place,*
religious humor in *Monty Python's Life of Brian,* critical thinking pedagogy, and posthumanism.

RICHARD BILSKER is Professor of Philosophy and Social Sciences at
the College of Southern Maryland, where he has taught since 1995.
He has broad teaching and research interests in philosophy, political
science, sociology, psychology, and the humanities. His books include
On Bergson and *On Jung.* His articles and book reviews have
appeared in the journals *Teaching Philosophy, Humanity and Society,*

Idealistic Studies, *ephemera*, *Hyle*, as well as in several volumes on philosophy and pop culture.

SCOUT BURCH studies Religious and Ethical Studies, Criminology, and Sociology at Meredith College in Raleigh, North Carolina. Her research focuses on the intersection of race and love in contemporary culture and ethical thought.

STEVEN BURGESS is an assistant professor of philosophy at Benedictine University where he runs an unauthorized philosophy club. He's really hoping to die a cool death someday, but knows it will probably just be table salt that does him in.

MARISA DIAZ-WAIAN is a public philosopher. Born in Santa Monica she spent the majority of her formative years along the coastlines of California, exploring tidepools, playing basketball and volleyball, body surfing, and getting into good-hearted mischief. As she grew older, Ennis and Helena, Montana, became her stomping grounds. After completing her MA in philosophy, Marisa moved to Montana to live off-grid as a resident-steward of Merlin Nature Preserve and founded Merlin CCC—a dope-ass philosophy in the community non-profit. Marisa also serves on the Board and Education Committee for The Philosophy Learning and Teaching Organization and is a speaker for Humanities Montana. Down to cut a rug (anytime, anywhere, and always with the "robot"), she digs elders, underdogs, laughter, art, jazz, reggae, wolves, ridiculous puns, hard work, good play, and ample room to wander.

DUNCAN GALE has a PhD in Philosophy of Religion from Claremont Graduate University. He is currently an adjunct professor of philosophy at a number of community colleges in the Inland Empire region of California. You can find other articles he has written on popular culture and philosophy in *Avengers Infinity Saga and Philosophy: Go for the Head* (2020) and *Indiana Jones and Philosophy* (2022). As a white guy, he is not offended by Dave Chappelle's impression of a white guy.

ALEX R GILLHAM is Assistant Professor of Philosophy at St. Bonaventure University, where he advises the Mock Trial team and runs the Diversity, Equity, and Inclusion Lecture Series. His research focuses on various topics in ancient philosophy, philosophy of religion, and ethics.

DRU GRAHAM is a graduate student in philosophy at the University of Guelph. His research focuses on phenomenology and philosophy of race. As one of the co-authors of "Does Hulk Have a Soul?" he makes just enough money to put food on the table to prove to his wife that, yes, you can make a living in philosophy.

CONOR HANSON graduated from the University of Wisconsin-Stevens Point with a BA in philosophy, and has a two-year technical diploma as an automotive technician from Madison Area Technical College. He is Lay Catechist/Campus Pastor at Immanuel Campus Fellowship at the University of Wisconsin—Whitewater. His main academic interests include moral philosophy, political philosophy, economics, hermeneutics, theology, and biblical studies. He is a father, a husband, and a lover of wood carving and automotive tinkering.

BRANDYN HEPPARD is an associate professor of philosophy at Raritan Valley Community College. He received his PhD in philosophy from the New School for Social Research in 2020. His areas of concentration are continental philosophy, critical phenomenology, intersectional feminist thought, and social and political philosophy. He's deeply interested in the intersections between comedy and revolution. He is also an emcee who performs under the name *Adeo* with the hip-hop reggae group *Universal Rebel*.

ROGER HUNT was an aspiring philosopher, then an aspiring psychoanalyst, then an aspiring . . . well, he just kind of gave up after that. Now he runs a boring fund in Boston, obviously watches too much Netflix, Hulu, Disney+, and Amazon Prime, but not HBO Max . . . yet. He co-edited *It's Always Sunny and Philosophy: The Gang Gets Analyzed* (2015), wrote *Freud: A Mosaic* (2012), and recently found supreme enjoyment as a troll on Parler.

CHRISTOPHER M. INNES got his PhD from Goldsmiths College. This is the coolest college in the University of London. This is where comedians such as Julian Clary, Ray Campbell, and others got their inspiration. The Goldsmiths' "Comedy Society" is also a place where many other comedians can come and perform. Goldsmiths has many degrees such as "About Drama: Comedy and Satire BA (Hons)" where it is made clear that comedy and satire is needed to comment on and critique the world around us. Chappelle could teach many courses for this degree. Innes now teaches philosophy at Boise State University in Idaho. He still finds the fundamentals of philosophy perplexing, but this does not stop him from revising his textbook, used in his undergraduate philosophy classes, which will soon be published. His specialization is in social and political philosophy where the questions about the mysteries of government and who should be in charge go unanswered.

"[TapTaptTap] . . . Testing, 1,2 . . . Can you all hear me out there? [*Audience applause*] Great! So, just last week, I was talking to JOHN V. KARAVITIS, he's one of those *philosophy student* types I know . . . [*rolls eyes upward while taking a hit of youknowwhat*] Anyways, he was at a school picnic with some fellow philosophy students. *Phil-o-so-phy* students! Anyways, I asked him how it went. He said, one fellow student was an idealist, and the other was a realist. Was? I asked. Yes. You see, the idealist said that 'reality' was all in his head—so the realist punched him. Knocked him cleantheyouknowwhatOUT! When the realist turned to John and asked him what *he* thought, John said,

'I'm a pragmatist—and 'I'm changing majors'. [*Dead silence*] Hello? Hello? [TapTapTap] You all still out there?"

CHRIS A. KRAMER has just completed his third year teaching philosophy at Santa Barbara City College after teaching for a decade in Rockford, Illinois. He had moved to Rockford after a professional career in rock music in San Diego inconceivably proved to be elusive. His interests intersect across the philosophy of humor, mind, religion, informal logic, existentialism and phenomenology, and oppression. He wrote his dissertation on "Subversive Humor", half about humor the other half about oppression. Readers will laugh and cry, but mostly cry, and mostly because they are reading a dissertation; what has become of their lives? He lives in Santa Barbara or "Saint Babs" with his partner Lynne, and his two diminutive philosophers, Milo and Lola, who continually test his epistemological prowess with their infinitely regressive queries.

DAVE LYREWOOD is a neuroethicist for hire, currently in the service of the ol' empire. His career had its humble beginnings in the study of analytic philosophy in northern Scandinavia, before he packed his bags and moved to the Netherlands and subsequently Germany. Here he earned his doctorate, focusing on the intersection of ethics, technology, and neurodegenerative diseases. He specializes in the analysis of moral conundrums relating to decision-making in sub-optimal and uncertain contexts, with a particular interest in divergences of autonomy-ascription. His contribution to this book has been written under pseudonym due to the nature of his current position, and the contents of the contribution.

MUKASA MUBIRUMUSOKE, Assistant Professor of Africana Studies, Claremont McKenna College.

LAUREN OLIN is an Assistant Professor of Philosophy at the University of Missouri—St. Louis. Her work is located broadly in the philosophy of cognitive science, with special emphasis on questions about the psychology of humor, knowledge, morality, and perception. So, naturally, she's also interested in Dave Chappelle.

NEHA PANDE has a BA in English from English and Foreign Languages University, and an MA in Women's Studies from Tata Institute of Social Sciences, India. She has worked as a Project Research Assistant at IIT Bombay where she conducted research and prepared the manuscript for Oxford Bibliographies to create a Trans Studies section, and conducted archival research on hijras- the popular transgender/transvestite population of South Asia. Neha has also worked with Maraa, a media and arts collective, and interviewed comedians to develop a comedy project for marginalized communities in Maharashtra. She has presented papers at two recent conferences, The Ethics and Aesthetics of Stand-up Comedy at Bucknell University, and at The Art of Being Human in Prague, Czech Republic. Neha is interested in understanding the nuances of gender, sexuality, casteism/classism, religion-oriented discrimination, patriarchal nations/nationalism through stand-up comedy (as a feminist lens).

RAYMOND E. PERRIER is an Adjunct Professor of Philosophy and Religion at Hinds Community College in Jackson, Mississippi. He spends most of his academic energy researching and writing about modern philosophy and religion, German idealism, German romanticism, and Kierkegaard. He has an additional passion for pop culture philosophy; he co-hosts, writes, and produces the Front Porch Philosophers Podcast, where he and two other scholars have informal discussions with guests on a variety of philosophical and pop culture topics. As any person from the American South will admit, he feels "genetically predisposed" to love fried chicken.

MARK RALKOWSKI is Associate Professor of Philosophy and Honors at George Washington University. He is the author of *Heidegger's Platonism* (2009) and *Plato's Trial of Athens* (2018), co-editor of *Athletics, Gymnastics, and Agon in Plato* (2020) and *Plato at Syracuse* (2019), and the editor of *Louis C.K. and Philosophy: You Don't Get to Be Bored* (2016), *Curb Your Enthusiasm and Philosophy: Awaken the Social Assassin Within* (2012), and *Time and Death: Heidegger's Analysis of Finitude* (2005). At George Washington, Ralkowski is also a Posse Mentor, a Learning Partner for GW TRAiLS, a Faculty Guide, and the Director of a study abroad program that takes students to Greece.

MONA ROCHA is an Instructor for the Department of Modern and Classical Languages and Literatures at California State University, Fresno. Mona is the author of many works of popular culture, with chapters in such books as *Psych and Philosophy: Some Dark Juju Magumbo* (2013), and *Westworld and Philosophy: Mind Equals Blown* (2018). She is the author of *The Weatherwomen: Militant Feminists of the Weather Underground* (2020) and co-author of *Joss Whedon, Anarchist?* (2019).

JAMES ROCHA is an Associate Professor of Philosophy at California State University, Fresno. James is the author of many works of popular culture and philosophy, with chapters in *Mr. Robot and Philosophy: Beyond Good and Evil Corp (2017), Veronica Mars and Philosophy: Investigating the Mysteries of Life (Which Is a Bitch Until You Die)* (2014), and *Psych and Philosophy: Some Dark Juju-Magumbo* (2013). Additionally, James is the author of *The Ethics of Hooking Up* (2020) and co-author of *Joss Whedon, Anarchist?* (2019).

BENNET SOENEN is a graduate student in philosophy at McMaster University. He has published in the fields of philosophy of religion, pop culture philosophy, and the philosophy of race in works such as *Marveling Religion: Critical Discourse and the Marvel Cinematic Universe* (2021) and *Philosophy of Forgiveness* Volume VI (2021). His love of Dave Chappelle started at far too young an age and Chappelle's comedy has affected his personality and sense of humor in ways that Soenen probably does not even know. If not for Dave Chappelle, he likely would have fallen for the old baby on the street corner trick at least a dozen times by now.

ZOE WALKER is a PhD student at Cambridge University, researching various issues in the philosophy of humor. She enjoys dissecting jokes and subjecting them to moral critique, and is very popular at dinner parties.

ANDY WIBLE is a philosophy instructor at Muskegon Community College in Michigan. He teaches the American standards such as Introduction to Philosophy, logic, and ethics. He does research in business ethics, bioethics, pop culture, and queer philosophy. Pastimes include golf, running, and impromptu dance parties when hearing the electric guitar.

ELIZA WIZNER is in her third year at the George Washington University, where she is pursuing a Bachelor's degree in Philosophy and Peace Studies with a minor in Sustainability. She enjoys reading philosophy and watching comedy, as you may have guessed, each of which is almost solely responsible for her (near) survival of quarantine thus far. Eliza has no idea what she wants to do post-grad and thinks about that constantly, which has been another fun way to pass time these days.

MIA WOOD, philosophy professor at Pierce College in Woodland Hills, California, is a middle-aged white woman who grew up in Malibu. Naturally, therefore, she is drawn to Dave Chapelle's comedy.

Index